HEINEMANN
AVCE

ADVANCED

Travel and Tourism

Janet Rodgers

HEINEMANN
AVCE

ADVANCED

Travel and Tourism

Janet Rodgers

Edexcel
Success through qualifications

Heinemann Educational Publishers,
Halley Court, Jordan Hill, Oxford OX2 8EJ
A division of Reed Educational & Professional Publishing Ltd

Heinemann is a registered trademark of Reed Educational & Professional Publishing Limited

OXFORD   MELBOURNE   AUCKLAND   JOHANNESBURG   BLANTYRE   GABORONE
IBADAN   PORTSMOUTH NH (USA)   CHICAGO

© Janet Rodgers 2001

First published 2001
2004 2003 2002 2001
10 9 8 7 6 5 4 3 2

A catalogue record for this book is available from the British Library on request.

ISBN 0 435 45592 3

Typeset by Tech-Set Ltd, Gateshead

Printed and bound in Great Britain by Bath Press Ltd, Bath

Tel: 01865 888058 www.heinemann.co.uk

Contents

Introduction   vii

Unit 1   Investigating travel and tourism   1

Chapter 1.1   Defining travel and tourism   2

Chapter 1.2   The development of travel and tourism   5

Chapter 1.3   Features of the travel and tourism industry   10

Chapter 1.4   Structure of the travel and tourism industry   22

Chapter 1.5   Scale of the UK travel and tourism industry   38

Chapter 1.6   Working in the travel and tourism industry   41

Chapter 1.7   Pursuing your own career aims   45

Unit 2   Tourism development   53

Chapter 2.1   Introduction   54

Chapter 2.2   The agents of tourism development   55

Chapter 2.3   The objectives of tourism development   60

Chapter 2.4   The impacts of tourism development   67

Unit 3   Worldwide travel destinations   77

Chapter 3.1   Research skills   78

Chapter 3.2   The location and features of the major travel and tourism destinations in continental Europe   86

Chapter 3.3   The location of major overseas destinations   96

Chapter 3.4   The features of major destinations   103

Chapter 3.5   Main travel and tourism gateways and routes   111

Chapter 3.6   The changing popularity of tourist destinations   116

Unit 4   Marketing travel and tourism   121

Chapter 4.1   How organisations grow through marketing   122

Chapter 4.2   Marketing travel and tourism   124

Chapter 4.3   The marketing mix   129

Contents

Chapter 4.4	Market research	138
Chapter 4.5	Marketing communications	152

Unit 5 | **Customer service in travel and tourism** | **161**

Chapter 5.1	Why excellent customer service is important	162
Chapter 5.2	Personal presentation	167
Chapter 5.3	Types of customer	173
Chapter 5.4	Dealing with customers	178
Chapter 5.5	Selling skills	183
Chapter 5.6	Customer service situations	190
Chapter 5.7	Handling complaints	196
Chapter 5.8	Assessing the quality and effectiveness of customer service	199

Unit 6 | **Travel and tourism in action** | **203**

Chapter 6.1	Feasibility of the project	204
Chapter 6.2	Teamwork	223
Chapter 6.3	Carrying out the project	230
Chapter 6.4	Evaluating the project	235

Further reading and useful websites | **237**

Index | **239**

Introduction

This book has been written to support students who are studying for a Vocational A-level in Travel and Tourism. The book is designed in six chapters, which cover the Compulsory units of the new Curriculum 2000 National Standards. The six compulsory units will form the core of the different Vocational A-level awards that will be offered by all awarding bodies.

These six units are:

Unit 1: Investigating travel & tourism
Unit 2: Tourism development
Unit 3: Worldwide travel destinations
Unit 4: Marketing travel & tourism
Unit 5: Customer service in travel & tourism
Unit 6: Travel & tourism in action

Each chapter of this book has been organised to follow the content specified for the corresponding unit of national standards. Headings are designed to make it easy to follow the content of each unit and to find all the knowledge and other details needed in order to achieve a high grade.

Assessment

Units will be assessed either by an assignment or by an external test, which will be set and marked by the awarding body. At the time of writing this book the author expected unit 2 and unit 4 to be externally tested. Units 1, 3, 5 and 6 are likely to be assessed through project work marked internally within the school or college delivering the A-level.

External tests are expected to involve giving short written answers to questions. These questions may often be based on case studies, or brief descriptions of situations.

Special features of the book

Throughout the text there are a number of features which are designed to be to encourage reflection and discussion and to help relate theory to practice in Travel and Tourism. Many activities may also help to develop **key skills** by practising numeracy, communication and ICT. These features are:

Check your understanding:
Thought provoking questions or dilemmas, which can be used for individual reflection or possibly for group discussion.

Did you know?:
Interesting facts or snippets of information about the Travel and Tourism industry.

Activity:
Activities to encourage the application of theory in practice.

Case studies
Brief stories or situations which help to explain the relevance of key issues and how theory relates to practice.

Other features, included in the book, are: Further reading, useful website addresses and an index.

Acknowledgements

The author and publishers would like to thank the following for permission to reproduce content and photographs.

Robert Bartlett (illustrations for map image on p.212)
Bluewater (photograph on p.170)
Boccon Gibod (photograph on p.235)
Gareth Boden (photographs on p.50, p.203 and p.223)
Bournemouth Tourism Visitor Information Bureau (photographs on p.53 and p.65)
British Tourist Authority (industry data and information)
Canterbury City Council and Canterbury Tourist Information Centre (photographs on p.26 and p.42)
Civil Aviation Authority (data and information)
Trevor Clifford (photograph on p.121 and p.133)
James Davies Travel Photography (photograph on p.57)
Digital Stock (photographs on p.161 and p.185)
Docklands Light Railway (photograph on p.114)
Nigel Embry, Farmstay (UK) / Julia Horner, Redmire Farm (photograph on p.12)
English Tourism Council (map on p.25 and information)
Format / Maggie Murray (photograph on p.176)
Sally and Richard Greenhill (photograph on p.121 and p.145)
Robert Harding Picture Library (photograph on p.88)
Hardlines (cartography and symbols for map image on p.212)
KPT Power Photos (photograph on p.91)
Stuart McCallum (photograph on p.45)
National Maritime Museum (photograph on p.62)
Julia and Christopher Naughton (photograph on p.102)
Ove Arup Partnership (photograph on p.60)
PhotoDisc (all other photographs)
R Smith (photograph on p.131)
Stone (photograph on p.200)
World Trade Organisation (information on p.39).

The publishers have made every effort to trace copyright holders, but if they have inadvertently overlooked any, they will be pleased to make the necessary arrangements at the first opportunity.

Investigating travel and tourism

The travel and tourism industry has often been referred to as the world's biggest industry. This unit offers you an introduction to one of the world's fastest-growing industries.

Through studying this unit you will have the opportunity to:

- investigate the reasons for the rapid growth in travel and tourism
- learn that the UK travel and tourism industry is made up of a wide variety of commercial and non-commercial organisations that interact with each other to supply products and services to tourists
- learn about the significance of the industry to the UK economy
- investigate the wide range of career opportunities available in the industry so you can identify the employment opportunities that match your aspirations, skills and abilities.

This unit supports the more detailed study of the travel and tourism industry you will undertake in other areas while working towards your Advanced VCE in Travel and tourism.

This unit will be assessed through your portfolio work only. The grade awarded will be your grade for the unit.

Chapter 1.1 Defining travel and tourism

The terms 'travel' and 'tourism' are so closely linked it is difficult to separate them when trying to find definitions of what these two words mean. Travel is very much about the methods and organisation of getting people to their chosen destinations. The reasons *why* people undertake journeys also need to be considered, however, as the travel and tourism industry is not just concerned with holidays but also travel for business and other purposes.

A dictionary definition of travel

Go from one place to another; journey along or through; n. travelling, especially abroad.

There are common stereotypes of tourism and tourists but the subject is much wider than these limited views!

Tourism takes place for leisure or recreation purposes and, in the majority of cases, this will be for a holiday. A widely accepted definition of a tourist is a temporary visitor who stays in a place for the purpose of a holiday for at least 24 hours. There are, however, exceptions to this and, indeed, any person touring by coach, cruise ship or car to more than one destination would not technically fit into this definition of a tourist.

A dictionary definition of tourism

Organised touring or other services for tourists.

Travel and tourism organisations similarly cover a very wide range of activities. There are differences that range from the ownership of the organisations supplying the travel or tourism to the types of services these organisations offer. Some travel and tourism organisations, however, fit very neatly into either the travel or tourism category, as shown in Figure 1.1.

Travel	Tourism
Travel agencies Tour operators Transport operators	Tourist boards Tourist information centres Guiding services Excursion companies (e.g. coach firms) Attractions (e.g. theme parks, museums, pleasure beaches, etc.)

Figure 1.1   Travel and tourism organisations

There are, however, activities that could easily be classified into both areas.

When considering tourism, we are very much looking at what happens at the *destination* (unless the product has been included as part of a travel package – for example, a tour operator's package that includes transport, coach transfer arrangements to the resort, and hotel and catering arrangements). This demonstrates how the link between travel and tourism makes it difficult to define the boundaries of each industry.

Why do people travel?

Activity	In groups of three or four, write up a list of the reasons why people travel. Then compare your list with those of your peers.

You should now be able to sort the ideas in your list into some of the categories listed below (you may need to add further categories):

- holidays
- business
- visiting friends and relatives
- excursions and sightseeing
- religion
- education
- conferences and exhibitions

Not all the items in this list would categorise these travellers as tourists and it is important when studying travel to consider the reasons *why* people travel. There are three essential conditions for travel to take place:

1 *Enabling conditions* Time and money are, usually, both essential requirements for travel to happen.
2 *Motivation for travel* People need either to have the desire to travel or to have a reason, such as attending a business meeting or conference.
3 *The availability of some form of transport*.

Within a particular society as a whole, for tourism travel to take place, there must also be:

- a reasonable level of political stability
- a minimum basic standard of transport and accommodation
- an environment that is attractive in some way in order to encourage visitors (e.g. good beaches or a warm climate).

Different types of tourism

Tourism can be divided into three categories: domestic, inbound and outbound.

Domestic

Domestic tourism takes place within the boundaries of the tourist's own country. For a UK domestic tourist, this would include holidays and short breaks in England, Scotland, Wales and Northern Ireland.

Inbound

When overseas visitors travel to the UK this is known as inbound tourism. Inbound tourism is very important to the British economy, both through direct spending on travel and tourism products (e.g. hotel accommodation) and indirectly through tourists spending during their stay (e.g. on souvenirs and meals out). Industries such as retailing, manufacturing and transport benefit from inbound tourists to the UK.

Outbound

The final category is outbound travel, which is what many people automatically think of when looking at tourism (i.e. people leaving their own country to visit overseas destinations). Outbound travel continues to increase in popularity, especially for northern European nationals who want to escape to the warmer climates of the Mediterranean and even further afield.

There have been many historical developments that have helped to shape the industry into what it is today. These are explored in the next chapter.

Chapter 1.2 The development of travel and tourism

The early days

Travel and tourism as an organised activity can be traced back to the ancient Egyptians when high levels of prosperity and a fairly stable social environment promoted the development of tourism. The Nile was a convenient method of transport to attractions such as the Pyramids and the Sphinx. Travel and tourism continued to evolve and, in the Roman Empire of the first two centuries AD, there are many references to travel in the writing of the time. There was a good network of roads and seaways and the average worker had 130 days holiday a year. The motivations to be a tourist were similar to those of today (e.g. the seaside, entertainment, art, architecture and visiting events such as chariot racing and boxing). Accommodation consisted of inns and private houses, there were innumerable couriers and guides and there was also a wide range of restaurants. Following the break up of the Roman Empire, travel was mainly for religious purposes, with people undertaking pilgrimages to such places as Jerusalem, Rome and Canterbury.

Figure 1.2 Travel and tourism were well-established by Roman times

Developments in the seventeenth to nineteenth centuries

Between the seventeenth and nineteenth centuries, wealthy travellers from Britain were influential in shaping the overseas travel market. The elite of society undertook the 'Grand Tour of Europe', developing their social, artistic and diplomatic skills while visiting Italy, Switzerland and Germany. As more of the middle classes started to travel, destinations in Greece, Portugal and the Middle East were added to itineraries.

The domestic market was not slow to follow, with development of spa and seaside resorts. The heyday for the domestic market was the 1870s, when the middle and lower classes started to travel on the railways. Spas at Bath and Buxton became famous for their health-giving waters. Sea bathing was considered very therapeutic and, with the rapid expansion of the railways opening up a mass market for travel, places such as Brighton, Cleethorpes and Margate became popular destinations. Rail services to ports and the introduction of the first cross-channel steamships made European and

Irish locations accessible, enhancing both the outbound and inbound tourism industries.

> ### Did you know?
>
> - Baedecker introduced the first guidebook for European countries in 1839.
> - In 1837 the first large hotels were built at railway stations and, by 1899, The Savoy, Claridges and the Carlton had all opened in London.
> - The first leisure cruises began when Cunard built its first steamship in 1840.
> - Thomas Cook took the first group of tourists on an excursion in 1841, from Leicester to Loughborough. Some 570 passengers paid a shilling each for the trip.
> - In the 1880s, Sir Henry Lunn started the first skiing holidays to Switzerland.

The turn of the twentieth century

Travel and tourism continued to develop into the twentieth century, particularly among the working classes. New resorts such as Blackpool and Skegness catered for the factory and millworkers of the north, the Midlands and the south of Scotland, who now had a little more money to spend and one or two weeks' holiday entitlement each year.

International travel continued to flourish, especially with the introduction of scheduled air services in the 1930s. These services, however, were unreliable, expensive and uncomfortable.

Developments since the 1930s

Domestic tourism as we recognise it today only really started to develop in the years up to the Second World War, when Billy Butlin opened his first holiday camp in Skegness in 1937. Apparently, while sitting in a bus shelter on a rainy summer's day, he overheard some holidaymakers complaining about the lack of things to do in Skegness. This prompted him to open a centre that had entertainment and other facilities suited to the British climate. This type of holiday accommodation expanded phenomenally and, by 1939, there were approximately 200 holiday camps in Britain, catering for 30,000 people a week at the height of summer.

After the Second World War, people's aspirations had changed. The war had given many people the opportunity to travel away from their homes, and some people had been overseas. They had mixed with a range of people from different classes and now had the desire to have what the 'upper classes' had had up till then. There was a new sense of equality in society, through the health service, education and social security.

National Parks were set up to protect the natural environment and to control the building of new facilities. These were established in 1949 as a result of the setting up of the National Parks Commission, which was later to become the Countryside Commission. The first park, the Peak District, was created in 1951.

Changing socio-economic circumstances (such as increases in car ownership, leisure time and disposable income for many people) have also had a considerable impact on travel and tourism.

Car ownership

The growth in car ownership has had a huge influence on the UK travel industry. Many people like the flexibility of being able to take to the road without being confined by timetables, advanced booking requirements, baggage restrictions, etc. Car travel is perceived as low cost, and accommodation can be selected to suit all budgets. Camping and caravan sites are very popular and facilities on sites have become more sophisticated, especially those for leisure and entertainment activities and for catering.

Other types of accommodation have also evolved from the traditional seaside guesthouse with its infamous landlady into a range of options including farmhouses, motels, pubs, boats, country houses and themed hotels such as the one at Alton Towers. Increased car ownership has enabled many people to take short stay motoring holidays, both within the UK and abroad. Approximately 3 million of the 15 million privately owned cars in Britain are now taken abroad each year.

Increased leisure time

Leisure time has increased for two major reasons. First, people are retiring at an earlier age and are becoming seasoned travellers (i.e. people are using their time to travel, in particular, taking long-stay holidays during the winter months). The second reason relates to workers' paid holiday entitlements, which have increased from the two weeks established through the Holidays with Pay Act 1938 to the four–five weeks' holiday over 77% of today's workforce now enjoys. More flexible working practices have seen the working week being reduced through flexi-time and job sharing schemes. This has enabled more people to take part in travel and tourism activities on a more frequent basis. They can travel outside peak travel times and make use of discounted entrance prices and hotel rates. As a result, people often take a second or even a third holiday. This desire to take more than one

holiday a year has resulted in the development of different types of holiday (e.g. skiing, adventure holidays and short-duration city breaks, etc.).

Air travel

Aircraft technology has also seen considerable developments since the Second World War, with aircraft travel becoming more comfortable, much safer, faster and more affordable. Following the end of the Second World War there was a surplus of aircraft and qualified pilots, which encouraged the growth of this sector of the industry. Runways and airports were built and many private airline companies came into being so that, by 1957, the number of passengers travelling across the Atlantic to America by air had overtaken the numbers travelling by sea. This trend in air travel has continued to develop, particularly since the rise of the package holiday (see below).

Although tour operators had been selling some form of package tours for many years, the most important development for the tour operations industry took place in 1950. This was when Vladimir Raitz of Horizon packaged the first tour that included a chartered air service, transfer and accommodation. In its first year of operation, this package took 300 UK travellers to Corsica. It did not take long for other companies to see the potential of this and, by the 1960s, chartered air travel had become the norm for most overseas holidays.

Disposable income

People now have more disposable income, and the holiday is the third most expensive item people spend their money on (second only to a house and a car). When the economy is buoyant, people have the confidence to spend money on travel – a product that is generally regarded as a luxury item. Increases in disposable income encourage spending on higher-value holiday products, such as cruises, all-inclusive holidays, and faraway and ski destinations.

Advances in technology

Technological advances have done much to enhance the industry. For example, computerised reservation systems (CRS) are now used to sell the majority of travel products. With this system, reservations can be confirmed instantly, and profits are maximised through this cost-effective way of making bookings. Prices and special offers can be updated instantaneously, ensuring the public has access to the best deals.

Package holidays

As we noted earlier, the package holiday market has continued to develop, with companies now offering a range of products and destinations. The travelling public who visited Spain in the 1970s and the Greek Islands in the 1980s are now established and experienced travellers. Demand for more exotic destinations has continued to rise and, throughout the 1980s and 1990s, the main package tour companies were offering such long-haul destinations as Florida and Jamaica. Tour operators continue to seek out even more exciting destinations, which is noticeable through trends in the popularity of such places as Mexico, Thailand and Australia.

Fashion and customer expectations

The popularity of destinations and holiday types changes as fashions and customer needs change. The introduction of a new mode of transport, such as Eurostar, or an attraction like Disneyland, Paris, can change the type of visitor to a particular destination. Television programmes and films have a huge impact on the popularity of a destination. As customers gain experience of travel, their expectations from the travel and tourism industry increase. Hence the industry has evolved enormously over the last 50 or so years into the one we know today.

CASE STUDY: Developments in the tourism and travel industry

One person's lifetime experiences of holidays will reflect many of the changes that have affected the tourism and travel industry. Take the example of Elizabeth Mellor, who was born just after the Second World War in a suburb of Manchester:

- In the 1950s Elizabeth and her family took the train for a week's holiday in Blackpool or Southport.
- In the 1960s Elizabeth went with her family in their new Ford Anglia car for holidays to Bournemouth, Cornwall and the Isle of Wight.

- By the 1970s Elizabeth was old enough to go on holidays with her friends. She and her friends went on package holidays to Spain, flying from Manchester Airport on charter flights.
- Now married, in the 1980s Elizabeth and her young family took package holidays to Greece, Turkey and Florida, staying in self-catering accommodation.
- In the 1990s the family rented gîtes in Normandy, Brittany, the Loire Valley and the south of France (taking their car across the channel by means of the Shuttle).
- In the early 2000s, now most of the children have left home, Elizabeth and her husband plan to travel further afield – perhaps to South America or Australia.

Interview friends or members of your family to see if they have experienced personally any of the developments that have affected the travel and tourism industry we have looked at in this section.

Check your understanding

Prepare a five to ten minute presentation about the development of the travel and tourism industry since the end of the Second World War. Remember to include:

- a description of the key developments since the war
- an explanation of the reasons for the rapid growth of the industry
- if you can, the factors that might affect the industry's future development.

Chapter 1.3 Features of the travel and tourism industry

Ownership of organisations

The travel and tourism industry can be categorised according to who owns a particular organisation (i.e. whether the organisation is in the private, public or voluntary sector).

Private sector

As in any industry, private sector companies will be owned either by an individual (a sole trader), a group of people (perhaps a partnership) or a larger company. In the travel and tourism industry, the majority of organisations in the UK are in the private sector, and many of these are part of large national or multinational companies. The main aim of these companies is to generate profit by selling products and/or services. The industry has tended to be dictated to and led by large private sector companies such as Thomson Holidays, Lunn Poly, British Airways and Whitbread.

Activity	As we have just noted, the holiday business is dominated by a few large companies. Find out as much as you can about these companies by searching their websites, studying the brochures/publications they produce and, perhaps, by visiting one of their travel agencies or branches.
	In particular, try to find out about:

- each company's turnover (how much money they generate a year)
- the other companies each of these organisations owns
- any other activities/businesses the companies are involved in.

The following web addresses might be useful:

Thomson Holidays: http://www.thomson-holidays.com/home.html
Lunn Poly: http://www.lunn-poly.co.uk/index.html
British Airways: http://www.british-airways.com/ecp_no_dhtml.shtml
Whitbread: http://www.whitbread.co.uk/html/whithome.html

There are, however, still examples of small and medium-sized enterprises within the travel industry (see pages 11–13), especially in the travel agency sector, where independent agencies can still be found in many of our towns and cities. Well-known attractions that are privately owned include Alton Towers, Sea Life Centres, Legoland, Madame Tussauds, Rock Circus and The London Dungeon. The dominance of the major players, however, is being challenged through Internet bookings; for example, by January 2000, lastminute.com had 800,000 registered users and ebookers had 700,000.

Free Admission	
Attraction	**Number of visitors**
1 Blackpool Pleasure Beach	7,200,000
2 British Museum	5,460,537
3 National Gallery	4,964,879
4 Palace Pier, Brighton	3,750,000
5 Seaworld, The Trocadero, London	3,454,690
Paid admission	
1 Alton Towers	2,650,000
2 Madam Tussauds	2,640,000
3 Tower of London	2,422,181
4 Natural History Museum	1,739,591
5 Legoland, Windsor	1,620,000

Table 1.1 Top UK attractions, 1999 (courtesy of English Tourism Council)

Public sector

Some aspects of the tourism industry fall within the public sector (i.e. they are subsidised or funded by the government through taxes). Many of these organisations are non-profit making and have been set up to provide a service that will either support local businesses or visitors to an area. Although they are not accountable to shareholders like most public companies, they are accountable to elected bodies and councils. On a national basis, such organisations as the national tourist boards and English Heritage are in the public sector. On a local basis, this sector includes most museums and tourist information centres (TICs).

It is worth noting that many of the support services for the international travel industry (such as immigration, air traffic control and customs and excise) are still within the public sector, but this situation is constantly changing. You need only consider how many support services have been privatised recently by looking at such examples as the British Airports Authority (BAA), Railtrack and National Express to realise that public sector services within travel and tourism are increasingly becoming subject to privatisation.

Voluntary sector

The third sector (and one that is not represented extensively within travel and tourism) is the voluntary sector. Voluntary sector organisations are funded mainly by their members through membership subscriptions, donations, grants, fund-raising activities and the sale of goods and services. Many of these voluntary sector organisations have come into existence to cater for the special needs or interests of their members. Very often, members of these organisations will work part time or full time on a voluntary basis, rather than being paid. The main examples of voluntary sector organisations within the travel and tourism industry are The National Trust and the Youth Hostel Association. On a smaller scale are battle re-enactments societies such as the Sealed Knot and some conservation groups like those that campaign to save the loggerhead turtles in tourist areas on Greek islands.

Small and medium-sized organisations

Within the tourism industry, there are many examples of small and medium-sized enterprises.

CASE STUDY: Small and medium-sized enterprises

In a holiday destination such as a seaside resort, the majority of guesthouses and hotels will fall into the small or medium-sized category: many of these businesses will be family run and owned.

An aspect of the tourism industry that has been successful recently is farm tourism. There has been considerable interest in such holidays from people who want to stay on farms and to take an active involvement in farming methods. Again, those farms are likely to be of small or medium size and to be family owned and run.

photo courtesy of Nigel Embry, Farmstay UK/Julia Horner Redmire Farm.

Within catering there are, again, some excellent examples of small and medium-sized companies, particularly when specialising in a certain type of cuisine, such as French, Chinese or Indian. There are, however, many fashionable chain restaurants and pubs that are moving into tourist areas and that are thus diminishing the number of privately owned establishments. For example, many of the recently established Travel Inns and Travelodges are linked to their own pubs and restaurants to maximise the profits made from customers staying in budget accommodation.

Small enterprises find it increasingly difficult to compete on price with many of the large organisations, and do not have large budgets for advertising and promotion. Similarly, although many tourist attractions (such as museums, parks and swimming pools, etc.) are still run by local authorities, an increasing number of privately owned attractions are being set up (e.g. theme parks, crazy golf courses and leisure resorts, etc.).

Finally, there are some small or medium-sized companies that offer 'niche' holidays. These companies specialise in selling holidays tailored to the needs or interests of particular groups of people (e.g. safari holidays in more remote corners of the world, holidays with a particular theme, such as learning how to cook in a particular way or how to paint, and holidays centred round a music or drama festival).

Activity	Visit a tourist destination with the main aim of looking at the types of tourist organisation that exist at the destination. While there, make notes of examples of organisations that fall under the three types of ownership:
	1 private sector 2 public sector 3 voluntary sector.
	Once you have completed this, consider whether these organisations are:
	• multinational organisations • large, UK-based organisations • medium-sized enterprises • small, family-run businesses.
	Produce a display that will show your findings, making use of pictures, graphs, charts and written explanations.

Extensive use of new technology

Until the 1980s, very little technology was used in the travel and tourism industry. Reservations were completed using wall charts that were updated when customers or travel agents telephoned to make a booking. Since then, there have been considerable advances in the use of technology (but the communication process remained fairly stable with customers visiting or telephoning travel agents, tourist boards, airlines, tour operators or hotels to make their booking – until the arrival of the Internet – see below).

The booking systems devised by tour organisers have gradually become more reliable and user friendly over the years, although some of the popular airline reservation systems (such as Galileo and Amadeus) still require extensive training before bookings can be made. With the growth in Internet bookings, however, the airline reservation companies are searching for ways in which the public can make reservations easily without the need for the technical knowledge currently required. Both Amadeus and Galileo are implementing point and click graphics aimed (initially) at making the travel agent's job easier but, in the long term, there are possibilities this service may be made available to the general public. For business travellers, in particular, it is easier and more convenient for them to plan and organise their own flights, accommodation and car hire over the Internet using a laptop or personal computer. Many other people are also making use of the booking services available on the Internet through such companies as Expedia, Top Class Travel and Connect Global, etc.

Activity	Find out what these Internet holiday companies can offer their customers by exploring their websites. Remember to make notes of the products they are selling and of any advantages you can spot for customers buying their holidays in this way. The following are the web addresses of a few of these companies:
	• http://www.expedia.co.uk • http://www.travel2. AmericanExpress.com • http://www.topclasstravel.co.uk • http://www.connectglobal.co.uk • http://www.travelon.com/

While in the past people relied on brochures, their previous experiences and recommendations from friends, the Internet can make it possible for a customer to view his or her flight, look at hotel facilities and services and see the resort he or she will be visiting. Hence there is the potential to eliminate the risk that is so inherent in the travel or tourism product. Opportunities to talk to staff who work overseas and to receive answers to questions a customer might have, plus greater prior knowledge about a product a customer is considering buying should reduce the complaints that inevitably arise from this very unpredictable purchase.

This new, fast-moving technology is certain to have a major impact on the way the industry will develop in the future.

Vulnerability to external pressures

The success of tourism in a particular area is very much dictated by external pressures. The four key factors that affect the industry are:

1 currency fluctuations
2 government legislation
3 climatic changes
4 war and civil unrest.

Currency

When calculating the cost of an overseas package holiday, a tour operator will work out the cost of the accommodation and the transfer costs in the local currency of the holiday destination. Contract rates (i.e. the charges to be made for the accommodation in the holiday destination) are usually agreed a year *prior* to the brochure being produced.

This means that a customer may be making a payment for a holiday possibly *two years* after the contract rates were agreed (i.e. *one year* after the rates were agreed and *another year* after the brochure was printed).

In countries where there are frequent changes in exchange rates, this can greatly affect the profit or loss made by a tour operator on a holiday package. In the 1970s and early 1980s, it was normal practice for tour operators to compensate for any loss they might make by adding a *currency surcharge* to the customer's holiday price. This meant the price offered in a brochure was not guaranteed until the customer finally paid for his or her holiday. Nowadays, however, after a great many complaints about surcharges, most tour operators have a 'no surcharge guarantee' they advertise on their brochures so that the price shown in the brochure is the one the customer will pay.

Activity	Look at the exchange rates for the following currencies for August 2000 and compare these with the rates for the same time the previous year:

£1 =		
	August 2000	**August 1999**
Japan	158.68 yen	177.43 yen
Greece	554 drachma	497 drachma
Turkey	958,938 Turkish lira	707,105 Turkish lira

Now calculate how much the following room rates would have cost in £ sterling in 1999 when the contract rate might have been agreed, and in October 2000 when payment was received for the booking:

18,000 yen

76,000 drachma

Where accommodation increases in cost, the difference will be absorbed by the tour operator from their profit margin rather than being paid by the customer. However, if the accommodation rate decreases in cost, the profit made by the tour operator will be higher than forecasted.

Next, look at the following example of a room rate of 35,000,000 Turkish lira. The room cost (using 1999 rates) would be £49.50. However, the 2000 rate would reduce the rate to £36.50, giving a £13 increase on the predicted profit for each holiday.

Currency rates can have a large impact on the tourism industry. For large tour operators, these currency fluctuations will balance out. However, if an organisation specialises in holidays to one country only, fluctuations can greatly affect profit margins.

The industry is affected by the legislation that affects all sales organisations, such as the Sale of Goods Act, contract law and the Trades Descriptions Act. Such legislation affects the way travel goods are described to the public. Obviously, such things as flight times, the facilities in a resort and services in accommodation do change, but a salesperson has to ensure the information given at the point of sale is accurate. Similarly, prices must not be misleading, particularly when advertising such products as reduced-price airline seats, as these must have been generally available at the higher cost prior to being offered at a reduced price.

Legislation has made travel and tourism organisations more accountable for the special offers they promote and for the prices and descriptions that appear in their brochures. Tour operators need to ensure that their prices are accurate and that, if any changes take place, these are passed on to the travel agent. Local representatives need to keep head offices informed about the properties they own or contract with, building work going on in the area and changes in the resort so the tour operator is not held responsible under either the Trades Descriptions Act or Sale of Goods Act.

Legislation

Legislation of all types has an impact on the industry, and not just UK legislation but also the legislation of overseas governments.

CASE STUDY: The Association of British Travel Agents

As well as government legislation there is also the Association of British Travel Agents (ABTA – http://www.abtanet.com/) code of conduct that sets out guidelines ABTA expects all its registered travel agents and tour operators to adhere to. The code covers such things as the relationship between ABTA travel agents and tour operators. It also explains the level of service a customer should expect and how complaints will be dealt with, including timescales for responses. The code of conduct also includes the things contained in the tour operators' brochures, their descriptions of the holidays on offer and booking conditions.

Since 1992 and the Single European Act, EU directives have also shaped the travel and tourism industry. The Act had three main aims: to remove physical, technical and fiscal (monetary) barriers to travel and tourism with the EU. This has mainly been done through harmonisation (i.e. ensuring that what happens in one country applies in other EU member countries). One example of where this has had an impact on the industry is the liberalisation of air and coach travel, with companies moving to being privatised and not dependent on government funding. This stimulates competition between airlines and coach operators and allows privately owned organisations to lead the way in both fares and routes offered. A more recent example has been the abolition of duty-free shopping within EU countries. This has already had a significant impact on both air and sea transport. Cross-channel ferry traffic has been particularly hard hit by this, and the marketing of day trips across the Channel is now focused on the destination and cheaper prices in French hypermarkets rather than the benefits of buying duty-free goods on the ferry.

It is now much easier for one firm to buy out another firm in the EU. This was demonstrated through the acquisition of the majority share ownership in Thomas Cook by the German tour company, Preussag, who then owned 50.1% of shares in Thomas Cook. Thomas Cook then had three major shareholders: Preussag, Westdeutsche Landesbank (a German bank), which held 27.9%, and US-based Carlson, which had a 22% share.

However, the directive that has most directly affected the industry is the EU Package Travel Directive, which came into operation at the beginning of 1993. The directive harmonised the different legislation that was currently in operation throughout Europe. As UK legislation, regulations and codes of conduct were already very rigorous, there was not much within this directive that was new to UK operators. However, since the introduction of the EU Package Travel Directive, tour operators have been made responsible for all aspects of the package tour, including the accommodation, excursions and transport. Prior to this directive, tour operators could pass on the problem of, say, a hotel overbooking to the hotelier, but now they have to accept this responsibility themselves.

Climate

The weather plays a big part in people's decisions about where to take their holidays. There are two aspects when considering climatic conditions: *predictable* (or seasonal) weather conditions and *unpredictable* changes in a particular area's weather conditions. We shall consider the predictable climatic changes first.

Check your understanding

What are the most popular months for tourism in the UK? At what dates do most UK tourist attractions (roughly) open and close?

Can you think of any UK destinations and/or attractions that have been able to *extend* this opening period? How have they been able to do this?

Most holiday destinations do not have an ideal, year-round climate for tourism and, indeed, when you look at northern Europe the tourist season is exceptionally short.

As a result, many tourist jobs are temporary or seasonal and income is generated only during a small part of the year.

The changing climate does, on the other hand, work to the advantage of countries

Skiing depends on weather conditions, predictable and unpredictable; too little snowfall means poor skiing and too much can spell danger from avalanches.

these countries. For example, Ibiza attracts mass tourism in the summer months but has no tourist industry in the winter. The winter climate in Ibiza is cold and rainy and, hence, there are virtually no winter package tours to this destination after the end of October.

Unpredictable climatic features (such as hurricanes or typhoons) can devastate the tourism industry of a destination. This is not just the result of the initial impact of something like a hurricane but more long-term problems, such as the destruction of hotels, attractions and the infrastructure (roads, railways, etc.) of the destination itself. In isolated, island regions such as the Caribbean, communications can also be affected, cutting the area off from the outside world. Sometimes the very weather that attracts a tourist to a destination can also be the root of the problem. When ski destinations have particularly heavy snowfalls, there is a higher risk of avalanches.

that have mountainous regions and can thus offer skiing. Spain, France and Italy are all able to benefit as countries that have long hot summers as well as ski areas that have reliable snow conditions in the winter. This does not, obviously, apply to all areas of

War and civil unrest

War and civil unrest is, in the long term, very damaging for a tourist area. People need to be assured of a reasonable level of political stability before they will visit a destination.

CASE STUDY: The former Yugoslavia

The most dramatic effect of war and civil unrest affecting a destination can be seen when looking at the former country of Yugoslavia as a holiday destination. Prior to the unrest, Yugoslavia was a very popular holiday destination, especially for British tourists. It was not as developed as areas of Spain and Greece yet offered good-quality accommodation, reasonable prices and a range of tourist attractions. It also offered not only beach destinations but also lakes, mountains, cities and ski areas. There was a year-round industry that disappeared immediately civil unrest broke out. Similar examples are Egypt, India and Sri Lanka.

Activity	Look through back issues of either a travel paper (such as the *Travel Trade Gazette*) or a large national newspaper (such as *The Times* or *Guardian*) for examples of how external pressures have impacted on the industry recently. Your examples can be either from the UK or overseas.
	Bring your examples to a group discussion so you can discuss how these pressures have affected the travel and tourism industry.

Positive and negative impacts on host communities

Tourism is often referred to as the 'smokeless industry' as, unlike other industries, there are no obvious effects on the local area. However, tourism does have a profound effect on an area and, although these effects may not be visible immediately, its impact on a host community can be just as powerful as any other form of industry. There are positive and negative effects on an area's:

- economy
- environment
- social and cultural life.

Economy

We have already noted the effects rates of exchange can have on the tourist industry. However, very often it is the tourists themselves who affect currency rates and whether or not a destination offers good value for money (as demand for currencies varies through the tourist season, rates will go up and down accordingly). One reason governments encourage tourism is to bring strong currencies into their own countries to help with their balance of payments (i.e. tourists bring with them money to spend that should go into the local economy and that should, thus, help to boost it).

However, this is not always the case. Positive economic advantages can often be cancelled out by negative ones (see Figure 1.3).

Positive	Negative
✓ Increased income for local residents	✗ Prices increase locally
✓ Increased employment within travel and tourism and within related industries	✗ The decline of traditional employment opportunities
✓ Improved standards of living for local residents	✗ Local people can no longer afford to live in the tourist areas
✓ The infrastructure of the destination is improved	✗ Increased taxes to pay for the new infrastructure
	✗ The money brought in does not stay in the local area but goes overseas to large multinational companies

Figure 1.3   The positive and negative economic impacts of tourism

Environment

The effects of tourism on the environment are much more difficult to assess as, very often, these cannot be measured in the same way as the financial aspects of tourism. However, the effects on the environment are usually more negative than positive and it is only where tourism is managed effectively that the negative impacts can be controlled.

Sometimes it is the very nature of the destination itself that invites its own destruction: unspoilt beaches, clear water, mountain scenery and animals living in their natural habitats. As more and more people are attracted to such places, they can only damage the very environment to which they were drawn. And once the damage is done it is very hard to rectify. Figure 1.4 summarises some of the main advantages and disadvantages of tourism on the environment.

Positive	Negative
✓ The restoration and renovation of derelict sites and buildings ✓ The money raised from tourism can be directed into environmental projects ✓ Landscaping could be improved	✗ The destruction of natural resources, in particular the landscape ✗ Increased pollution ✗ Litter ✗ Traffic congestion

Figure 1.4   The positive and negative impacts of tourism on the environment

CASE STUDY: Skiing and the environment

To most of us, skiing may seem a fairly harmless pastime: it takes place in remote areas when the ground is frozen and when most wildlife is asleep for the winter, and it does not involve a great deal of motorised equipment that could pollute the environment. However, consider the following facts:

- In some ski areas, the visual attractiveness of the landscape has been marred by the construction of ski lifts, hotels and car parks.
- The use of bulldozers to construct pistes damages the soil and vegetation.
- When the covering of snow is thin, skis can cut into the soil, which damages the roots of over-wintering plants.
- In time, footpaths that are used regularly become worn out and difficult to negotiate. People then tend to walk along the edges of these paths to follow the route to the top of the mountain, the car park, etc. and, in so doing, they widen the path and cause further damage to the landscape.
- Birds often collide with and are killed by the overhead wires of ski lifts.
- Dogs taken by walkers to ski slopes can disturb birds, particularly in early spring at nesting time.
- Carelessly discarded litter (particularly food scraps) attracts scavenging animals, which may also steal birds' eggs at nesting time.
- The increased amount of road traffic at peak skiing times can have a damaging effect on small towns and villages.

Can you think of any more examples, either in the UK or abroad, of tourism adversely affecting the environment? You may need to do a little research here. Keep your eye out for newspaper reports or programmes on the television, which often cover this sort of issue. You could also visit your college or local library to see if they have any books on the topic.

Social and cultural life

The lives of local people are bound to be affected by the advent of a tourist industry, and the impact of tourism will be different on those who have never experienced tourists before from those who have known tourism all their lives.

While tremendous opportunities arise from tourism for the exchange of ideas and views with people from different backgrounds, there can also be problems for the local community. In more extreme cases, tourists and locals do not live happily together and there can, therefore, be considerable antagonism.

CASE STUDY: Tourism in the Caribbean – the Flying Fish resort

Holidays in the Caribbean are often presented to us as some far-off, romantic, idyllic dream: beautiful, clean beaches, clear warm water and locals who are only too friendly and keen to help us. This can, however, often be far from the truth.

The Flying Fish company is looking for a destination to build its next all-inclusive resort in the Caribbean. Flying Fish resorts are always developed on remote islands where tourism is not fully established. The American-owned company believes in creating a 'home from home' environment for tourists from the USA. It imports the majority of materials from the USA and Canada for the buildings and because it has had problems in the past with local builders, it uses its own staff to build and landscape the properties. All its resorts have nine-hole golf courses, extensive gardens around the accommodation and private beaches. Flying Fish recruits British and American citizens for management, reception, entertainment and customer service roles in the restaurants and bars. The company prides itself on its ability to provide high-quality food and drink, importing meat, vegetables, wines and spirits it can rely on.

Flying Fish is having problems with one of its resorts – a problem that has been going on for five years. The Caribbean Tourism Action Group has used the resort as an example of how life on an island has been drastically affected by tourism, giving the following as the main areas of concern:

- Local inhabitants are not given worthwhile jobs in the building or running of the resort. They tend to be offered cleaning, gardening or washing-up jobs. There are no opportunities for them to be promoted within the Flying Fish resort as these jobs go to outsiders.
- Any profit made by Flying Fish goes back to America. Very little is bought locally for the tourists. Seafood and fruit are occasionally bought, but the demand for the year-round availability of fruit is not satisfied by the island.
- Because the resort is all-inclusive, tourists tend not to venture outside. There are souvenir shops and a car rental office within the resort. Some local people have started to set up cheap trinket stalls on the beach and tourists rarely go into the town.

- Agricultural land has been used for the golf course and for landscaping the resort.
- Local people are restricted on when they can use the beach. They can now only fish before 09:00 and after 20:00.
- Valuable resources (such as water and electricity) are becoming scarce. The resort is placing a high demand on these. A private health clinic has now been set up and many of the qualified doctors and nurses have transferred to this clinic to work. Crime has increased, including muggings and theft. The police resources are now being stretched by this increase in crime.

Questions

1 What sort of client would appreciate a holiday like this?
2 Can you think of any other instances where holiday makers and local people are kept apart like this? You do not need to look as far afield as the Caribbean!
3 While we may consider ourselves to be open-minded, fair people, have you ever been in a situation as a holiday maker or tourist when you have felt you were being prevented from seeing 'behind the scenes'?

Figure 1.5 summarises the positive and negative effects of tourism on an area's social and cultural life. (The impacts of tourism on the host community are studied in more detail in Unit 2: 'Tourism development'.)

Positive	Negative
✓ The preservation of customs and crafts ✓ Increases in public services ✓ The development of community facilities ✓ The opportunity for local people to find out more about different people and to develop language skills	✗ An increase in taxes to pay for the development of the infrastructure ✗ Increases in crime, particularly theft and violent crimes ✗ Areas become destabilised as youths move away from traditional areas to seek jobs in tourism ✗ Local customs and religions become trivialised ✗ Conflicts with the host community

Figure 1.5   The positive and negative impacts of tourism on an area's social and cultural life

Chapter 1.4 Structure of the travel and tourism industry

The travel and tourism industry is made up of a number of different components that complement each other to form an overall tourist product. Although these components are very closely linked, they are quite individual in themselves. In this chapter we will consider these components separately and will also look at examples of how these components work together to form the travel and tourism industry.

Tourist attractions

The success of a tourist destination relies on a balance of attractions, amenities/ facilities and the accessibility of the destination itself. The attractions can be classed either as a site attraction (i.e. a country, region, city or resort, or a specific building or place e.g. Canterbury cathedral see photo) or an event attraction (such as a festival, sports event or conference). Here we are mainly concerned with site attractions that are either natural or built (or in some other way human made). A destination could have a combination of both types of attraction. For example, Chatsworth House is human-made but its grounds (although extensively artificially landscaped) are, in the main, natural. Figure 1.6 gives examples of the types of attractions that fall into the human-made (or built) category and those that would be classed as natural.

Human-made (or built)	Natural
• Stately homes • Cathedrals and abbeys • Ancient monuments • Theme parks • Entertainments (theatres, concert halls, etc.) • Museums • Industrial heritage sites • Holiday centres (e.g. Center Parcs and Butlins Holiday Worlds)	• National parks • Areas of Outstanding Natural Beauty • Beaches • Forests • Lakes • Mountains • Wildlife reserves

Figure 1.6 A classification of attractions

In addition, leisure activities can be categorised as tourist attractions if the leisure activities bring tourists into a particular area. Examples include outdoor pursuits (e.g. Aviemore), shopping (e.g. Covent Garden), health clubs (e.g. Champneys) and sports (e.g. Twickenham rugby ground).

<table>
<tr><td>

Activity

</td><td>

For your own county or region, obtain a map that gives details of the county's or region's attractions (the majority of tourist information centres will have a map showing the attractions for their regions).

Find as many human-made and natural attractions as you can that fall into the categories given above (you may find additional categories of attraction that fit under the two main headings).

Now look at the type of attractions within your county or area. Do they tend to be human-made or natural? Discuss what local factors may have affected this.

Next, consider if there are any types that are missing. Is there scope for this type of attraction to be promoted, or are there barriers to such development?

</td></tr>
</table>

Accommodation and catering

Accommodation can be divided very simply into *serviced* and *self-catering* accommodation. Serviced accommodation will often include some sort of meal arrangement, either bed and breakfast, half board (dinner, bed and breakfast), full board (bed, breakfast, lunch and dinner) or all inclusive (all meals, snacks and drinks). However, within this sector there are examples of where no meals are provided, but what places this type of accommodation within the serviced sector is that it will generally be within a hotel, inn or lodge that offers optional meal arrangements.

Self-catering accommodation does not always include cooking facilities, although there are many examples of cottages, apartments, caravans and chalets that will provide this facility. In Mediterranean resorts, self-catering includes what is known as a 'room-only basis', where rooms can be rented that contain no catering facilities and where visitors must make their own arrangements for meals.

Examples of *serviced accommodation* include the following:

- hotels
- lodges
- inns
- pubs
- guesthouses
- resorts and clubs.

Serviced accommodation will generally be *graded*, and there are different grading systems depending on either the country or the organisation that is providing the grading scheme. An example of this in the UK is the star system, with one star being a small hotel with few facilities and a five-star hotel having considerable amenities, both within the room and the hotel. The English Tourist Board uses the crown system where the accommodation is 'commended' or 'highly commended', which provides an endorsement of the quality within that particular crown banding. It also has a 'listed' category which covers accommodation that has not been graded, either because it is a new property or it has not achieved the requirements for one-crown accommodation.

<table>
<tr><td>

Activity

</td><td>

Obtain from your local tourist information centre lists of the accommodation available in your area. If you can, try to obtain lists that grade the accommodation in some way (e.g. the five star and/or the crown systems).

</td></tr>
</table>

Study the accommodation carefully and try to work out what qualifies particular hotels and/or guesthouses for the grading they have been given. You may also find it useful to study individual hotels and/or guesthouses' advertising material to see what sorts of facilities they offer their customers (such advertisements are sometimes to be found in brochures published by individual resorts and by many towns and cities throughout the country).

Greece uses an A, B and C classification to grade its hotels, with A being the most luxurious and C being the lowest grade. There are also grades awarded by the tour operators themselves, many of whom use their own symbols (for example, Thomson, who use T ratings, and Virgin, who use banana symbols).

Examples of *self-catering accommodation* include:

- cottages
- apartments and studios
- chalets
- boats
- camping
- caravans
- youth hostels.

There are grading systems within self-catering accommodation and, in the UK, this tends to be done through a key system. Self-catering accommodation has increased in popularity recently, especially in destinations such as Greece and Turkey where it is inexpensive to eat out in restaurants. The self-catering option also allows the customers the flexibility to eat when and where they want and, for many holidaymakers, this represents a major factor when deciding on accommodation type.

For families, self-catering has been exceptionally popular, for two reasons. First is the opportunity to receive maximum child discounts by having the whole family in one apartment rather than having to book several rooms in a hotel. The second is again to do with food. Although there are hotels that cater for children in their meal plans, the majority do not offer the type of food children want to eat.

Self-catering accommodation is an important part of the overall hospitality industry, especially in the opportunities it gives to locally owned cafés, bars and restaurants to benefit from the visitors' custom.

Tourism development and promotion

The tourism development and promotion sector within the UK is, currently, government funded and is thus in the public sector of the industry. The 1950s and 1960s saw a rapid growth in tourism within the UK, and the governments of the day recognised the need to set up a framework to regulate this growth. This framework was established through the Development of Tourism Act 1969. This Act had three parts:

1 The setting up of a structure to promote the tourism industry, including the four national tourist boards and the British Tourist Authority (BTA).
2 Providing financial assistance for hotel development through grants and loans. This allowed for construction and improvements to take place to improve the hotel stock and the quality of hotel bedrooms. However, most of this development took place in the London area. This part of the Act was also a short-term project that ended in 1973.
3 The compulsory registration of tourist accommodation. This part of the Act was

never fully implemented. Instead, a voluntary system of grading and classifying accommodation was introduced.

The British Tourist Authority (or BTA – http://www.visitbritain.com/) is the overall organisation with responsibility for promoting incoming tourism to Britain. It operates overseas with the main objective of increasing the number of visitors to the UK and of encouraging them to spend more money while they are here. While promoting London as a major tourist attraction, the BTA is very much involved in persuading visitors to explore less well-known areas of the UK. As the UK is perceived as being a seasonal destination, one of its aims is to encourage people to visit Britain all year round.

The tourism councils and tourist boards

Tourism promotion within the UK is divided into the English, Welsh, Scottish and Northern Ireland areas, with each being funded separately and holding responsibility for setting up tourist boards and information centres.

CASE STUDY: The English Tourism Council

To understand how the tourism industry is organised in one area, we will look at the English Tourism Council (http://www.englishtourism.org.uk/) as an example (see Figure 1.7)

Figure 1.7   The structure of the English Tourism Council (by courtesy of the English Tourism Council)

The English Tourism Council was launched in July 1999, after being renamed from the English Tourist Board. The council has direct reporting responsibilities to the government's Culture Secretary. The English Tourism Council has a relationship with tourist organisations and agencies throughout the country and sees the following five areas as being key to development: technology, policy and strategy, research, public affairs and quality standards.

The regional tourist boards are the link between the tourist boards and the tourist information centres. They will hold responsibility either for very large areas of the country (for example, the West Country Tourist Board) or for a smaller, yet very busy, region (such as the London Tourist Board). Regional tourist boards have responsibility for overseeing the tourist information centres and for ensuring the relevant publicity materials are distributed within the region. They have objectives for their particular areas and produce a guide that promotes the region as a whole to encourage tourists to spend as much time as possible there.

Activity	Find out which regional tourist board covers your particular area. Look at the counties that are included within this region and the attractions *you* think should be promoted to encourage a wide range of tourists to visit your region. Next, obtain your regional tourist board's guide and compare your own notes with what is being promoted. Discuss what types of attractions are in the guide and why these have been identified as being important to your region (for example, what types of tourist they are trying to attract). From your own notes, are there any attractions you consider are missing from the guide?

With thanks to Canterbury City Council and Canterbury Tourist Information Centre.

Tourist information centres

Tourist information centres (TICs) are located throughout the UK in places such as town centres, railway stations, airports, ports, town halls, libraries and major tourist destinations. They provide information that covers up to a 50-mile radius of the centre. Most of the TICs are funded by local borough councils and they receive support from the tourism councils in the form of signs, literature, books and staff uniforms. TICs make money in three different ways:

1   A bed booking service. They make 10% commission through selling accommodation either locally or through the 'Book a bed ahead' service, which allows people to book accommodation at other locations.
2   Through the sale of goods and services within the TIC, which will include maps, books and souvenirs. Many TICs also sell sightseeing excursions and tickets for events, including concerts and plays.
3   Promoting guided tours and walks, some of which are free of charge but many of which are sold on a commission basis by the TIC staff.

Because of the nature of this type of work, staff within TICs tend to speak more than one language. Many TICs also offer guiding services, and these are often provided by volunteers who have an interest in the local area's architecture or history.

Tourism development overseas

The type of tourism development initiatives found in different countries will depend on the system of government within a particular country, alongside that particular country's reliance on tourism as an industry. In a country such as the USA, tourism development tends to be privately funded by the major tourism companies. This means that sectors of the industry (such as accommodation, transport, tour operators and attractions) fund the promotion of tourism to a particular area. In some areas, promotion is very much centred on one small part of the country or a specific destination as the stakeholders prefer to promote tourism to their own regions rather than to the whole of the USA.

On the other hand, if we look at an example of where the state has more control (such as in Russia), we find the government has more say over policy-making and planning. Many tourism facilities will be state run (e.g. hotels, transport, package tours and sightseeing). If a country is very dependent on tourism (such as Spain) it will usually have a minister of state responsible for tourism to ensure tourism issues are discussed at parliamentary level.

Transportation

Transport plays a very important part in the travel and tourism industry. Without the ability to get to a destination easily, there would be limited opportunity for travel and tourism, as an activity, to happen. When considering transport it is important to bear in mind the following points:

*   Generally, transport provides the means of travel to the destination and back again, which will usually be at the beginning and the end of the holiday or trip.
*   Transport can be the means of travelling around the destination, either on organised excursions or through the traveller finding his or her own way around the area.
*   It could be the main feature of the trip (for example, a cruise ship, the Orient Express or a coach tour).

Travel can be further split into the following different modes of transport:

*   air
*   sea and river
*   rail
*   road.

Air travel

Air travel can be divided into *scheduled* or *chartered* flights.

Scheduled flights operate to a published timetable, and the fares that are quoted by scheduled air companies will have been agreed with the IATA (International Air Transport Association). Very often, the scheduled airlines are known as the flag carrier of a particular county (for example, British Airways, Swissair or Lufthansa). They will offer more than one class of travel to accommodate business and leisure travellers and will include meals and drinks within the cost of the fare. More recently, several low-cost airlines have set themselves up as offering a 'no frills' service that is still scheduled but that frequently cuts the fares charged by the traditional airlines. These companies usually fly out of less popular airports such as Luton and Stansted, have one class of travel and charge for such services as food and drink. Examples of these types of company are Ryanair, Go (owned by British Airways) and Easyjet.

Chartered travel is different as it does not operate to a published timetable and the flight might operate once a week and for certain weeks of the year only. Chartered flights are offered by a company that either owns the aircraft or that makes a block booking of seats on a plane, usually through a tour operator. The tour operator might publish a price but this could be affected by the date the passenger actually travels (for example, it could be reduced nearer the date of departure if there were many unsold seats). Examples of charter companies are Britannia, Air 2000 and Monarch. Some of these charter companies have attempted to offer a scheduled service alongside the charter product, but this has not been too successful. Charter companies usually offer one class of travel and, although a meal will be included in the price, drinks tend to be extra.

Sea and river travel

Sea and river travel includes ferry journeys, mainline voyages and cruises. *Ferry travel* has become extremely popular with the increase in car ownership and because of people's desire to have the flexibility of their car while on holiday. There are now ferry ships that resemble cruisers with their high levels of comfort and, on some of the longer routes, the facilities offered include swimming pools, gyms, cinemas, discos and numerous bars and restaurants. Newer forms of transport (such as hovercraft, hydrofoils and high-speed catamarans) have reduced the journey times on some of the routes, and faster loading and unloading systems have cut down waiting times for car travellers. Until the abolition of duty free to EU destinations, very cheap rates were offered to foot passengers, and there were many promotional offers of fares of £1.00 return. Even though ferry companies still sell cut-price tobacco and alcohol, ticket prices have been forced up to compensate for this loss of duty-free revenue. Examples of ferry companies include P & O Stena Line, Hoverspeed, Seafrance and Brittany Ferries.

Mainline voyages on *ocean liners* have declined over the last fifty years, having been affected by the competition of increased and cheaper air travel. The ships have become old and outdated with expensive operating costs. There are, however, still examples of successful mainline voyages. The *QE2* service between Southampton and New York operates regularly, with cruises sometimes added in between the voyages. Some of the cargo shipping companies will book cabins on their routes to fare-paying passengers, but the facilities offered onboard cargo ships are very limited as the ships were not designed for passenger travel.

<table>
<tr><td>Activity</td><td>Use the Internet to find information about what the ocean cruise liner companies offer to customers:

1 What sorts of facilities do they offer their customers onboard the ship?
2 How do you think these facilities compare with similar facilities offered by top-class hotels?
3 What sort of client do you think the cruise liner companies are trying to attract?

You could use the following websites.

• http://www.atlantistravel.co.uk/
• http://www.POSL.com (P & O Stena Ferries)
• http://www.qe2.org.uk/ (for details of what is on offer aboard the QE2).</td></tr>
</table>

There are three types of *cruise*: traditional ex-UK cruises, fly cruises and river cruises. Ex-UK cruises will visit such areas as Scandinavia, the Atlantic regions of the Canary Islands, Africa and Portugal or the Mediterranean. Fly cruises can either consist of flying to and from the point at which the cruise starts, or flying one way, either outbound or return and cruising the other way. Areas that have proved very popular for fly cruises are the Caribbean and Mediterranean. However, there are itineraries that include the Far East, Alaska and the Indian Ocean.

River cruises can be supported by air, road or rail travel. Two of the most popular rivers to cruise are the Rhine and the Nile. Cruising has seen considerable changes since the mid-1970s and is now the fastest growing sector of the travel industry. The cruise market in the UK between 1990 and 1995 grew by 88% to 352,179 passengers. Since 1995, these changes have been made even more evident with both Thomson and Airtours launching their own cruise programmes. This has made the cruise product more accessible to the mass market through price, the layout of the brochure and the way in which the product is sold.

This new business has also had a positive impact on the more traditional cruise companies as, once people have taken a cruise, they tend to repeat book on that type of holiday. Many move up to the next category of price and ship rather than travelling on the same ship next time. There are now some exceptionally large cruise companies, including names such as P & O, Princess, Royal Caribbean, Carnival and Festival.

Rail travel

The first half of the twentieth century was the heyday for rail travel as there were very few cars and rail services were quick and frequent. Most European travel took place by rail, and ski resorts and tourist cities were serviced by a good train network. The UK nationalised its rail service in 1947 and, since the 1950s, train services have been reduced considerably with many branch lines to villages having been closed down.

There are now many privately owned rail companies within the UK, including Virgin, GNER and Thames Trains. Within this category of travel it is also appropriate to include the Eurostar and the Shuttle channel tunnel services, which take passengers and vehicles under the English Channel in approximately thirty minutes.

Coach travel

Coach travel within the UK was once a nationalised industry with one main company, the National Bus Company, dominating the main routes and local bus companies controlling services within our towns and cities. However, all that changed with the Transport Acts of 1980 and 1985, which brought about deregulation to the coach and bus industry. Following deregulation, regional companies formed British Coachways to compete with National, and low prices were introduced as a result of the increased competition. New companies were formed and a wider range of services were offered.

The coach touring market is still important for incoming tourists to the UK who want a reasonably priced touring or tour and stay holiday, and also for UK tourists who want low-cost holidays to France, Spain and northern Italy. If you broke down long-distance coach travellers by age, half would be in the under 35 years of age category and the other half would probably be 55 years of age or older. The reason why older citizens enjoy coach travel is because of the low prices, door-to-door travel when touring, no baggage or transfer problems and the couriers, who provide a service throughout the holiday.

Travel agents

The travel agency is the retail part of the industry equation. All travel agencies in the UK are within the profit-making (or private) sector. Travel agents have three main responsibilities:

1. selling travel products to the consumer
2. providing advice about a range of products, destinations and modes of travel
3. promoting products through brochure racking, late offers and advertising.

Travel agents differ from tour operators in that they do not usually package the different travel products together but act as an intermediary between the operators and the public. Although a package tour brochure will offer a price for a holiday, it is now customary for travel agents to discount these prices by offering either a percentage reduction, free insurance or additional benefits (such as a taxi to the airport).

Activity	What does a typical travel agent sell? Have a look in your local agencies to obtain a feel for what they sell. The following list should give you an idea of the range of products on offer:

- Tour operators' packaged products
- Independent tours or travel
- Air tickets
- Cruises
- Ferry tickets
- Rail and Eurostar tickets
- Coach travel
- Car hire
- Insurance
- Hotels and accommodation
- Theatre bookings and tickets for other events
- Travellers cheques
- Currency
- Guide books and maps
- A passport and visa processing service
- Airport car parking
- Sightseeing and excursions

As you can imagine, offering all these services means travel agency staff must have considerable training and knowledge. There are, however, agencies that do not offer this full range of services but instead focus on one product such as package holidays (which make up 80–85% of what most agencies sell). This allows staff to specialise in selling one particular type of product and, hence, to maximise the profit made. Travel agencies are paid a commission for selling a company's product, which can range from 10 to 15% for package holidays up to 35% for car hire and 40% and over for insurance. Because the travel agent's main role is selling, travel agencies tend to be located in high streets.

There are basically four different types of travel agency:

1 *Multinationals* Travel agencies that are represented in many different countries. They will usually have offices worldwide and, for the staff, this can offer the chance to work overseas and to progress in their careers on an international basis. American Express and Thomas Cook are both examples of multinational organisations.

2 *Multiples* These are national companies that have branches throughout the UK. They are very often part of a much larger organisation that might not be a travel company. Examples of multiples are Lunn Poly and Going Places.

3 *Miniples* These are agencies that normally have more than six branches but that are still small or medium-sized enterprises. They are very often based in a particular region and, for this reason, are very vulnerable to takeover by larger companies that want outlets in that particular area.

4 *Independent travel agencies* These are often a single retail unit but could be a small organisation with up to six agencies. These types of agencies often specialise in destinations or products or will simply excel through the customer service they provide. While independents can be located in high-street locations, they are often found in suburbs or villages.

(*Note*: It is very difficult to give examples of miniples and independent travel agencies as their names tend to vary in different parts of the country.)

Activity	In your local *Thomson Directory* or *Yellow Pages*, look up the entry for travel agencies. Once you have done this, divide them into four headings: multinationals, multiples, miniples and independent companies.

While we have focused on retail travel agencies that deal with the public, there are two other types of agency we need to consider: *telesales* and *business travel companies*.

Telesales

The telesales area has seen considerable growth recently. People very often do not have the time during the day to visit a travel agency. By contacting telesales companies in the evening or weekend, they can make their reservation without leaving their home or office. Telesales companies often offer good discounts as many telesales companies are owned by multiple or multinational companies (for example, Thomas Cook Direct).

Business travel companies

Business travel companies are also often part of a multinational (such as Thomas

Cook or American Express), although they may also be well established independent companies. Some companies specialise in this type of business (e.g. Hogg Robinson, Portman, Uniglobe and The Travel Company). Unlike retail agencies, business travel agencies do not need to have a high profile in the high street; they are usually located in out-of-town locations or in business parks, where the rent will be lower. When business travel organisations hold large company accounts they will often set up their own office within a particular company, which is known as an *implant*.

Business travel agents tend to be allocated specific clients so they can develop a link with that company and can offer a service that meets the needs of its business travellers. They can offer the same range of products as a retail agent but their main business is transport (air, rail and car hire) and accommodation. Many products are high value, and there can be a steady flow of business throughout the year instead of at the peak months when the retail agencies are busy.

Business travel agencies offer a 24-hour service to cater for last-minute travel arrangements. They often deliver documentation to the company through their own courier service and many have VIP services, such as lounges and airport services.

Tour operators

A tour operator is a company that creates a holiday by negotiating contracts with airlines, accommodation providers, coach companies and attractions, and then packaging these products together into the holiday. This holiday is then priced and will appear in a brochure. If a customer wants to book a holiday that is not in a brochure, for example for a different duration, flight or hotel, this can be organised by a department within the tour operator called the 'tailor-made' department. This department will put together an individual package for the customer and then quote a price for the holiday. The customer benefits from the bulk buying rates of the tour operator and the ease of having someone else making the bookings and calculating the costs.

Brochures are often produced one to two years in advance and so the information within them is constantly being changing and updated. The tour operator has a responsibility to inform the travel agent and the customer about these changes.

The tour operator accepts the reservation from a travel agent on behalf of the customer and will send confirmations and invoices to the travel agent. The tour operator does not usually have contact with the customers until they arrive at their destination, although some companies like Panorama have a representative who will travel on the flight with the customers to ensure customer service is provided throughout the holiday.

Just as there are different types of travel agent, there are also different types of tour operator (see Figure 1.8).

Mass market tour operators

These are the main tour operators and are household names, such as Thomson, Airtours and First Choice. Between them, these companies carry the majority of the leisure travel market. They are able to compete with each other on price because they can negotiate lower contract rates as a result of the numbers of people they take to a destination. These companies tend to dictate what happens within the industry.

They own their own airlines and many also have their own cruise ships and accommodation. (The next section on integration gives examples of how these companies are linked with travel agencies.)

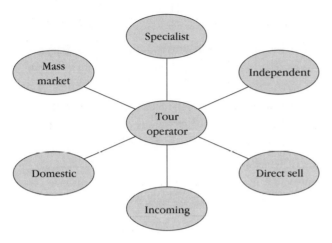

Figure 1.8   Types of tour operator

Specialist tour operators

These companies sell products that are very specialist, either in the geographical area they cover, the activities they offer or in their target customers. Geographical area could mean offering holidays to one particular destination (for example, Balkan specialise in holidays to Bulgaria). Specialist operators such as HF Walking Holidays focus on activity holidays and Club 18–30 gears its products at a specific age range.

Independent tour operators

This category is becoming smaller each year as more of the larger, mass-market companies take over the independent ones. Independents can be either large-scale companies, such as Cosmos and Kuoni, or much smaller, such as Travel 2.

The British National Travel Survey is published on the British Tourist Authority website. The survey of 1997 showed that 27.25 million holidays of four nights or more were taken overseas, with an average cost of £611. Individual tour operators publish details of tourists who travel with their companies in their annual reports and in the trade papers, such as the *Travel Trade Gazette (TTG)*.

In the twelve-month period to March 2000, ten tour operators controlled 59% of the overseas market, and this figure is dominated by the top four companies who carried 46% of the licensed capacity from the Civil Aviation Authority.

Position	Tour operator	Licensed capacity	% of total	% change on March 1999
1	Thomson	4,172,570	16	−6
2	Airtours	3,106,646	12	+5
3	JMC Holidays	2,915,009	11	+5
4	First Choice	1,895,469	7	−4

Source: Consumer Protection Group, CAA

Figure 1.9   The top 4 tour operators

Companies such as Travel 2 carried far fewer passengers: 176,104 in the 12 months to March 2000.

Domestic tour operators

These tour operators offer holidays or tours purely within the boundaries of their own country. In the case of the UK, this includes coach tour companies (e.g. Wallace Arnold), holiday centres (e.g. Butlins and Haven Warner), boat operators (e.g. Blakes), holiday cottages (e.g. Hoseasons) and short break companies (e.g. Superbreak).

Very often there is no transport element to this type of holiday, as people will make use of their own cars to get them to and from their destination. Bookings for domestic products are rarely done through travel agencies, as customers tend to contact the company direct.

Incoming tour operators

Incoming tour operators are companies that specialise in packages for overseas visitors who want to prebook their travel and accommodation within the UK. These operators frequently offer coach tours, although rail travel is also available. Accommodation is often prebooked by visitors, especially if they are coming at a very popular time (for example, the Edinburgh Festival).

Some of the brochures are priced in US dollars to enable US and Far East customers to calculate the costs more easily. One company that deals purely with incoming visitors is Insight International, although others (such as Kuoni) also have an outbound product as well.

Direct sell operators

These can be either part of a large organisation such as Portland (part of Thomson) and Eclipse (part of First Choice), or an independent tour operator. Many of these companies advertise on Teletext and in the Sunday papers as retail travel agencies do not represent them. The prices offered by direct sell operators can be low but, as some of these companies may not be members of an organisation such as ABTA, the customers' money could be at risk.

Integration between tour operators and travel agencies

As you will have realised by now, the UK travel and tourism industry consists mainly of extremely large organisations that own a number of smaller companies. Over the years, companies have combined one with another to form even larger companies. This has lead to the 'integration' of the industry (i.e. through amalgamations and takeovers, what are seemingly separate organisations are in fact integrated under a common ownership). Integration can take either a *vertical* or *horizontal* form.

Vertical integration

Vertical integration is where the holiday company (the main company) owns some or all the links *down* the buying chain (for example, airlines, accommodation, tour operators and travel agencies). Vertical integration maximises profits. By owning a range of organisations throughout the buying chain, the holiday company can retain a high percentage of the profit made. There are also other benefits of vertical integration – from both a marketing and customer service point of view. A company can ensure its brand name is visible at all stages of the holiday, from the brochure to the point at which a booking is made, carrying this through to the airline and then completed with the staff based in the resort. From a customer service point of view, the company can also set service standards that apply to all aspects of the customer experience, and so have greater control over these aspects.

An example of a vertically integrated company is shown in Figure 1.10 (similar structures link Thomson with Lunn Poly, JMC with Thomas Cook, and First Choice with Travel Choice and Bakers Dolphin).

Figure 1.10   A vertically integrated company: Airtours

Horizontal integration

Companies can also be horizontally integrated in that they have bought up companies *across* their own particular sector of the industry. This has happened to some extent in the travel agency sector although, generally, the companies that have been purchased change their names to the purchasing company's name (for example, when Thomas Cook bought AT Mays, the new branches were renamed Thomas Cook).

More recently, there have been instances where the buying organisation has retained the names of the companies it has acquired. For example, when First Choice purchased the Bakers Dolphin chain in the south west of England, the original Bakers Dolphin name was retained. This meant a town could have at least two travel agencies with each having a different name. This could potentially increase the number of sales made by the two agencies as customers perceive them as being different companies.

However, most horizontal integration has been in the tour operations sector. In the last few years, many of the smaller tour operators have been bought by larger tour operators who want to build up the range of products they offer. They want to gain a hold on as much of the travelling public as possible by offering a wide variety of travel companies and holiday types. A good example is the Thomson model.

Activity	The following are just *some* of the tour operators that form part of the Thomson group:
	Thomson Holidays; Portland Holidays; Magic Travel Group; Simply Travel; Skytours; Blakes; Crystal; Jetsave; Jersey Travel Service; Austravel.
	Each company offers a number of different products. Collect a sample of the brochures produced by the companies in this list and, after studying these, answer the following questions:
	1 What sort of holidays do the different companies offer?
	2 Can you identify the particular market segment each company is trying to attract?

There have been investigations by the Monopolies and Mergers Commission into the types of integrated organisations that now exist within the UK travel and tourism industry. The concerns raised are about consumer awareness of the ownership of the products they are buying, and the way in which travel agencies within a vertically integrated structure promote their own company's tour operator products rather than offering an impartial and unbiased service. As a result of these investigations, travel agencies that are vertically integrated must now display in a prominent place details of who owns them.

Differences between commercial and non-commercial organisations

Non-commercial organisations like the tourist boards, The National Trust and London Zoo do not have 'profits' but usually aim to operate with a 'surplus'.

In *commercial* organisations, the organisation's objectives will have been set by the owner or, in the case of large organisations, through the board of directors. The types of business objectives a commercial organisation might have include the following:

- profit or sales targets
- customer service targets
- expansion or developmental plans.

In a non-commercial organisation, the objectives will depend on whether the organisation is in the public or voluntary sector. In the case of public sector organisations, objectives will probably first be set by the government and then by regional offices (or possibly by local councils). Many voluntary organisations have structures similar to those of private sector organisations and, indeed, decision-making often takes the same form as in private sector companies.

Objectives could relate to a specific project or a group of projects and may focus on a common interest or target. Objectives for non-commercial organisations could include:

- securing grants or donations
- ensuring the interests of members are achieved
- obtaining sponsorship deals
- raising public awareness about a project.

Funding or revenue generation is the key difference: the commercial sector is reliant on sales of products and services to make a profit. This means commercial organisations have to be very aware of the profitability of what is sold and must increase sales of those things that generate a higher profit. If you think back to the earlier section on integration you will see that by keeping sales within one organisation profits are maximised, and there is no need to pay commission to competitors.

In the non-commercial sector, the need to maintain costs within the level of funding available can determine how successful an organisation is. Once the money from grants or donations has been allocated (unless alternative funding methods are identified), it is unlikely an organisation will be able to generate additional funding. Occasionally, however, fund-raising activities or sponsorship might raise money to help with cash flow or to fund specific events or activities.

The owners or stakeholders of commercial and non-commercial organisations will have different expectations of how funding or profits are put to use. In the commercial sector, when a shareholder has invested money in a company, he or she expects to see a return on that investment, either in an annual return or in an increase in the value of the shares. In the non-commercial sector, the stakeholders expect to see that the interests of a group of people are being met, and that their money is being used appropriately. They do not expect to see a return on the money put into the organisation. Where a surplus is made, they would expect to see that money being used for reinvestment in the organisation or for its members.

Activity	Select two organisations: one from the commercial sector and the other from the non-commercial sector. Identify the differences between these two organisations, especially their objectives and funding. Where possible, arrange to interview a manager from each organisation so you can illustrate your findings. Prepare a verbal presentation to be given to the rest of your group.

Chapter 1.5 Scale of the UK travel and tourism industry

The travel and tourism industry is constantly changing, and any statistics tend to be at least two years old by the time they are actually published. For this reason, it is always recommended you use the most up-to-date information available. Any figures given here were the most up to date at the time of publication. A really useful source of information is the website for the British Tourist Authority (http://www.visitbritain.com/), which contains the major tourism facts and figures about Britain.

UK travel and tourism revenue

According to British Tourist Authority statistics, 25.7 million overseas visitors came to Britain in 1998 and these visitors spent more than £12 billion. They also estimate that, by the year 2003, this spend figure will have risen to £18 billion, which is a rise of more than 44%. The spend from domestic tourists is even higher at over £14 billion, taking the total spend on tourism in 1998 to £26.7 billion.

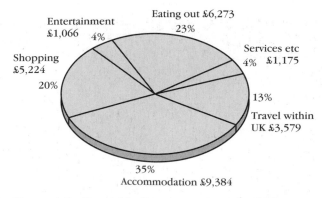

Figure 1.11   Tourist spending in the UK, 1998 (£ million) (information supplied courtesy of BTA)

It is interesting to look at what this money was spent on and Figure 1.11 identifies tourist spending broken down into different products.

By now you will probably appreciate the importance of the hotel and catering industry to the overall travel and tourism product in the UK. Notice also how shopping benefits from tourism. While there will be naturally a big spend on souvenirs, other retail outlets also benefit from tourists.

The spend on additional services is fairly low at 4%, but other services will receive income from the hotel and catering industry (for example, goods and services bought in by the accommodation sector, such as laundry and food and drink, etc.).

Employment statistics

Tourism in Britain supports around 1.7 million jobs and is one of the fastest-growing industries. Currently, one in every five new jobs created is within the tourism industry. Because much of the employment will not be directly within the tourism sector itself, but indirectly supported by the tourism sector (e.g. people who work in restaurants, bars, shops, etc., in tourist destinations), it is very difficult to get hold of exact statistics relating to employment.

If we consider the times of the year when tourists visit the UK, we will start to realise why much tourism employment is seasonal and why cash flow within the industry is such a big issue (see Figure 1.12).

Month of trip	UK residents' trips (%)	Overseas visits (%)
January	6	6
February	7	5
March	7	7
April	9	9
May	9	9
June	7	8
July	9	11
August	12	12
September	7	9
October	8	9
November	7	7
December	11	8

Figure 1.12   Tourist trips in the UK, 1998 (information supplied courtesy of BTA)

Incoming tourist numbers to the UK

Earlier we noted that the number of incoming tourists to the UK in 1998 was 25.7 million. It is also interesting to look not just at current statistics but also at the trends that have occurred in the last ten or so years (see Figure 1.13).

Year	Visitors (millions)	Nights' stay (millions)	Spending (£ million)
1988	15.8	173	6,184
1989	17.3	187	6,945
1990	18.0	196	7,748
1991	17.1	186	7,386
1992	18.5	186	7,891
1993	19.9	190	9,487
1994	20.8	192	9,786
1995	23.5	220	11,763
1996	25.2	220	12,290
1997	25.5	223	12,244
1998	25.7	231	12,671

Figure 1.13   Overseas visitors to the UK, 1988–98 (information supplied courtesy of BTA)

What is encouraging for British tourism is that the increases are steady and consistent, year upon year. There was a slight decrease in numbers and spend in 1991 due to the Gulf War, and it is often necessary to look for any reasons in the UK or worldwide that may have caused a drop in one particular year.

It is also useful to know where the tourists come from. The top-ten countries for visitors to the UK are listed in Figure 1.14.

Country of origin	Visitors (thousands)	Spending (£ million)
USA	3,880	2,482
France	3,274	750
Germany	2,830	882
Irish Republic	2,310	824
The Netherlands	1,718	407
Belgium	1,183	225
Italy	1,090	555
Spain	900	396
Sweden	676	310
Canada	673	319

Figure 1.14   Numbers of visitors to the UK in 1998 by country (information supplied courtesy of BTA)

What is interesting from these figures is that France (the country that supplies the second highest number of visitors to the UK) has a low figure for spending. There are many factors that affect spending and, in the example of French visitors, length of stay in the UK may be a major determinant in the amount of money spent.

Statistics are also collected by the World Tourism Organisation (WTO – http://www.world-tourism.org/), which releases figures concerning incoming tourist numbers for each year for each country. The organisation also identifies the percentage growth or decline for a particular year and highlight any factors that may have influenced this trend (for example, sporting events or business activity). The WTO also comments on travel trends generally, and whether travel as a worldwide activity is increasing. It also makes a prediction for the year to come (for example, it predicted a growth in tourism of between 4 and 5% worldwide by the end of the year 2000).

Travel statistics for UK residents (domestic and outgoing tourists)

The 122 million UK domestic tourist trips made by residents of the UK contribute around £14 billion to the economy (this figure is for UK residents who stay overnight). There is also a considerable amount of day-trip traffic that contributes over £31 billion to the economy. The majority of these trips will be for holiday purposes (65.1 million), with visiting friends and relatives accounting for 38.4 million trips. UK domestic trips for business purposes account for 13.7 million trips, with other purposes making up 5.1 million.

Figure 1.15 shows figures for the distribution of tourist trips by tourist board regions for 1998.

Tourist board region	Trips (millions)	Spending (£ million)
Cumbria	2.9	380
Northumbria	4.2	340
North West	8.4	970
Yorkshire	9.2	940
Heart of England	16.8	1,160
East of England	13.0	1,290
London	11.6	1,055
Southern	10.9	1,245
South East	10.5	825
N. Ireland	0.8	200
Scotland	9.8	1,540
Wales	9.8	1,100

Figure 1.15   UK tourist trips by tourist board regions, 1998 (information supplied courtesy of BTA)

Activity	Using the statistics in Figure 1.15, try to answer the following questions:
	1 What could influence these statistics?
	2 What is likely to affect visitor numbers and spend in these areas?
	3 Do high numbers of visitors mean high spend figures?
	4 What could some of the areas do to improve on their statistics?

Chapter 1.6 Working in the travel and tourism industry

The travel and tourism industry has a wide range of different employment opportunities for people who have the right skills, knowledge and personal qualities.

The range of employment opportunities

You will realise by now that there are many different sectors within the travel and tourism industry, each of which offers a wide range of job opportunities. It is a good idea at this stage to look at all the employment possibilities available.

Activity	To get an overall idea of what employment possibilities there are in the travel and tourism industry, think through the process of selecting, booking and going on a holiday. In pairs, go through each stage and write down all the workers you will be involved with in all the stages of your holiday. Remember that some people might not have direct contact with you (for example, the people who put together the brochure and the contractors who negotiate the rates for the hotel room or the airline seat).
	Once you have produced your list, compare yours with those of the rest of your group.
	You might already have some idea of the types of job you would like to do – but are there any additional possibilities you might have identified through this exercise?

Now we have looked at possible jobs we need to consider the nature of some of this employment.

Working hours

Employment in travel and tourism can be on a full-time basis (for example, working in a retail or business travel agency, a tourist information centre or for the reservations department of an airline or tour operator). However, while the hours worked each week will be set, these hours may not be on a nine-to-five, Monday-to-Friday basis. Most organisations in travel and tourism also employ part-time staff, particularly to cover their busiest times (for example, lunchtimes or Saturdays). This is one way many women who have left the industry to start a family often return to work. Also, the hours when travel agencies tend to be busiest fit in well with the hours when children are at school.

Employment basis

While much travel work in the UK is on a permanent basis, overseas work tends to be temporary, covering the length of the holiday season sold by the tour operator. Most overseas representatives start off by signing up for a summer season and are then given the option to work either the first or second half of the winter season. This can mean staying in the same resort or moving to different areas or products, such as winter sun or ski destinations. Quite often, the following jobs are temporary: airline crew, tourist attraction staff, holiday camp employees, guides or event workers.

We also refer to this type of work as being *seasonal* – it fits the main tourist seasons.

The nature of employment

Many workers in the travel and tourism industry work anti-social hours. While often considered one of the more glamorous sectors of the industry, working for an airline requires staff to work on a roster system. This means very early starts, late finishes and night flights. While a flight might depart at 0630, the crew would need to be at the airport much earlier than that and, as check-in would probably open at 0400, staff would need to be available very early in the morning to start this process. Frequently flights are delayed and, when this happens, it is obviously not possible for staff to finish work at the agreed time. This type of work usually involves long hours and times of working that change on a daily basis. If you think this lifestyle would suit you, it would mean you are off work when many people are working, and this can bring flexibility to your working and leisure time.

The industry is very much a people-centred one, and the majority of organisations have customer service as one of their key objectives. People going into the industry need to ensure they really like working with people, and they must have a genuine desire to make the experience an enjoyable and memorable one for the customers. There is now so much competition in the travel and tourism industry it is very difficult to maintain customer loyalty. In many of these jobs you will be permanently on display to the public, and will need to give a positive impression of yourself and of your organisation. This is not just in your outward appearance and smartness but also in the actions you take and in the way you

communicate with the public, other members of staff and suppliers.

With thanks to Canterbury City Council and Canterbury Tourist Information Centre.

Personal and technical skills and qualities required by employers

Think of a really good experience you had as a customer and you will start to realise what personal skills are essential for the people who work in the travel and tourism industry. The following are some of the personality traits that could be useful for someone working in travel and tourism:

- flexibility
- sense of humour
- good communication skills
- common sense
- being well organised
- smart appearance
- patience
- team worker, or being able to work independently.

Other personal qualities will be required, depending on the particular job (for example, the last item in the list would depend on your working environment). If you were working as part of a cabin crew team or in a retail travel agency, teamwork would be essential. If, however, you were working as a chalet staff member or as a guide, you would be very much working alone. One personal quality you might not be able to do much about is your age, height or weight. It is worth while finding out now if there is anything that could restrict you from going into a particular career, such as a minimum or maximum height restriction.

Technical skills may be something you already possess or could be an area for you to develop in the future or while you are working. Again, the technical skills required will depend on the type of career you wish to pursue, but could include:

- being computer literate or able to use specific reservation systems
- air fares and ticketing skills, including qualifications like BA I and II
- language skills
- selling skills
- experience of handling money and foreign currencies
- a driving licence
- a first aid certificate
- travel and tourism geography knowledge

You are unlikely to have all these skills at this time. However, by looking at these lists now you can start to consider what skills you currently have and how you can develop your skills further. Some of the technical skills can be developed through attending specialised courses or training programmes. One example of this is the NVQ (National Vocational Qualification) offered at Levels 2 and 3 in Travel Services or Tour Operations.

There are many travel agencies that offer apprenticeships that incorporate an NVQ as part of the training scheme, giving you the opportunity to develop your skills in geography, selling and product knowledge for the industry. Air fares and ticketing courses are often offered by colleges and might form part of the course you are currently taking; alternatively, these courses can be studied by distance learning.

How to find jobs in travel and tourism

There are many specialist sources of help, but your first port of call should be your local careers office, many of which have information about training courses and general information relating to careers in travel and tourism.

ABTA will be able to give you further information about careers in the travel sector, including companies that offer NVQ training programmes. They produce a very good guide that can be purchased through the Travel Training Company (The Cornerstone, The Broadway, Woking, Surrey GU21 5AR – http://www.tttc.co.uk). This will give you a general idea about such job areas as resort representatives, tour operators, travel agents, airlines, tourism, guides and tour managers.

The English Tourism Council and the Scottish, Welsh and Northern Ireland Tourist Boards will be able to supply you with information about working in the tourism sector generally. However, for more specific information, try contacting the companies or organisations that own or run tourist events, attractions or museums, etc.

If you already have a clear idea about the type of employment you would like, the best course of action is to contact companies directly for information. Many organisations (such as airlines, tour operators or travel agents) have an information pack they send out to potential employees, explaining job roles, availability, recruitment processes and the personal and technical skills and qualities required. Make sure you contact either the head office or the human resources office of large organisations as it is unlikely this information will be held at local branch offices.

The most up-to-date source of employment vacancies is the travel trade press, the two main papers being *TTG* (*Travel Trade Gazette*) and *Travel Weekly*. A whole range of jobs is usually advertised at the back of both papers. You might find these journals in your college or local library. However, as these papers are purchased on a subscription basis only, it is not possible to buy them from a newsagent. Your local newspapers will often advertise specific jobs available in your area, and national newspapers will often carry advertisements concerning the large recruitment drives of the major airlines and tour operators.

The other source of information is the people who already work in the industry. If you take part in work experience, this is a good opportunity to speak to people about how they started in the industry and about the types of jobs they have done. There are now many specialised employment agencies for the travel and tourism industry and, while they deal mainly with people who are currently working in travel and tourism, they do occasionally handle vacancies suitable for people who are just starting out in their careers. It may be that your nearest agency

is in a large city but agencies are quite happy to deal with initial enquiries over the telephone.

Occasionally you will come across recruitment organisations advertising for cabin crew or for vacancies aboard cruise ships. Take care when dealing with such organisations as very often they will charge you for the service they are offering and, sometimes, will not supply you with much information that is of value. Most airlines run their own recruitment campaigns and will train you specifically in the working practices of their own particular companies and fleets.

Activity	Before moving on to the next chapter, you need to ask yourself the following questions:
	1 What are my personal strengths and weaknesses, and what are my interests?
	2 What sectors of the industry could I feasibly work in?
	3 What job opportunities exist – in both the short and long term?
	4 How can I improve my employment prospects?
	Some of these questions you will be able to answer through self-reflection; others will require you to research jobs that interest you to find out what you need to do or achieve to become eligible for such work.

Chapter 1.7 Pursuing your own career aims

How to plan your own career development

The answers to the questions you have just asked yourself should form the basis of the work you do for this section of the course. Now you have an idea of the job opportunities available, start to map them out in the following way:

- Which jobs would you be eligible for on completition of your Advanced Certificate in Travel and Tourism?
- Which jobs require further training or the devclopment of your skills/qualities (including your age)?
- What would you like to be doing in ten years' time? (This question is important as you need to consider what you would like to be doing in the long term.)

For example, you might want to work as an overseas representative, but this type of work has a minimum age requirement of 21. What you could do in the meantime is work for a tour operator in the UK in reservations or administration, work for a travel agency or as a hotel receptionist or work at a UK holiday centre. Alternatively, you could undertake a further course of training (e.g. a CACHE Certificate or Diploma or an NVQ in Early Years Care that would qualify you as a nursery nurse and that would mean you would be eligible to be a children's representative when you reached the age of 19. This could then lead on to you becoming an overseas representative).

It is also likely there will be some aspects of your personal skills you need to develop to ensure you meet the criteria for a

Jobs in travel and tourism cover a wide spectrum. Leading guitarist Stuart McCallum developed his career as a professional musician by playing to tourists on a cruise ship.

specific career. This could involve you taking up a foreign language or improving on your current language skills. Alternatively, you might be able to develop your skills by obtaining (or changing) any part-time work you do (for example, in order to demonstrate your abilities to work in a team or as a salesperson). In some cases, your development might be very much a personal issue (for example, losing weight or improving your level of fitness to increase your stamina).

Activity	Identify two jobs in the travel and tourism industry that you would like to go into when you leave school or college. Then consider where this job could take you, and what your second job in the industry might be. For example, you might decide that your first job will be a retail travel agent, and your second job an overseas representative. Now discuss in pairs what skills and qualities will be required for each job you have chosen and enter these on the grid.

First job in travel and tourism: 1 2	Skills and qualities

Second job in travel and tourism: 1 2	Skills and qualities

Whatever career you have in mind, it is important you find out as much as you can about what it entails *now*.

Employment, training and educational opportunities and obtaining the right information and advice

Do not narrow down your options to one single thing – look at a range of employment, training and educational opportunities. Consider *all* the alternatives: it may be that, to achieve your long-term goal, you cannot rely purely on experience alone – you may need to obtain a degree or an HND in a related subject.

If you haven't already done so, organise a careers interview. As a result of this interview, you will be given further information and an action plan to help you plan your career. You will also probably find it useful to talk to your travel and tourism tutors at this stage as they will be able to give you additional advice about what your options are.

If training programmes are an important part of your action plan, find out *now* what will be involved and how to apply for the training. Some training programmes are very popular and there is strong competition for places.

Find out what you will need as a *minimum* to be eligible for your chosen employment, training or education, and make sure you are working towards that minimum. If you need an Advanced VCE with a Merit or Distinction grade, ensure you are achieving those grades from now on. If it is unlikely you will achieve that grade, you may have to reassess your career choices.

Curriculum vitae, letter of application and application forms

Curriculum vitae

A curriculum vitae (or, simply, a CV) is a summary of who you are and what you have achieved so far. A prospective employer will usually see your CV before he or she sees you. Therefore you should make every effort to ensure your CV gives an employer a very good impression about yourself.

A CV should include the following information about yourself:

- *Personal details* – your name, address, telephone number and date of birth.
- Current and/or most recent *place of study* with *qualifications* achieved (including grades and year) and those courses you are currently studying.
- *Work* (including current, part-time and work experience jobs). You should also supply a brief description of what this work involves – try to focus on those things that are most relevant to your potential employer.
- *Personal skills and qualities*. Write this in the present tense ('I have, I am', etc.) and use active words ('success', 'achieved', 'awarded', 'gained', etc.) to describe yourself and the skills and qualities you possess.
- *Achievements*. Things you might think are not important could be interesting to an employer (e.g. being captain of a football team, a fund-raiser for a Children in Need event, being a prefect at school, etc.).
- *Interests and hobbies*. Think very carefully about this. Saying you enjoy reading might be true but could give the impression you are very quiet. On the other hand, saying you enjoy socialising might give the impression you are wild and unreliable.

CV tips
- Always wordprocess your CV and keep it on your own floppy disk so you can update it as and when required.
- Keep your CV brief (generally, it should not be longer than two pages of A4).

- Spell check it and get someone else to read it. Listen carefully to any advice this person gives you.
- Use good-quality paper.
- Before making each job application, make sure your CV contains accurate information that is relevant to the position you are applying for.
- However tempting it may be, don't tell lies on a CV. You will probably be caught out at the interview.

Figure 1.16 is a template you could use as a guideline for your own CV. Alternatively, look at the software on your computer as these often supply examples of CVs that could be useful to you.

Curriculum Vitae

Name:
Address:
Telephone number:
Date of birth:

Education

Date   Place of study:
        Qualifications working towards:

Date   Place of study:
        Qualifications achieved:

Date   Any additional qualifications achieved:

Employment

Date   Name and address of employer:
        Job role and types of tasks undertaken:

Date   Name and address of work experience:
        Types of tasks undertaken:

Personal skills and qualities

Use this opportunity to sell yourself, using your own words and getting across why you are the ideal person for the job.

Achievements

Hobbies and interests

References

Available on request (or provide the names, titles, addresses and telephone numbers of two referees).

Figure 1.16   A CV template

Letter of application

When you send in your CV, you should always accompany this with a letter of application. This letter should explain what it is that interests you about the job and why you feel you would be suited to it. Make sure you spell the names of people and the company's name correctly as you will not get off to a good start if you misspell any of these.

Activity	Study the three job advertisements carefully and choose one job you feel most suits you and that you are most interested in.
	In *draft form* (if you have not already done so), produce a CV and letter of application you could send in reply to this advertisement. Before you finalise your CV and letter of application, get someone else to read these and ask this person for his or her comments.
	In the light of what this person has said, work on your drafts to improve them before producing them in their final form.

Junior Retail Travel Consultant
A great start if you've just finished a travel course. You will need good customer care skills, enthusiasm and will be a team player. Good communicator who wants to succeed in the travel industry. Must be computer literate and have a good knowledge of major travel destinations.
Apply with CV in writing to Mr George, City Travel, London SE13 9JN

Ski Tour Operator
Plenty of variety working in reservations, ticketing and administration. You will need to have good telephone and organisational skills. The ability to speak a second European language is an advantage.
Apply with CV in writing to Mrs Blades, Ski House of Manchester, Manchester M23 3HH

Hotel Receptionist
Excellent opportunity to join a major hotel group working in a busy airport hotel. We are looking for a confident, lively and friendly person. You will need to have a willingness to work shifts and have a flexible approach to work. Communication and numeracy skills are essential.
Apply with CV in writing to Human Resources Manager, Flight Path Hotel, Heathrow Airport TW16 4DF

Application forms

Most companies these days now require you to complete an application form rather than send in a CV. If this is the case, do *not* send in your CV as the company has probably requested you complete an application form for the following reasons. To:

- process the information quickly, especially if there are likely to be a large number of applicants
- look at how neat you are and how easy your handwriting is to read
- ensure certain questions are asked to help process the applications (for example, there may be questions about health or nationality)
- enable comparisons to be made through the answers different applicants have given to the different questions.

The steps involved in completing an application form

1 Apply for the form in plenty of time. It could take up to two weeks to send off for the form, to receive it, to fill it in and then to return it back to the company.

2 Always photocopy the form *before* completing it. Use this as a practice and then copy what you have written *neatly* on to the original.

3 Read the questions carefully, especially when you are asked to place things in date order (e.g. is it current/most recent educational establishment first or last in the list?).

4 Only answer the question – do not give irrelevant information. This could be a test of how you write information concisely on to a form.

5 Once completed, photocopy your completed application form so you can check what you wrote prior to being interviewed.

6 If you are asked to submit a photograph, look at the instructions (is it passport or full size?). If you have applied for a job that will require you to wear a uniform, try to get a photograph of yourself wearing a smart suit or your current work uniform (if appropriate).

7 Always check the postage by getting your completed form in its envelope weighed: application forms can often cost more to send than standard first-class letter post.

How to prepare yourself for an interview

Once you have been selected for interview, it is important you reduce the amount of stress you are likely to experience on the day of the interview, and there is only one way to do that – to prepare yourself!

Find out as much as you can about the organisation prior to the interview:

- What do they do, sell or promote?
- What is their mission statement?
- Who owns the organisation?
- How do they link in to other sectors of the travel and tourism industry?

Check the date, time and location of the interview. Find out exactly how you will get there and aim to be early. If you must take anything with you (e.g. certificates) locate these well in advance. Try on what you are planning to wear for the interview well in advance. Will this create the impression that you want to put across? Make sure your outfit is clean and ironed a few days before the interview.

Read through the photocopy of your CV or application form: an interviewer will often refer to this in the interview and will ask questions about what you have written. Try to anticipate the types of question you might be asked:

- Why do you want the job?
- What can you bring to the organisation?
- What do you think are your own strengths and weaknesses?
- Are there any areas of the job in which you feel you would need further training?
- What aspects of your studies at school or college have you enjoyed the most/the least?
- How do you feel about working as part of a team?
- If left on your own, do you think you would be able to deal with matters efficiently and effectively?
- What is it about the travel/tourism industry that appeals to you most?

- What do you see yourself doing in five years' time?
- You say on your application form that you were a prefect/sports captain at school/college. Do you think this has helped you in any way?
- In what ways will the part-time work/ work experience you do/have done help you in this job?
- Does it concern you that you may be asked to work unsociable hours/over the weekend?
- Are there any particular features of our company/organisation that appeal to you?
- Have you applied for any other jobs apart from this one?
- How do you see yourself progressing within our organisation?

If your answer to the last question suggested you intended to use this job as a stepping stone to better things, this would not go down well with an employer. Consider what opportunities there could be if you stayed within that organisation.

Similarly, prepare questions you could ask the interviewer. This will show you are genuinely interested and have given some thought to actually doing the job. For example:

- Does your company/organisation offer training courses I could attend?
- Does your company/organisation have any plans for expansion in the near future?
- Please could you tell me more about (a point raised earlier in the interview)?

And practise shaking hands with people – this might be the first thing an interviewer does on meeting you.

On the day of the interview, smile and look enthusiastic. Sometimes nerves can affect the way we communicate with people. If you need to organise your thoughts, do not be afraid to take a short pause before answering a question.

Group interviews are often used to shortlist candidates within a short space of time and to look for the strong personality types within a group. If you are ever in this situation, do not make the mistake of overperforming: act naturally and try to include members of the group in conversations – especially people you have not met before.

Activity	You have applied for one of the following positions:
	1 A retail travel agent with a large multinational company.
	2 An administration assistant with a local ski specialist tour operator.
	3 An assistant at your local tourist information centre.
	4 A management trainee with a large theme park.
	5 A receptionist at an airport hotel.

You will need to work in groups of three for this activity. Role play an interview situation in which one person is being interviewed by a manager, one person is interviewing and the other person is observing the interview. Prepare for the interview using the guidelines given in this chapter, ensuring you keep the situation as realistic as possible.

At the end of the interview, the manager will give feedback, initially to the interviewee. This should then be followed by feedback from the observer. Rotate the roles and, at the end of the activity, discuss what you feel you have learnt from this exercise.

Tourism development occurs throughout the world and, as someone who hopes to work in the travel and tourism industry, you will need to understand the reasons for and implications of this development.

Through studying this unit you will have the opportunity to learn about:

- the organisations involved
- the objectives of tourism development
- the impacts of tourism development and how these can be managed effectively.

This unit builds on the introductory work you did in Unit 1 about positive and negative impacts of tourism. It also links with Unit 3 ('Worldwide travel destinations').

This unit will be assessed through an external assessment only. The grade you achieve in this assessment will be your grade for the unit.

photo by courtesy of Bournemouth Tourism.

Chapter 2.1 Introduction

Check your understanding

Before setting out on this unit, make sure you are comfortable about the sectors that make up the travel and tourism industry as we will be looking at how important these different sectors are in the process of tourism development.

The term 'tourism development' is very wide ranging. We could be talking about the development of tourism in a country, a region in a country or in one single specific resort or town. Alternatively, we could be discussing the setting up of a new tourist attraction.

When researching tourism development, you must be clear about exactly what the scope of your research is going to be. Similarly, if you are studying one particular destination rather than a country, make sure there is sufficient information for you to complete the work before you start.

Activity

In groups of four or five, study the outline of Cantaloupe Island shown in Figure 2.1. Currently, there is no tourism development on this Caribbean island. Think about what you would need to develop to encourage a range of different tourists to stay for a holiday on the island. Mark these features on the map. (*Note*: Apart from the inactive volcano, the island is flat – it has no cliffs or hills, etc., and the only major settlement is Cantaloupe Town itself, which is a port with a small industrial area.)

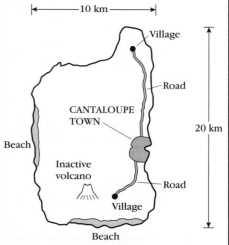

When you have finished, compare your map with those created by the rest of your group.

Chapter 2.2 The agents of tourism development

Tourism development is usually the result of a national or regional government policy initiative that has identified the need to develop tourism either generally throughout a country or in a specific region. Once a policy has been established, different organisations will become involved in putting it into practice. However, as we saw in Unit 1, different types of organisation have different reasons for becoming involved in tourism development.

| Activity | Look back at the activity you did previously about Cantaloupe Island. Now consider the types of organisation (e.g. building contractors, tour operators, etc.) that will be needed to develop the island. Divide these into the three categories of public, private and voluntary organisations. Select one organisation from each list and identify what the reasons might be for that organisation being involved in the island's development.

As a group, discuss your findings. Are some of the reasons for the organisations being involved the same across all three sectors? (You may find there are common themes among all the organisations, such as the generation of income or the creation of jobs.) |
|---|---|

For example, a private sector accommodation company will want to buy up land to build hotels and restaurants, whereas local groups within the community may want to preserve the natural landscape. Public sector organisations (such as the local council) may want to set limits on the type of building that takes place while, on the other hand, wanting to ensure the interested parties are able to develop the destination in a way that will encourage tourists to visit the area. The various people involved in tourism development will also view the issue of tourism differently. For some, it will be a big part of their lives while, for others, it might have a minimal impact and be considered of little importance. For larger organisations, the reasons for becoming involved in tourism development might be purely for profit. This would mean personal feelings would not affect the decision-making process, only business or strategic objectives. However, if you were living in the area being developed, your reactions to the proposed scheme could be extremely emotional.

We will now look at some of the types of organisation that are likely to be involved in the tourism development process and their reasons for becoming involved in these projects.

Private sector enterprises

In the initial stages of tourism development, the main private sector enterprises involved will not be tourism organisations. *Development agencies* take on the initial work of looking at the feasibility of tourism development. Such an agency will provide a report about what could be achieved through tourism and the likely costs and benefits to the area. Development agencies do not necessarily have local knowledge of the area but will probably have been involved in similar enterprises in the past. It is highly unlikely local people would participate in this stage of the development.

The actual physical development will start with the buying up of land. At the beginning of the development, land is likely to be relatively cheap but, as more and more people and organisations buy up sites, prices will rise and good plots will become scarce. The incentive of high financial returns can make people greedy about the prices they can charge for their land, which might result in bad feelings among local residents. Problems often occur when land is developed close to where people are still living or working. It is not unusual to see hotels being built next to farms or on the edges of residential areas.

Sometimes the land is purchased and handed over to a *development company*, who will take on sole responsibility for the project. This is to ensure there is an integrated approach to the whole development. It also means there is more control over the development. For example, it might be agreed that a development will have a set number of self-catering apartments and/or hotels and that the entertainment will be varied to complement the range of accommodation. Alternatively, there could be a decision that the development consists solely of luxury-class hotels, with suitable amenities to suit this type of clientele. The development agency will make sure the project fulfils these clearly defined and agreed guidelines. If a development company is brought in, it will probably also be responsible for the sale of the units to other companies and organisations.

Consultants are often employed to conduct a range of tasks, some of which include:

- marketing
- budgeting
- local research
- legal issues
- transportation
- building and surveying
- organising travel and tourism suppliers.

It is unlikely local people will have this expertise and, if one of these areas is overlooked or not covered in sufficient depth, the consequences for the development could be disastrous.

Sometimes these consultants will form consultancy groups (for example, if you were developing a remote island in the Pacific, you would need the advice and support of a wide range of organisations in the travel and tourism sector). Such organisations would include tour operators, airlines, cruise companies, local transport operators, hoteliers and travel agents. If organisations identify a long-term benefit from being involved in the project from the start, they are usually more than keen to become involved. For example, a tour operator might be able to negotiate favourable rates with organisations it had worked with as part of this consultancy process, and a transport operator might be able to benefit from extra business gained as a result of working with tour operators, airlines and cruise companies.

Leisure and entertainment organisations are also a key part of tourism development. This might be in the form of companies that already exists in the area or could be through the setting up of new organisations. What is important is that the leisure and entertainment provided match the client target group. There will also likely be an interesting mix of businesses, some that will be exclusively for the use of tourists and some that will also serve the local community.

Activity	What leisure and entertainment might appeal to the following client groups: 1 elderly visitors 2 families 3 young couples 4 single people? Make a list of the leisure and entertainment organisations that might be needed to ensure these people are happy with the tourism development of a particular destination. Now consider the example of Disneyland, Paris, and how the company addressed all client groups within the one development. Was this successfully achieved? You will probably need to research this through brochures (available at travel agencies), websites (try http://www.disneylandparis.com/disney/smain.htm) or by interviewing people you know who have been there.

Disneyland Paris is one of the most significant tourist developments in recent times.

Some of these organisations might be very small enterprises, such as family-owned restaurants or excursion companies. However, they are just as important to the destination and to the attraction of tourists as the very large companies that set up hotels, casinos and larger attractions.

Public sector organisations

Local authorities make many of the decisions involved in tourism development (despite the fact that the policy and planning initiatives will probably have been taken at a national or regional level). Local authorities are responsible for ensuring that some of the more tangible aspects of the tourism product are readily available for the visitor. These will include some of the following:

- tourism information and publicity
- local authority-owned attractions (e.g. beaches, piers, parks, gardens, museums and other public buildings)
- roads and footpaths
- signposting
- health, security and safety provision
- sanitation
- access to the destination (including the development of road, rail, air and sea transport).

The destination's economy greatly affects how much of this provision comes from the local authority. In some more wealthy destinations, much of the above will be privatised but, in poorer, developing areas, they will still be very much under the control of the local authority. The way funding is obtained is usually a big problem. Grants might be available to help with development; alternatively, local people will find their taxes and business rates are increased to pay for the development. If there is a large interest from private sector enterprises, these companies are often keen to subsidise the development.

While national governments will often have set the policies that stimulate tourism development, they are unlikely to have much involvement at a local level. They are more likely to co-ordinate the developments that are taking place within their countries. In the UK, decision-making will probably result from EU directives or from British Tourist Authority policies. Nationally, the government might be responsible for providing funds to help pay for the development. This could come in the form of grants or loans that must be repaid following the completion of the development.

Tourist boards can also be involved in the development. National and regional tourist boards will promote the destination both to overseas visitors and to the country's own residents. If the development is of a high profile, this will involve liaising with the main private sector companies (such as tour operators and airlines). They will be involved jointly in promoting the destination, which will be done through brochures, leaflets and awareness raising. Promotional events and educational visits will ensure travel agents have sufficient knowledge to sell the destination and to give advice to potential visitors.

Voluntary sector bodies

Very often, voluntary sector bodies will be made up of local people who have an interest in how the development will affect their lives. They often form local community groups made up of volunteers. Some examples of such groups include:

- religious groups
- amateur dramatics groups
- natural history societies
- sports groups
- Neighbourhood Watch or community police.

Some community groups will be against the development (because of more traffic, more noise, pressure on local amenities, the destruction of local wildlife habitats, etc.), although occasionally some groups push for a development to take place (for example, if there is high unemployment in a specific area). These groups will have objectives that have been agreed by the groups' members or the residents of the area. Funding for any activities will come from donations or through fund-raising in the locality. Local groups should be given the opportunity to be represented at discussions or planning meetings. However, they are very often overlooked as contributors at this stage of the development. When this happens, community groups usually evolve into pressure groups.

Pressure groups are much more vociferous and forceful in their actions and can be either from the local community or part of a much larger national organisation. Very often, local pressure groups start with one or two people who will recruit more members through word of mouth, advertising and public meetings. They rely on recruiting prominent local people (such as vicars, lawyers, politicians or celebrities) who can raise awareness of their cause and the likely problems that will occur as a result of the development. Most pressure group activities involve posters, petitions and demonstrations. However, there may also be opportunities to lobby local MPs to persuade them to become involved in the cause.

Activity

Sun Parks is a large holiday centre. It has recently applied for planning permission to build a new year-round holiday village at a lake close to where you live.

Your group will role play a meeting about the development that will include people from the public, private and voluntary sectors.

The roles from the private sector include the following.

- The chief executive of Sun Parks, who is keen to get started on the project and who wants it open within a year.
- The owner of the farm next to the lake, who is hoping to sell the farm to Forward Development, the company responsible for buying up land for Sun Parks.
- The negotiator from Forward Development, who will receive a large bonus if all the land is bought within two months of planning permission being granted.
- The regional manager from an entertainment company who has a franchise with Sun Parks to provide catering, cinemas, shows, bars and discos within their villages.

The roles from the public sector include the following.

- The chief executive of the local council, who is worried about who is going to pay for all the extra amenities and infrastructure needed to support the Sun Parks' development.

- The manager of the local tourist information centre, who personally thinks the development is out of character with the area but who will be able to take on extra staff to work in the information centre at Sun Parks.
- The regional tourist officer, whose idea it was to include Sun Parks in the tourism development strategy for the region.

The roles from the voluntary sector include the following.

- The head of the local angling group, who has been advised that none of the group's fishing licences will be renewed after this season – thus making it illegal to fish in the lake.
- A member of the pressure group 'Save our Sanity', which has been set up to stop the development. Members do not want tourists to spoil the 'laid back' atmosphere of the town.
- The head of the local chamber of commerce who is representing that organisation and who is keen to see the development go ahead as local businesses will benefit from the extra people coming into the area.

The meeting should allow all parties to be involved in the discussion, and you must take note of the views of all participants.

Simply because an organisation is in the private, public or voluntary sector does not mean it will be for or against a development. It is also important to consider what each individual organisation's objectives or agenda are for the development.

Chapter 2.3 The objectives of tourism development

The first question to ask is: why develop tourism? Some of the main reasons a destination will be interested in developing tourism are as follows.

- *To attract visitors*:
  - by improving accessibility
  - by raising awareness about the destination
  - through the 'familiarity' (or, alternatively, the 'exclusivity') of the destination.
- *To retain visitors*:
  - through offering an all-round, quality product
  - by planning the development of the destination
  - by addressing seasonality issues.
- *To increase the visitor spend*:
  - by looking at how the resort's superstructure can be improved
  - through creating new markets to visit.
- *To preserve assets*:
  - through conservation and preservation
  - through the charging of sensible admission fees.
- *To increase assets*:
  - through development and planning.

Tourism development takes place in both the developing and developed countries of the world, and for all sorts of reasons. We will now consider some of the main reasons why organisations choose to become involved in tourism development.

Economic objectives

Economic objectives include:

- employment creation
- increased foreign currency earnings
- increased income
- economic development and regeneration.

The new City of Manchester Stadium owes much to the 2002 Commonwealth Games (artist's impression courtesy of Ove Arup).

Employment

Tourism creates many jobs, both directly and indirectly. Initially, industries such as construction, manufacturing and transportation will benefit from the development of tourism. However, once a project is nearing completion, there will be a demand for tourism workers themselves. The challenge for any organisation is to find staff who are suitably qualified to deal with tourists. A destination will need staff with language, customer service and tourism skills to work in hotels, attractions and other facilities.

To begin with, it is unlikely the local workforce will be suitably trained or experienced for all the jobs needed. This could result in a labour shortage, and workers may have to be brought in from other destinations or from overseas. There will, however, be a need to train and develop local workers as imported workers are likely to be expensive to relocate, employ and retain. Because of the nature of the industry, organisations will need to employ large numbers of specific groups of people (for example, part-time workers on a temporary basis to service accommodation during the peak season). Not all the jobs will be attractive, and many will involve shift work and the need for workers to move nearer to the resort areas. Where members of the same family work in tourism, it is not unusual for the family unit to break up or to become fragmented.

As the destination's infrastructure continues to develop to support the increased number of tourists, indirect employment will be created in other industries such as security, health and sanitation.

Foreign currency earnings

An increase in foreign currency earnings is particularly important for destinations that have a weak economy or that may need to import goods and services from other countries to keep the tourists happy. In many developing countries, acquiring strong currencies such as the US dollar and Deutsche Mark will enable them to purchase more than they otherwise could with their own currency.

Some governments impose very strict currency regulations that restrict or forbid the import or export of local currencies. Very often, these countries have exchange rates set by the government, and tourists must exchange their currency at official state-run exchange bureaux. This enables the government to build up its reserves of foreign currency.

As we saw in Unit 1, to maximise their earnings from both foreign and local currencies, it is important for destinations to ensure the money spent by tourists goes into locally owned organisations rather than large international companies. There may still be some leakage of the earnings, however, particularly if restaurants and shops have to import goods to encourage the visitors to spend money. It is also important for destinations to attract visitors who are going to spend money locally. If a destination encourages the establishment of hotels that offer all-inclusive and full-board arrangements with all entertainment on site, tourists are not likely to spend much money in the destination. Self-catering accommodation and hotels offering half-board, room-only and bed and breakfast rates are important for destinations in order to ensure the local economy thrives as a result of tourism.

CASE STUDY: Foreign currency

Think back to the Flying Fish case study given in Unit 1, where tourists rarely leave the resort and can use their credit cards to make purchases for such things as souvenirs or car hire. Most of the money earned from this spending will be used to buy American products (American food and drink, for example) rather than to buy locally produced commodities. Any profit is repatriated to Flying Fish and its American shareholders. Resorts like these do not benefit the local economy and it is difficult to identify any advantages tourism of this nature brings to developing countries.

We can contrast this type of resort with the Greek Islands, where the majority of the accommodation is self-catering or bed and breakfast. Most are small, family-run businesses and even the largest of the hotels are owned by Greek companies. These resorts also have many locally owned restaurants, tavernas, bars, shops, car hire and excursion companies. People often pay in local currency and exchange their travellers cheques at hotel receptions and local bureaux de change. This type of destination maximises the amount of money that can be generated from foreign currencies.

Similarly, the majority of resorts on the Spanish mainland and Balearic Islands have this well-balanced combination of different types of accommodation. In the case of both Greece and Spain, while the local economy does well from foreign currency earnings it is not, at the same time, over-dependent on foreign currency earnings.

As a result of tourism, some of the money generated can be invested into the local area to develop facilities and amenities for local people. Overseas companies are often taxed to make sure that any money that is leaked out of the economy is maximised and a return re-invested in the destination. In some places, tourism development has totally regenerated areas, turning destinations that were once run down into successful and thriving attractions that are once again making money.

Examples of now thriving attractions include Thorpe Park in Surrey, where disused gravel pits have been transformed into a popular theme park that employs many local people and has made the area attractive again. Similarly, the docklands areas of many cities (such as London and Salford) have been regenerated. Developments such as the Dome and the National Maritime Museum attract many visitors to the dockland areas of London, as does the Lowry Centre in the once run-down port of Salford. The canal area of Birmingham has also been regenerated, and now has such amenities as restaurants and bars that are used by both local residents and tourists alike.

Environmental objectives

Environmental objectives include:

- habitat preservation
- environmental education
- environmental improvements.

There were environmental benefits to Greenwich by developing the Dome on a derelict site.

Habitat preservation

Habitats need to be preserved, particularly when it is a habitat that is attracting tourists to the destination. Examples include the safari parks in Kenya, the Great Barrier Reef in Australia and the National Parks in the UK. Tourists can harm a local habitat and controls need to be introduced to restrict the numbers and types of visitors.

Tourist spending can be fed back into the area by channelling fees charged for admission, car parking or souvenir purchases into preservation projects. Habitat preservation also aims to minimise the effect tourists can have of causing animals, birds or sea creatures to move away from the areas they would normally inhabit.

Environmental education

Environmental education applies both to the local population and to the tourists visiting an area. Very often, the local population does not recognise the potential harm from tourism development until it is too late. If local people have started to benefit from the positive economic effects of tourism, they might feel the environment is something they can afford to neglect. However, environmental education is a very powerful force if used effectively. This is particularly true when tourists become involved. Examples include the protection of the loggerhead turtle in Turkey and Greece and the opening up of whale-watching areas along the southeast coast of Argentina. This later example has many benefits. The tourists who come to watch the whales bring money to the local economy. At the same time, they learn about whales and may go on to campaign for the worldwide abolition of whaling.

Similarly, money is generated for the study and preservation of whales and the whales are protected while they are in the area: diving is banned and shipping is kept clear.

Environmental improvements

Environmental improvements can benefit both local people and wildlife. Where conservation and preservation projects have taken place, areas that at one time might have been run down and disused are given a new lease of life (see photo opposite). People will start to visit these places again and wildlife might also return if the project is sensitively handled.

One initiative in the UK that has resulted from tourism is the blue flag beaches scheme, which publishes a list of clean, high-quality beaches with good bathing water. The continuation of tourism depends on the protection of special places, which is why environmental improvements not only benefit local people but also tourists.

Environmental projects and improvements also include many human-made attractions. The following are examples from the UK.

- Conservation areas (such as Bath's Royal Crescent, the seafront at Llandudno and many historic town and city centres – for example, York, Lincoln and Brighton).
- The blue plaque system that identifies buildings in London and other cities where important or famous people lived.
- Heritage centres (such as at Chester and the White Cliffs Experience in Dover).
- Industrial attractions (such as Iron Bridge Gorge, Castlefields area of Manchester and Liverpool's Albert Dock).

Socio-cultural objectives

Socio-cultural objectives include:

- promotion of understanding of other cultures
- improvements to the quality of life
- provision of community facilities.

Understanding other cultures

Through the development of tourism, it should be possible to promote an understanding of the different cultures of both the destination community and the visiting tourists. Too often in the past, however, there was an unbalanced relationship, with the host country providing services for tourists and the tourists having a greater, and negative, impact on the local population. An understanding of other cultures can develop a local population's awareness of the outside world and can raise expectations.

Tourists are far more likely to remember the exchanges they have with local people as these are unique and fascinating experiences. Local people, on the other hand, are likely to have many such meetings throughout the tourist season and will come to regard them as quite mundane.

Quality of life

Generally speaking, the quality of life of the local population should improve. Those going into tourism jobs will have time off and more money to spend. For many local people, tourism opens up a way of life they might not have imagined possible. For some there will be an opportunity to travel and to see more of their own country and other destinations. There might also be more money available in the local community for better educational opportunities and health care.

Community facilities

Better roads will be built to enable people to move around the destination, and sewerage, water and electricity services might be improved. The facilities used by tourists (including restaurants, shops and entertainment and leisure amenities) will also be available for the local people. People will probably find they have a choice about what they use or do which they did not have before the arrival of tourism.

Political objectives

Whenever a country, region or resort develops its tourism industry, there will always be some political objectives that are quite distinct from any of the other objectives we have considered so far:

- image enhancement
- the creation of a regional or national identity.

These two objectives are very similar to each other, and both depend on how the destination managers have decided to market their destinations. The most important thing is to make sure the correct image is conveyed about the destination, and that it reflects what is actually happening in the resort. Very often, resorts that have received bad publicity or have an image for a certain type of holiday will work on how to create a different image.

CASE STUDY: Bournemouth

This change of image happened recently in Bournemouth – a resort with a rather old-fashioned image and that was not attracting young visitors. The town underwent a major development plan that included:

- partnerships with such companies as Harry Ramsden, Oceanarium, Vistarama, Brewers Fayre and other leisure companies
- developing the seafront area
- the development of all-weather and year-round attractions.

The result was the reinvention of the destination as one for a much younger age group, and the creation of the 'Bournemouth is Best' image.

Find out more about Bournemouth by collecting brochures from your local travel agency or visit its website (http://www.bournemouth.gov.uk/index.asp).

Can you think of any more UK destinations that have undergone similar transformations in image recently? (Do not limit yourself to seaside resorts!)

photo by courtesy of Bournemouth Tourism.

Creating regional and national identities happens all the time in tourism, and this will have an impact on the local inhabitants who will acquire some sense of the identity that has been adopted by their home. The majority of advertisements that appear on television and in the newspapers continuously employ slogans to describe a region, country or place. Regionally, The English Riviera is used to describe Torquay and Paignton. Nationally, most countries have an identity, and some of these are easily remembered (such as 'Indiaaah') while others are not so memorable. Places, too, have their slogans: 'Skegness is so bracing' and 'Edinburgh: the Athens of the north'.

Check your understanding

Write a report that:

1 identifies the people and organisations involved in tourism development
2 describes and explains the objectives these people and organisations might have for tourism development
3 explains the conflicts in the objectives between these different people and organisations
4 explains how these different people and organisations could be inter-related.

Chapter 2.4 The impacts of tourism development

Tourism has a considerable impact on the destination and the people who live there. To begin with, tourism is felt to bring only benefits as land is sold, jobs are created and all the rest of the positive impacts of tourism development become apparent. However, it does not take long before the negative impacts start to emerge and, very often, these can outweigh the positive ones. We first look at the positive and negative impacts of tourism development and then consider how the benefits can be maximised and the negative impacts minimised.

Check your understanding

As a group, find out how much you already know about the positive and negative effects of tourism. Use the themes of economic, environmental and socio-cultural impacts to help you.

What do you consider to be the *key* issues for tourism development?

Economic impacts

In Unit 1 we noted that economic impacts are relatively easy to measure because they relate to hard facts that provide statistics about, for example, money generated, jobs created, improvements in infrastructure and increases in foreign currency earnings. You will also probably find when you go on to research destinations that most research that has been done has been on the effects of tourism on the local economy. These studies are also likely to give a very positive view of what tourism will do or has done for a particular locality, with the aim of raising support for tourism and of promoting its continued development.

The positive impacts to the local economy will only be experienced to the full if the money raised by tourism remains in the local area. When this income goes to small and medium-sized enterprises that employ local people and use local produce, the money has a greater local benefit than when the money is spent on internationally owned fast-food chains which employ local staff for unskilled work only and which import most of their produce.

What the local workforce does with this money is also important: it is essential it remains within the local economy. If it is spent in the fast-food chains and other internationally owned businesses, it will once again leave the local economy. In tourism, this circulation of expenditure is known as the multiplier effect, and will demonstrate how self-sufficient a destination is. Unfortunately as the destination continues to develop the balance of local and international organisations tends to change, with larger remote companies buying up small local ones. This often leads to more money being taken out of the local area.

The negative impact on the economy is that, as spending increases, so do prices and, as a result, the cost of living rises. For the majority of tourists this is not a problem as most newly developing destinations will still be much cheaper than the tourists' home countries. However, this will create problems for the local people because, although they will have increased incomes from the wages they receive, the prices of local and imported goods will also have risen.

Eventually, if inflation continues to rise, the local currency will become so unstable it will have little worth. Some countries end up devaluing their currencies to reduce the exchange rate rises, while others impose strict controls on currency exchange. When a destination's prices rise this will ultimately impact on the visitors, who might feel they are being 'ripped off'. Eventually, visitor numbers will be affected as tourists find new, less expensive destinations to visit.

Employment generation is often regarded as one of the key reasons for developing tourism, particularly where the destination has little or declining industry. Employment in tourism covers the full spectrum, from unskilled to skilled labour. There will be considerable investment in training and developing staff to meet the needs of tourists. Once they are trained, local workers will have a greater range of employment opportunities in the destination. Many people will also work exceedingly long hours during the holiday season because, once the season ends, there may be little or no work.

There will be a decline in the destination's traditional employment as a result of tourism. Many young people, in particular, will not want to continue working in such jobs as farming or manufacturing when there are opportunities to work in the tourism industry at higher rates of pay and with better conditions. As a result, businesses that could make the destination self-sufficient will go into decline, which will have an adverse impact on the multiplier effect.

There is likely to be a shift in the ages of those people who live in the more remote areas away from the tourist destination as young people move to the tourist areas. However, some of the employment will not be very attractive for unskilled workers who might find they are working long hours for low pay, being treated poorly by managers and then having an extensive period of unemployment during the non-tourist season.

Tourism development will bring an increase in the amount of taxation raised. This revenue will be raised through direct taxation on employment, tourism enterprises (international and local businesses) and from fees and services charges. Indirect taxes will also be raised, including customs duties, tax on goods consumed, interest payments and loan repayments. On the positive side, these taxes will pay for additional amenities and services necessary to support increasing tourist numbers. On the other hand, the taxes are likely to create bad feeling from existing business owners who feel they have been caught up in the development.

Activity	You work as a researcher at Flying Fish resorts and have been asked to write a report on the possibility of the company opening a new, all-inclusive Flying Fish resort on Cantaloupe Island.

Write an unbiased report that:

* identifies the agents needed for tourism development on Cantaloupe Island
* describes and explains the objectives these agents might have for tourism development
* outlines the possible conflicts in the objectives of these different agents
* shows how these various tourism agents will have to co-operate with each other in order to get the development up and working.

Use the information contained both within this unit and in Unit 1 to write your report for Flying Fish.

Environmental impacts

Tourism should help to pay for the upkeep of the environment that is attracting the visitors (this could be a natural landscape or human-made buildings). Conservation areas and national parks might be created that will limit a region's development. In some areas there will be very strict limitations on building heights and locations. The reuse of derelict or disused buildings as hotels, museums or heritage centres will also have a very positive impact on the local area.

Giraffes enjoy a well-managed environment in Kenya.

The development can be carefully landscaped to blend in with existing buildings and the natural environment.

An example of where this has been done effectively is on the island of Lanzarote, where the height, colours and styles of all the buildings are regulated to ensure that any new development is in harmony with the existing environment.

When compared with other industries such as mining and manufacturing, tourism does in fact have a very low level of pollution. However, the increase in people visiting a destination is inevitably going to impact in a negative way on the environment. Although each area is different, some common environmental impacts are:

- pollution of the air and water
- increased levels of noise
- damage to the skyline and a destination's overall architecture
- little use of local building materials
- the destruction of natural eco-systems
- negative effects on wildlife and breeding patterns
- increased litter.

Impacts on the environment are worse because they cannot be seen until it is too late. Some damage may be very slow to rectify or even irreversible.

There are also a great many indirect negative impacts on the local fauna and flora. For example, in the national parks in Canada, bears have found it far easier to eat the food people throw away in rubbish bins than to hunt. This has also resulted in the bears not being wary of humans as they see them as a source of food. The impact on natural habitats from people constantly walking across grassland has resulted in tighter restrictions on access in national parks to try to stop the erosion.

Activity	Select a destination on which you can complete a case study of the positive and negative impacts of tourism. If possible, choose a destination that is close to you or that you have a good knowledge of through a recent visit.
	Prepare a talk to give to your group about the positive and negative impacts of tourism on your chosen destination.

Socio-cultural impacts

The destination's culture is likely to be one of the features that attracts tourists. Culture can include art, craft, dance, events, festivals or carnivals. It can also be an aspect of everyday life (for example, Greek men playing backgammon outside a local taverna). Tourism can preserve this culture: traditional arts and crafts will be something people will want to see as part of their visit. Experienced tourists will also want to experience the lifestyle of the locals and to eat local dishes.

Culture, however, has become a commodity and, in many places, has been commercialised and trivialised. Cheap and nasty souvenirs are sold in markets and in beachside shops. Traditional designs disappear to make way for mass-produced trinkets that can be sold cheaply and in high volumes. Events such as weddings can form part of a weekly excursion trip offered to tourists, taking away the spontaneity of the event and making it nothing more than an evening's entertainment. Customs and religious beliefs might not be respected but seen as a source of amusement.

Exchanges between tourists and host communities can broaden the outlook of both parties, allowing greater understanding of each other's cultural backgrounds. Tourism can also encourage emigration and movement, giving people the opportunity for positive lifestyle changes.

Tourism can have dramatic impacts on the host community, with traditional religious and family values and beliefs being the first to disappear. In many cases the hosts will see the tourists as people they want to emulate, with their more relaxed way of life and relaxed attitudes to drinking, enjoyment and sex. The hosts may not be aware that the tourists behave very differently for the rest of the year. The hosts often want to be as wealthy as the tourists and see ways of achieving this through either overcharging the tourists or through crime.

Community services and public facilities may improve, with transportation, health services and leisure and recreation facilities increasing in both quality and quantity. The standards considered necessary for the tourists' needs are likely to far exceed what the local people are used to. The negative aspect of this is that local people must share these facilities with the tourists, and this may result in overcrowding, queuing or the need to make appointments for services that were previously easy to access.

We also need to consider the reasons why some of these services are needed and, in the case of security, this is as a result of an increase in crime. With the arrival of tourism, the locals' moral conduct may change and, where once there may have been no theft, jealousy of tourists' possessions may inevitably lead to an increase in stealing. As tourism continues to develop, other 'services' tend to be demanded, causing problems with prostitution, gambling and drugs.

As we have already seen, initially, tourists will be welcome for bringing new wealth and for opening up opportunities. As the flow of tourists becomes more regular, the tourists are taken for granted and the local inhabitants become apathetic towards them. Once tourism starts to reach the mass stage, tourists become an irritation and the local people probably do not want them any more. The local people may become less generous and may start to exploit the tourists. If tourism continues to escalate, the visitors are unlikely to be welcomed at all, and there will be hostility from the local community. While it is not inevitable that tourism development will lead to this worst-case scenario, if there is no systematic planning there is every danger it might develop. The final part of this chapter identifies the strategies that can be implemented to prevent these problems.

Maximising the positive impacts

It is the job of tourism professionals to *plan* for the long-term benefit of destinations. This section suggests ways in which these positive impacts can be maximised. While it is unlikely a destination will implement all such possible activities, considering how the positive impacts can be achieved will ensure tourism development happens in a controlled way.

If the planning strategy ensures local companies are involved in the development, this will retain tourism earnings within the host community. The plans must also ensure that as many people from the local community as possible are able to work in the tourism industry. This will probably mean training staff to carry out skilled jobs as well as the unskilled ones. Training needs to include more than just the basics of the job – it also means training staff to understand the expectations and behaviour of the visitors.

Maintaining a balance of different types of tourist is important. If a destination attracts only the very poorest tourists, who perhaps lie on the beach all day and spend no money, there will not be much new money entering the economy. Similarly, if it sets out to attract the ultra-rich only, these visitors may demand French champagne, Russian caviar, etc., and may consider local produce in the shops below their taste. These tourists will not help the local economy much either. Instead, destinations need to maintain a balance. Visitors with a high disposable income will ensure there is sufficient spending within the destination. There should also be enough variety in the shops and in the entertainment to stimulate spending and to keep the tourists within the confines of the destination.

To make sure local people feel positive about the development, it is important they can see how the income is being reinvested in the local infrastructure. Building schools, hospitals, roads, community centres, libraries and homes is a wise form of investment of tourism money. Investment in community projects and groups will help the host population to maintain its identity and to keep in contact with their own people.

The improved facilities and assets that come from tourism development must be easily accessible for the local population. It is essential residents are not penalised in allowing visitors to use these resources. Controlling visitor flow will ensure this does not happen but more positive methods can be used (for example, by offering local residents discount rates to attractions). Looking after the locals' needs when it comes to issues such as car parking and residents' permits will ease problems during peak times.

The key investors and organisations must take on the responsibility for training staff. There must also be some form of staff development so the need to import trained staff can be reduced once the development has got off the ground. There must similarly be opportunities for permanent, long-term employment. The training and development of front-line staff who have direct contact with the tourists can create a sort of 'cultural broker' whose job it is to deal with the tourists and who will ensure they have minimal contact with the worst effects of tourism.

Training and education start at an early age and it is important this knowledge comes through a reputable source, such as a school, college or training organisation. There is a danger that, if this is not achieved, tourism knowledge will be passed on through families and friends. Language training needs to include a range of situations rather than just the language needed to sell or to 'chat' to tourists.

Technical training in tourism and hospitality skills can be given through specialist courses at colleges (in some countries such as Cyprus and Tunisia, there are now colleges that focus on the tourism or hospitality industry). Higher-level education, however, will still tend to occur away from the tourism destination, but student sponsorship should ensure the students bring their new skills back to the destination rather than seeking employment elsewhere.

Minimising the negative impacts

Planners can reduce the negative impacts on the physical environment by regulating development. If careful planning does not take place, development will be left to the vagaries of market forces, and conflicts of interests between local residents, tourists and environmentalists are likely to occur. Planning should result in an adequate amount of legislation and control to counteract some of the negative impacts of the development on the physical environment.

There are many destinations where building heights and architectural styles are controlled. Similarly, tourist development is often encouraged away from populated areas (as in Tunisia), which can reduce impacts on the local community but which, at the same time, can alienate the tourists from the local population. A requirement that bars, entertainments and duty-free shops must be licensed can help to regulate the development of such amenities within resorts. Taxing the profits made by hotels and other forms of accommodation can discourage some owners and, therefore, reduces the problem of excess capacity.

Sustainable tourism identifies the best carrying capacity for a destination and ensures this is not exceeded. If it is exceeded, there is likely to be an unacceptable change in the physical environment and a decline in the quality of the tourist experience. Carrying capacity includes the following factors.

- *Physical considerations*. How many beds, restaurants, bars, etc., there are within the destination. This will dictate the maximum number of people who can be accommodated comfortably.
- *Ecological constraints*. What the environment can take comfortably (for example, people walking on the grass and disruption to the local wildlife).

- *Numbers of visitors*. At what point will a visitor say a certain place is now too crowded and therefore unattractive to visit? Visitors expect a certain number of other people to go to a destination but their satisfaction level will decline as tourist numbers increase.

Visitor management means establishing a destination's carrying capacity and restricting the number of visitors coming in by air or sea. However, controlling the number of people entering the destination by road and rail is more difficult. Restricting car parking places and using the media to inform potential visitors about overcrowding can go some way to controlling visitor numbers. Signposting can similarly direct visitors away from areas that are already full and towards those areas that still have spare capacity.

CASE STUDY: Zoning

Zoning tries to ensure that only the right types of visitors have access to certain areas within a particular destination. This can be illustrated through the case of the Boundary Waters Canoe Wilderness area, which is located on the US/Canadian border.

This area (which covers some 420,000 ha) includes many rivers (e.g. the Rainy and Pigeon Rivers) and also parts of Lake Superior. As an area, it was once exploited for both its timber and mineral deposits but, early in the twentieth century, it was realised this outstanding area of forest land should be preserved and made accessible to all. It was therefore turned into a National Park.

Today, the area has become even more accessible with the rise of the motor car. Two zones have been created inside the park to control how the visitors make use of the many rivers and lakes inside the forests. The first wilderness area deep inside the park is reserved for canoeists only, while the outer zone can also be used by motorboats. It is this outer area, needless to say, that attracts the crowds.

Environmental auditing considers the current impacts of tourism on the environment and makes recommendations on how to lessen these. It emphasises the reinforcement of positive impacts and suggests ways the negative impacts could be lessened. Environmental auditing may lead to restrictions on future planning and may recommend an *environmental impact assessment* is carried out in a particular area.

Environmental impact assessments (EIAs) are now essential procedures in the approval of some projects and could become much more common in the future. In such countries as Australia, the USA, Canada and Peru, they are used extensively to avoid some of the problems encountered in the past and to make sure new tourism developments are sustainable. An EIA is conducted either by the organisation responsible for the development or by an outside consultant. It analyses what the impacts of the development are likely to be and the findings are published as a report. The usual way to conduct an EIA is through a checklist of concerns, which could include the following:

- noise
- land use
- agriculture
- traffic
- air pollution.

On the basis of this checklist of concerns, proposed development schemes are scored and the totals added up. The scheme with the lowest total is the one proposed to run. At the moment, there is no one person or government body this proposal is submitted to, but many countries have environment ministers who take on the responsibility of studying the results. The results are also made public so that people who are likely to be affected by the development are able to see the EIA's findings. EIAs are, currently, not employed widely within Europe but there have been discussions about implementing EIAs to bring consistency across EU practices.

The strategies discussed in this section are not exhaustive, and there may be additional methods you will come across that can enhance the experience of the destination, both for the tourists and the host community.

Activity	Produce a leaflet entitled 'How to Ensure the Success of your Development' to help future developers of tourism projects. The leaflet should give details of how to maximise the benefits of tourism development and of how to minimise the negative impacts.

In this unit you will improve your knowledge of the major continental European and worldwide tourist destinations. We tend to refer to non-European destinations as 'long-haul' destinations, and you might sometimes hear the term 'medium haul' being used, which covers the Middle East and north African destinations. You will be looking at different destinations and what their appeal is to the visitor and to different tourist groups. One of the important factors in providing information is knowing where to look, so the starting point for this unit is the research skills you will need to develop.

The unit builds on the work you completed in Unit 1 ('Investigating travel and tourism') and has links with Unit 2 ('Tourism development'). It also relates closely to optional units, including Unit 7 ('UK travel destinations'), Unit 8 ('Travel agency operations') and Unit 10 ('Tour operations').

This unit will be assessed through your portfolio work only. The grade awarded will be your grade for the unit.

Tourists travel throughout the world for many different reasons.

Chapter 3.1 Research skills

Having good research skills is an important attribute for anyone who wishes to work in the travel and tourism industry as customers rely on our abilities to provide accurate, relevant and up-to-date information. The first thing we must establish is what a particular customer wants information about. Questioning the customer politely will establish his or her particular needs and should direct you to the information the customer requires.

Activity	Imagine you are considering visiting a destination you have not been to before. Make a list of all the possible things you might need to know about that destination before making your decision to visit it. Do not include such things as flight times or cost – we are focusing here on the destination rather than the travel details.
	Compare your list with the rest of your group. You will probably find some things you have listed are identical but others are different. This shows that, even with a group of similar people (in terms of age, education, background, etc.), individuals have different information needs. If you look at an even wider age range or client group, these needs will vary even more.

What happens if you do not have a customer in front of you to double-check on what he or she wants to know? Then, you will have to set the objectives of your research yourself.

Always start off by asking yourself why the journey is taking place and then produce a list of what a traveller would need to know (i.e. what is *essential*), what he or she would probably like to know (i.e. *desirable* information) and what you could add as supplementary information that would probably be interesting to the traveller (i.e. *additional* information). In other words, put yourself in the position of the traveller and use your professional skills to establish what the traveller would need to know.

Once you have produced this list it should act as a checklist for your findings. And make sure you keep the focus of your research on the items that are essential and desirable rather than on the additional information.

Searching for information

You should now have an idea of the information that could be useful to a tourist visiting a new destination and so your next step is knowing where to find the information. Many of the information sources you have used in the past might not be very helpful to you: an encyclopaedia or geography textbook might touch on tourism but is more likely to give you a lot of information that would be in the category of additional rather than essential information. There are, however, many specific travel and tourism sources that will supply you with the information you require, and these can be split into *primary* and *secondary* sources.

Primary sources

Primary sources of information are first-hand sources of information (i.e. information obtained directly from someone with first-hand experience of a destination). In the travel and tourism industry, there are many people who can provide this sort of information.

Most overseas countries have a tourist board office in the UK and the staff in these offices should have a very specialist knowledge of the particular country they represent. Many of these staff will have lived or worked in the country or will have made many visits there. They should be able to answer specific questions about destinations or provide recommendations if a customer is unsure which is the right location for him or her. Tourist board staff should also be able to provide up-to-date information about particular local circumstances and events.

Staff in travel agencies are generally very well travelled and, in one agency, you are likely to find a good range of destinations has been visited. This will have been done through a combination of personal holidays and educational visits. Educational visits are often organised by tour operators, tourist boards or airlines to promote travel to a particular resort or region. Many travel agencies often list in a prominent place the destinations their staff have visited so that customers know who would be best able to advise them about travelling to a particular destination.

Activity	As a group, create your own list of destinations visited. This can be displayed either on a map of the world or in list form by country and should be a useful primary source when you are completing your own portfolio work.

Tour operators will have staff who have visited the destinations in their brochures. Reservations staff will also have visited many of the places and should be able to give advice and make recommendations to both travel agents and customers. Tour operators are also in regular contact with their resort staff and so specific questions (for example, about the suitability of a resort for disabled guests, the location of churches or facilities for large groups) should be answered very quickly.

The final primary source is the customer him or herself, either through commendation or complaint. Unfortunately, it is the complaints that seem to be the responses that most frequently are fed back to travel agents and tour operators. If you do not have a good knowledge about a destination, a complaint could alert you to an issue that might affect your visit (for example, if there was extensive building work going on in the destination or if hygiene standards were particularly poor). Occasionally, customers do come back with positive stories about their holidays and it is worth remembering the positive comments made about destinations. Also bear in mind that what was quite acceptable to one customer may not suit all people – go back to the questioning techniques to find out what the customer's needs are.

Secondary sources

Atlases and maps

Secondary sources are the published information you can use to find out more about a destination and, initially, these may be your first port of call. It is a good idea first to use an atlas to find out more about the locations of destinations and the type of climate they enjoy. If you use a tourism atlas, this will also give you information about airports, resorts and attractions. Alternatively, you might be able to find a map of a specific destination or acquire one directly through a tourist board.

Brochures

Brochures are the main selling tool used by tour operators and travel agents. However, make sure you use the information contained in brochures carefully as the prime objective of brochures is to sell holidays. Information in brochures can give you a great deal of good background information about attractions, climate, cost of living, hotels and quiet, medium and busy resort areas. Some of the long-haul brochures are very useful for finding about specific weather conditions (such as the rainy season or humidity) and also about visa and inoculation recommendations for specific destinations.

Gazetteers

Travel agencies use a set of guides called 'gazetteers' which are written by independent industry specialists about resorts and hotels. A gazetteer is often referred to as a 'truth book' because it gives a very frank and honest opinion about destinations. If a gazetteer says something is good, this is generally a very reliable indication of the quality of a resort or hotel. Gazetteers are published for different holiday types, including Mediterranean, ski, villa and apartment, etc., holidays. Your school or college library may have copies of these or, alternatively, you could contact your local travel agency to see if they will let you use their gazetteers.

Guidebooks

There is now a considerable range of guidebooks you can buy but you must consider the type of customer you are dealing with before recommending which guidebook he or she should use. For the tourist traveller looking for sight-seeing or relaxation, the *Berlitz*, *Baedecker* or *Insight* guidebooks are usually adequate. For the more independent traveller, the *Lonely Planet* or *Rough* guides would be more applicable. Guidebooks contain a wealth of useful information and, as they are usually published independently, they are generally very reliable.

Textbooks

Textbooks should be used with caution as some of the information they contain might be slightly outdated. Some good textbooks, however, have been produced to support AVCE and BTEC National courses specifically for travel geography and tourist destinations. One book published especially for the travel industry is the *World Travel Guide*, produced by Columbus Press and also available on CD-ROM. This guide contains a wealth of information about every country in the world, including tourist board details, passport and visa requirements, climate, money, holidays, health considerations, resorts and excursions, and social and business profiles. The guide is also well illustrated and has information about the industry's trade associations at the back.

The Internet

The Internet is rapidly becoming the easiest method of finding information quickly and, in the case of travel and tourism, it can provide you with a link to the majority of the tourist offices throughout the world. Much of the information available will be of use to you when you require information about a specific destination. However, you can also request information about a particular area or region. When using the Internet, always find out whether the information is coming from a tourist office or a tour operator. Some of the companies that have websites have their country names within their own names. This does not, however, mean they are that country's official tourist office (for example, Swiss Travel Service is a tour operator whereas Switzerland Tourism and Travel Centre is the name of the tourist board based in London). If you are unsure of the address of a particular website, try looking in the *World Travel Guide* as most sites are listed there.

Activity	With a partner, decide on a tourist destination to research. You might want to choose an Italian ski resort or a Spanish Mediterranean resort, the Great Barrier Reef (see photo above) or New England. Separately, search the Internet for information you think would be useful for a young holiday-maker and make notes of this. Now compare what you have found with what your partner has found. Did you find different information? Were some Internet sites more informative than others? What were the best strategies for finding the information?

Newspapers

Most newspapers have travel sections or supplements and, if you are lucky to find an article about your chosen destination, this should provide you with supplementary information to help you. Alternatively, your school or college database may contain copies of articles you could use. While you are on this AVCE programme, try to read the weekend travel articles and keep a file of those that are the most interesting or useful.

Trade papers

The two main trade newspapers (*Travel Weekly* and *TTG* (*Travel Trade Gazette*)) feature articles on specific destinations or on particular holiday products such as ski holidays. These articles should provide you with up-to-date information and they may also refer you to contacts mentioned in the articles. Trade papers are generally useful for reporting newsworthy events that are happening overseas, particularly if there has been civil unrest or troubles with the climate.

Videos

Videos are usually produced as selling tools for a particular destination but they may also give you some insight into the destination involved. Videos can often be loaned from tourist boards, travel agencies or tour operators, or you may find your library has a stock of these.

Whatever your source of information, the important thing to remember is to use a variety of different sources. In so doing you should be able to establish that the information you are using is reliable as it has appeared in a number of different places. You should also be able to select the most relevant points for the task you have in hand.

Deciding what might be useful

When you research a tourist destination, you might find you have too much information or, alternatively, not enough information relevant to your needs. When deciding what is relevant or useful you should go back to your original checklist. Is the information:

- essential
- desirable
- additional?

Sort your findings into these three sections and then look at the balance of information you have found.

If you feel you have too much information about a particular topic, you may need to ask yourself the following questions.

- Can I summarise this information?
- Is the information duplicated?
- Is all the information relevant to my needs?
- Is some of the information out of date?
- Is the information relevant to the particular traveller I am dealing with or have in mind?

If you have too little information, it may be the information sources you have selected are not the most appropriate ones for the task in hand. Look back at the sources you have used to make sure you have not missed out any important ones.

Collecting and presenting relevant information

Once you have decided what might be useful, you must prepare the information ready for presentation. Take particular care with descriptions given to you by other people. Rewrite these in your own words. Do the same with any information you use from brochures. Remember, you are presenting an independent piece of research based on a number of different information sources, not one person's or company's view of a particular destination. Above all, when assessing your information, always bear in mind whether it would be suitable to give to a customer (i.e. is it fit for its purpose?).

Most written correspondence these days is done using computers. There are several advantages in presenting information this way.

- You can change the information should you decide this is necessary at a later stage.
- You could add additional information or even pictures should these become available.
- You can use the computer's tools to help you present the information (e.g. spelling and grammar checks) but, remember, the computer may not pick up misspelt place-names or the names of people or customers – it is up to you to make sure these are correct.
- The finished product will look far more professional and informative.

As part of your AVCE course, you will learn how to improve your information communication technology skills (e.g. your skills in word processing and desktop publishing). Make the most of these opportunities!

While a great deal of the information you provide will be presented as straightforward text, there may be occasions when you could make use of other ways of displaying the information. For example, some things look better if they appear as a list, and a list may be even more informative if it has small pieces of text to accompany the keywords. The following might be things you feel could be shown as a list:

- attractions
- public holiday dates
- vaccinations or health risks
- tour operators serving a resort or destination.

(Remember to make use of your word processing program's facilities to make your list more attractive - bullets, numbers, etc. - but do not overdo this: too much 'clutter' could make your information unreadable.)

Charts and graphs (see Figure 3.1) can be used to show climate patterns - for example, hours of sunshine, average daily temperatures, snow depth, rainfall, humidity, etc. With a bit of thought it is possible to show various types of information on the same chart (for example, one graph or bar chart showing both temperature and humidity). Comparisons could also be made to average UK temperatures or sunshine hours. Pie charts can be used to demonstrate the availability or range of different categories of accommodation or of the different types of visitor to a particular destination.

Maps should always be used to show a destination's location and accessibility. You may need to supply several maps to show the location of a destination within a continent (such as Europe) and then within a country (such as Greece). You may then need to identify airports, ferry ports and rail or bus terminuses. Major road links could

also appear on the same map. If you are explaining a specific resort or resort area, you might also locate specific attractions or destinations.

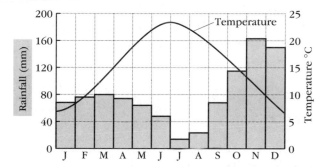

Figure 3.1   Graph and chart of climate in Marseilles

| **Activity** | Start getting used to handling maps now! Obtain a map of your area or region from your local tourist information office or a travel agency. Study this carefully, paying particular attention to: |

- the points of the compass (which is north, south, east, west)
- the scale (how many kilometres/ miles to the centimetre/inch)
- the key (what do all the symbols on the map represent?)
- the communication links in the area (e.g. roads and railway lines, airports, etc.).

Ask a fellow student or friend to imagine he or she is a stranger to the area. Demonstrate to him or her how to get about your region, where the attractions are, how far it is from point A to point B, all the time using the map. Now ask him or her for questions about the area – and try to answer these by means of the map.

A well-chosen photograph can be very effective in a presentation. This combination of spectacular scenery and enjoyable activity would be irresistible!

Clip Art available on your computer or photographs will help to make your work attractive. Pictures will help to demonstrate the heights of mountains and/or the types of ski runs in winter sports destinations. Sometimes you may need to hand draw things but brochures may contain diagrams you could adapt or annotate. Always ensure, however, that you use pictures carefully and that you select only those that are relevant to the topic and that enhance the information you wish to give, rather than just making it look nice.

Drawing conclusions about your findings

Once you have written up your findings about the destination, you need to draw together your key findings into a conclusion. The purpose of a conclusion is not to repeat what you have already written but to focus the reader on what you feel are the important features of that destination. While the contents of your conclusion will vary depending on the destination you have chosen and any specific information that has arisen from your research, as a rough guide, the following might be included in your conclusions:

- The appeal of the destination for UK holiday-makers.
- Routes and gateways to the destination.
- Any changes in the destination's popularity over the last ten years or so.

Above all, your conclusion should demonstrate what the destination can offer your customer.

Acknowledging your sources

Throughout your research it is important you maintain a record of the sources of information you have used and that you acknowledge these sources. Make sure you update this record as your research develops, and ensure you provide sufficient information for the person reading your work to be able to check the sources you have used or to judge how appropriate they were for the task that was set.

When using primary sources, you must acknowledge the person or people who helped you in your research. Your tutor will need to know what this person or people do and their relationship to you as a student. Very often, acknowledgements are given as straightforward text but sometimes a list might be more appropriate.

Whatever format you use, make sure you include the following:

- the name(s) of the person (people) who have provided the information
- if employed in travel and tourism, this person's (people's) job role and the name of his or her (their) company
- if *not* employed in travel and tourism, the reason why this person (people) was used as a source of information
- a brief summary of the information this person (people) was able to supply
- how you made sure this was a reliable source to use for your research.

When you produce a record of the secondary sources of information, you may find this fits very easily into a list format and that, by using a table or the tab keys on a computer, you can record the information neatly.

For secondary sources, record the following information (where appropriate):

- the name of the author or company who produced the literature

- the name of the publication, brochure or leaflet itself
- the year of its publication
- the page numbers used in your research
- the edition number, where applicable
- how you checked the validity of this source as suitable for your research.

You will have noticed that the last point in each list is to explain why you considered this a suitable source of information. The reason for this is that an outsider reading your work may not feel a particular source was valid for the task in question. However, if you can explain the reasons why you used this source it will show the thought process you went through when deciding to use it.

When you quote something directly from the source, always acknowledge this immediately after the quotation. This is usually done by including after the quotation the author's name and page number(s). Occasionally if you have used the same author or company twice, you could do one of two things: either note each publication with the letters a, b, c, d, etc., or include the year of publication to identify the specific source used.

Chapter 3.2 The location and features of the major travel and tourism destinations in continental Europe

Continental Europe comprises many diverse countries stretching from France in the west to Finland in the north, Russia in the east and Turkey in the south. There is a wide variety of destinations that can be categorised under the following headings:

- towns and cities
- seaside resorts
- purpose-built resorts
- countryside areas
- historical/cultural destinations.

majority of tourists visiting them during the autumn, winter and spring months. Because of the different cultures and characteristics of European countries, each city has its own special appeal.

Paris, Amsterdam, Bruges, Brussels, Munich, Barcelona, Dublin, Venice, Rome, Prague and Athens are some of the most popular destinations. Look at your original list of cities: are there any more you now want to add to your map of Europe?

| Activity | For each of the five headings given above, give five examples of destinations from across Europe that fit into each category. Try to select destinations from the whole of Europe rather than from just one particular country. |
| | Now draw on a sheet of A3 paper a map of Europe and mark on this each of your destinations (use a colour code to identify each of the categories). Keep this map as it will be something you will build on throughout this section of the course. |

The canals and sights of Venice make it a popular travel and tourism destination.

Towns and cities

City holidays have become increasingly popular recently, particularly with couples as a second holiday to supplement their main summer holiday. For this reason, cities tend to be seasonal destinations, with the

We now need to consider the type of person who would visit a particular city or town as a holiday destination. The following is a brief outline of the types of people who tend to take this type of holiday (you may be able to add more to this list).

Couples

Couples of all ages and, in particular, those celebrating a special occasion such as a honeymoon or an anniversary like to visit towns and cities. This explains why Paris (which has always been perceived as a romantic destination) continues to be at the top of the list for city holidays.

Although Vienna is perhaps best known as a city of culture, it also has many other attractions.

Young people

Young people (either in groups or singly) are attracted by the nightlife offered by such cities as Amsterdam and the more liberal attitude of the city's inhabitants. Very often a major sporting event such as a football or rugby match will be the attraction or a particular city might be chosen as a suitable venue for a hen or stag party.

Culture

Many cities have very extensive cultural attractions or events, such as music festivals, museums, art galleries and the like. Destinations such as Vienna, Venice and Athens fall within this category. These cities also attract visitors on educational or study tours, many of whom will stay in hostel accommodation.

Conferences and business

While business travellers may not be attracted to a town or city because of its range of tourist facilities, a business event or conference may bring them to the town or city. Some towns and cities have developed extensive facilities for business and other types of conference (e.g. Harrogate, Blackpool and Brighton).

Tours

The final group of people who typically visit cities or towns are the tourists on an all-inclusive tour of different European countries and, indeed, Paris, Amsterdam and Brussels traditionally feature on these types of tour. These types of tour very often take place throughout the year.

Activity	Look back at the map of Europe you have just drawn. Have you marked any cities or towns on your map that have not been discussed above? What is the appeal of these places? What sort of person is likely to visit them?

Seaside resorts

Europe (in particular the region surrounding the Mediterranean) has a vast range of seaside resorts that attract both domestic and international visitors. This great variety of resorts means you have to be very careful when making recommendations, although most tour operators are now much more honest in their definitions of what is a quiet or busy resort. The skill is to match the resort to the visitor. Do not make assumptions. Just because someone is young does not mean he or she will want a busy nightlife, and some older people prefer a very active holiday.

Some of the most popular seaside resorts in Europe are discussed below. You will notice they are all in southern Europe – which probably says something about European weather!

Activity	Get hold of one of the main tour operator's summer sun programmes for the Mediterranean region. Then, from your favourite soap opera, pick four different characters, families or couples and try to identify a suitable resort for them to visit. Present your recommendations to your group.

Spain

Spain has many resort areas: the Costa Brava, Costa Dorada, Costa Blanca, Costa Almeria and Costa del Sol. While some of the Costa names may not be familiar to you, the resorts of Benidorm, Torremolinos and Marbella will be well known. The Spanish seaside areas also include two important island groups: the Balearics in the Mediterranean (including Majorca, Ibiza and Menorca) and the Canary Islands in the Atlantic (including Tenerife, Lanzarote and Gran Canaria).

Spanish resorts include the black volcanic sand beaches of Tenerife in the Canary Islands.

Greece

Greece, with its mainland resort areas of the Athenian Riviera and Thessaloniki and its many islands, continues to attract vast numbers of visitors throughout the summer months. Greece is the second most popular destination after Spain for British tourists. It has over 300 islands and these groups of islands attract both single-centre visitors and island hoppers alike (island hoppers are holiday-makers who make use of the extensive ferry networks between the Greek islands).

The most popular islands are Crete, Rhodes and Kos (in the Dodecanese), Corfu and Zante (in the Ionian group) and Skiathos (in the Sporades). The reason for the popularity of these specific island groups is their ease of access (each island has an airport), whereas some of the smaller islands require a boat or hydrofoil transfer from the point of arrival.

Turkey

Although only 3% of Turkey is actually in Europe, it is included in this section as its seaside resorts border the Mediterranean. Even though the beaches of many of its resorts are poor, Turkey's culture and reputation for good value for money encourage many tourists to visit the country. Some of the most popular resorts are Bodrum, Marmaris, Kusadasi, Side and Alanya.

Italy

Italy has many resort areas, many of which are close to major tourist towns and cities, giving visitors the opportunity to combine a beach holiday with sight-seeing. For example, the Neapolitan Riviera resorts of Sorrento, Positano and Amalfi are close to Pompeii and Vesuvius, and Venice is in easy reach of the Venetian Riviera resort of Lido di Jesolo.

Portugal

The other country that is popular with tourists is Portugal, with its resort areas of the Algarve, Lisbon, the Estoril coast and Costa Verde. Portugal has many fine

beaches but these border the Atlantic, which tends to make the temperatures slightly cooler than in the Mediterranean. The south-facing Algarve has beaches that stretch for 100 miles, which are complemented by exceptionally good sporting facilities, particularly for golf and tennis. Popular resorts on the Algarve include Albufeira, Lagos and Vilamoura. Estoril and Cascais on the Estoril coast are well-established resorts that can also offer the visitor the sights of the capital city, Lisbon, with its cathedral, museums and castle. The Costa Verde in the north of the country is relatively undeveloped, and the weather can be cool early and late in the season.

Other countries

There are also many more traditional resorts around the European coasts and these tend to be 'fashionable' (for example, Nice and San Tropez). Some of these fashionable destinations are very well established and have well-developed infrastructures to support visitors. However, as they tend to be more 'exclusive', they attract the rich and famous and, as a result, are expensive resorts to visit. Some of these resorts, on the other hand, are not far from much more reasonably priced destinations that often form the basis of self-drive or campsite holidays for visitors.

Activity	Look back at your A3 map of Europe. If the five seaside resorts you chose are all in the Mediterranean, add two other resorts from other areas.

89

Purpose-built resorts

Purpose-built resorts originated in northern Europe where the unreliable weather meant tourists would not necessarily visit destinations all year round or, indeed, even during the summer months if the weather was poor. The idea is that these resorts provide indoor activities and entertainment facilities that are all within a short distance of where the visitor is staying. These resorts also generally offer a range of catering establishments to ensure visitors do not need to leave the resort for their meals.

The following are a few examples of purpose-built resorts.

Disneyland Paris

At Disneyland Paris (**http:// www.disneylandparis.com/disney/ smain.htm**) there is the main attraction of the Disneyland theme park, an entertainment zone and a range of accommodation. Obviously, it is the theme park that attracts visitors to the destination, but the opportunity to stay in a purpose-built resort with all amenities on site encourages many visitors to stay at Disneyland rather than in Paris or in one of the near-by towns. The accommodation on site has been themed to appeal to different tourists (for example, the Cheyenne Lodge is aimed at families and people on a budget). Each hotel has its own entertainment and catering facilities themed to that particular accommodation. The entertainment area, again, has a range of fast-food and other restaurants to cater for all tastes. There is also a variety of entertainment in the main area, including cinemas, discos, shows and bars.

Center Parcs

Center Parcs (**http://www.centerparcs. com/**) has three sites in the UK that are modelled on established, purpose-built resorts in The Netherlands and Denmark. These resorts are slightly different from the Disneyland model in that they have a covered dome area where the facilities are clustered together, the accommodation itself radiating out from this dome. The locations selected for resorts in the UK have made use of, for example, attractive, natural local scenery (e.g. Sherwood Forest) or local built attractions (such as Longleat).

Although the accommodation is self-catering, many visitors make use of the restaurants on site. Prices at Center Parcs are based on the size and number of rooms within each accommodation type and accommodation is not themed as at Disneyland Paris.

Theme parks

There are also many examples of purpose-built resorts that have developed from theme parks. However, most of these comprise accommodation and attraction only rather than being self-contained resorts. Examples are Alton Towers (**http:// www.alton-towers.co.uk/default1.asp**) and Legoland (**http:// www.legoland.co.uk/default.htm**), which may be developed further into self-contained resorts.

Butlins

Butlins (**http://www.butlins.co.uk/**) (with its 'holiday world' product) has developed holiday centres that could be classified as purpose-built resorts but these centres are located close to major tourist destinations.

For example, would you classify Southcoast World (Bognor Regis) and Somerwest World (Minehead) as purpose-built resorts or as attractions within the main resort?

Countryside areas

Forests

Although forest regions are not usually considered tourist destinations, there are important forest areas that are famous enough to be included here. The most famous forest within Europe is probably the Black Forest in Germany, with its thick woodlands and scenic lakes. The Black Forest is associated with cuckoo clocks and chocolate gateaux, but many people visit the forest to enjoy such activities as walking, riding and hunting. The other forest region that could be classified as a tourist destination in Europe is the Ardennes Forest in Belgium – an area that is also noted for its fine food.

Mountains

The mountains of Europe are tourist destinations both in the summer and winter but have fewer visitors in the spring or autumn. The visitors who come in the summer are very different from those who come in the winter as they will have selected mountain destinations for their beautiful scenery and for their suitability for walking or hiking. Resorts that are popular summer destinations generally have lake areas as well, and many tour operators feature these destinations in lakes and mountains brochures. The same accommodation is used in both the winter and summer, and the ski lifts and cable cars remain open to take visitors to the mountain peaks.

Resorts such as Davos and Interlaken are popular in Switzerland, while Seefeld is popular in Austria. It is the more traditional resorts rather than the purpose-built ones that tend to have successful summer seasons.

Wintersports regions

The continuing popularity of wintersports ensures that resorts in France, Austria, Switzerland and Italy benefit from considerable numbers of visitors in winter. There are also less well-established skiing resorts in Spain, Andorra and Bulgaria that offer cheaper skiing holidays than the more traditional resorts but, generally, the ski conditions are less reliable.

Switzerland

Some 61% of Switzerland is covered by the Alps and the country has 250 ski resorts, the most famous being Crans Montana, Zermatt, St Moritz and Davos. As a country, Switzerland is the most expensive of the ski destinations, its resorts attracting a very up-market clientele including many film stars and members of the royal family.

Austria

Austria has excellent ski resorts that are particularly well suited to families, with good children's facilities being available in such resorts as Mayrhofen and Seefeld. There are also some extremely lively resorts in Austria, such as Kitzbuhel which caters for all grades and types of skier.

France

France has five main skiing regions (two resorts from each region are given in brackets below):

1 Portes du Soleil (Avoriaz and Morzine)
2 Trois Vallées (Meribel and Courcheval)
3 Central France or the Cévennes Mountains (Le Puy and Clermont Ferrand)
4 Pyrenees (Font Rómeu and Luchon)
5 Savoie (Tignes and Val D'Isère).

The first two regions are both in the French Alps, where there are many examples of purpose-built resorts, including Les Arcs (which consists of three self-contained resorts of varying altitude, each one named after its height). These resorts are very well organised and contain a great deal of self-catering accommodation that is particularly attractive to families.

Italy

Italy has good snow conditions and a lively nightlife. It also has a mixture of very traditional, well-known resorts such as Cervinia, Courmayeur, Livigno and Cortina D'Ampezzo, and more modern resorts such as Sauze D'Ouz and Bardonecchia.

Other countryside attractions

Lakes have already been mentioned as part of the overall lakes and mountains package, but there are destinations where the lake is the main reason people visit. Italy has a number of lake resorts, including Garda, Maggiore and Como. Other destinations that attract visitors for their lakes are Geneva in Switzerland and Lake Balaton in Hungary.

There are other countryside destinations that attract visitors for a specific reason, including rivers such as the Rhine and the Danube, the fjords of Norway, the Arctic Circle of Sweden, Finland and Norway, and the wine regions of France, such as Bordeaux, Champagne and the Loire. In the UK there are many countryside areas that have their own appeal (for example, the National Parks, ranging from the Peak District with its caves and rugged landscape, to Dartmoor with its famous ponies).

Activity	Choose one of the following countries as an example of a destination that has a range of countryside attractions: • Switzerland • France • Austria • Italy • Germany. Produce a brochure to show what the country can offer visitors who want a countryside holiday.

Historical and cultural destinations

Historical destinations can either attract visitors for a short period (e.g. a sight-seeing trip) or may form the main focus of a holiday. Historical sites can date back to early times (such as the Roman Empire) or can be more recent (such as sites associated with the Second World War).

Italy has long been recognised as a country full of historical and cultural attractions and, very often, visitors will tour Italian sites on either a multi- or two-centre holiday. Rome (the Eternal City) contains the ruins of the Roman Forum and Colosseum as well as the independent state of the Vatican City with its famous Sistine Chapel. Naples is close to the ruins of Pompeii and Herculaneum, and most tourists will also visit Vesuvius. Florence has been a centre of the arts since the fourteenth century, and has many museums and art galleries along with the Pitti Palace and Ponte Vecchio. Many people visiting Florence also take a trip to Pisa to see the famous leaning tower or to Sienna to see its ancient piazza and cathedral.

The area around *Athens* contains many well-known historical sites, such as Delphi (the religious centre of ancient Greece), Marathon (where the Persians had their famous victory) and Olympia (the site of the original games and of the statue of Zeus). Athens itself has many historical attractions, including the Acropolis (with the Parthenon and Temple of Zeus).

Spain has a mixture of historical and cultural sites. Its most visited historical site is Granada with the Alhambra Palace (home of the Moorish kings over 700 years ago). Madrid, which has been the capital of Spain since 1606, has the famous Prado art museum.

More recently there has been a growing interest in sites associated either with the Second World War or the breakdown of the barriers between the east and west. Places of interest associated with the Second World War include the battlefields of the Ardennes region of France and the Auschwitz concentration camp in Poland. The site of the former Berlin Wall still continues to attract tourists, as does the wall in Nicosia, Cyprus, that still divides the island into Greek and Turkish Cyprus.

Traditional city destinations (such as London, Paris, Amsterdam and Vienna) are widely recognised as places where there is a vast range of cultural activities and attractions. The cultural importance of cities has been strongly emphasised over recent years, with the award of European City of Culture being allocated to one European city each year. This helps to raise awareness of the city's cultural attractions to tourists.

Activity	Find out which city is European City of Culture this year, and then identify what that city has to offer tourists.

Features

There are many things that will influence a tourist's decision as to which of the major travel and tourism destinations in Europe he or she might visit, including the:

- food and drink available
- types of entertainment on offer
- transport facilities
- accessibility of the destination
- climate.

When selecting a holiday, food and drink are likely to be one of the main factors tourists will consider. Indeed, the food and drink available in some destinations is often a destination's most powerful attraction. Just consider the following:

- In the Greek islands there are tavernas and bars with tables that overlook harbours or beaches. The ambience of these tavernas and bars is often enhanced by the music of bouzouki players. A variety of starters will be served, including olives, dips and Greek salad with feta cheese. This might be followed by more simple food that has been grilled, barbecued or cooked in a clay oven. All this washed down with Greek wine, ouzo, reasonably priced brandies and strong Greek coffee.
- Nice, on the other hand, is often considered as being more formal, with expensive menus and French food. Exotic dishes, such as snails and frog legs, might be followed by steak tartare (served raw) and seafood. Excellent French cheeses and expensive French wines and champagnes contribute to the *haute cuisine* of the top restaurants in the South of France.
- In Spanish resorts, alternatively, it is often difficult to find local cooking. You are more likely to find international restaurants serving Chinese or Indian food and pizzerias rather than traditional paella or tapas bars.

Food and drink might also be a key factor in the selection of short-break holidays (for example, Belgian beer, the Indonesian restaurants of Amsterdam, and Parisian bistros and street-side cafés). However, entertainment might be a more important consideration when tourists select a short break. Brussels, Amsterdam and Paris all have considerable amounts of entertainment:

- Brussels has its uptown Porte Louise entertainment area and similarly, downtown areas between Place Roger and Place de la Bourse (which have many bars, discotheques, jazz clubs and nightclubs).
- The Moulin Rouge and can-can girls of Paris are a tourist attraction in their own right.
- Amsterdam has its infamous red-light district and some of the liveliest nightlife in Europe.

In other short-break destinations, such as Prague, Budapest, Vienna and Rome, the main cultural attractions are the theatre, opera and concerts. There are, however, still nightclubs in these cities but these tend to be much more low key and are often located in hotels.

Transport is a big consideration for many people who are planning to visit European destinations. Air journeys to Paris, Brussels and Amsterdam are very short and there are many regional connections, which makes travel from local airports simple and easy. Low-cost airlines (such as Buzz, Easyjet and Go) offer cheap air fares to most European destinations. It is now commonplace to see fares of £39 to the majority of European cities. And the opening of the Channel Tunnel has made rail travel from central London to these destinations as quick as air travel.

Some types of holiday are significantly affected by a destination's accessibility. For example, there are often long transfer journeys at the end of flights to reach certain ski destinations. Although flight times may be only $1\frac{1}{2}$–3 hours, the journey to the resort might often be the equivalent length of time as the flight itself, if not longer. Resorts in the Innsbruck area of Austria (including Innsbruck, St Anton and

Kitzbuhel), on the other hand, benefit from the short transfer from Innsbruck airport. Resorts in Andorra (where there is no airport), alternatively, have long transfers, and the majority of tourists take the cheaper option of travelling the whole journey by coach or rail.

Transfers to some of the quieter resorts of the Mediterranean are also lengthened by the need to travel to the destination from the airport by boat. The journey to Athens is relatively short, but the transfer to the islands of Evia and Andros can make the journey a whole day or overnight event.

The weather is just as important for city breaks as it is for ski or beach holidays. There are, however, very few destinations in Europe that have reliable year-round weather. Cities that are pleasant in the winter, (such as Seville, Florence and Athens) are stiflingly hot in the summer. The Scandinavian cities of Copenhagen, Oslo and Stockholm are beautiful in the summer but suffer from short days and long nights in the winter, along with cold weather. The southern Mediterranean resorts on Crete, the Algarve, Cyprus and Malta have reasonably good climates throughout the spring, summer and autumn, while the season in the more northerly resorts of Nice, Corfu and the Costa Brava is much shorter. The weather in some of these resorts can be very unpredictable at the beginning and end of the summer.

Chapter 3.3 The location of major overseas destinations

Non-European (or long-haul destinations) have seen a considerable growth in visitor numbers since the 1980s, fuelled by cheap air travel and by travellers becoming more experienced and mature and, hence, starting to seek more exotic, different destinations. Some areas have witnessed a constant, solid growth, while others have been affected by events external to the industry (e.g. political instability, terrorism or natural disasters) and have, thus, had more erratic trends in visitor numbers. (Remember, when studying trends in visitor numbers for a country you are less familiar with, make sure you understand the reasons for any changes.)

The city of New York is one of the principal destinations in North America.

The three main areas that continue to be popular with UK visitors include:

- North America (the USA and Canada)
- the Caribbean
- Australia and New Zealand.

The main features of these three areas are considered briefly here but to study one of these destinations further would require you to conduct your own research into that specific destination.

North America (the USA and Canada)

North America covers a vast area containing many time zones, climate patterns and a huge range of tourist attractions, both natural and built. We will focus here first on specific areas of the USA and will then go on to consider the main features of Canada.

The USA

Florida

The most popular state in the USA for UK visitors is Florida, with a summer climate that reaches over 30°C, mild winters and wet tropical months of July–October. Miami is one of the main entry points for visitors, either by air or as a cruise port. Miami Beach itself has excellent beaches with a variety of accommodation from motels to luxury hotels. However, many buildings along the coastline tend to be high rise. The resort has many museums and art galleries, a seaquarium, and it is the starting point for the Florida Keys (160 miles of coral reefs and diving centres).

The nearby resorts of Fort Lauderdale (with its canals, rivers and lagoons) and Palm Beach (with its fashionable, palm-lined boulevards) are also popular. The Everglades (North America's largest subtropical wilderness) can be explored by boat trips or guided tours. Tampa (on the Gulf Coast) has a very good sunshine record and a thriving tourist industry. Much of this can be attributed to the nearby location of Busch Gardens (the African theme park) and by Tampa's close proximity to many islands that are easy for tourists to visit.

However, the one big attraction that brings people to Florida is at Orlando: Disneyworld, with its many themed hotels (including the Polynesian Village, Fort Wilderness Camping and the Caribbean Beach Resort). Disneyland is complemented by a wide range of additional built attractions, including EPCOT (Experimental Prototype Community Of Tomorrow), Seaworld, Cypress Gardens, and Universal and MGM film studios. Very few visitors actually visit the town of Orlando as there is so much happening in Disneyworld they tend to remain within the resort.

Activity	Find Florida on a map of the USA. Draw an outline of the state showing bordering states and seas/oceans. On your map locate the following: • Miami • the Florida Keys • Palm Beach • Fort Lauderdale • the Everglades • Tampa • Orlando.

Florida is visited by all types of tourist but particularly attracts families with young children. The majority of visitors take a fly-drive arrangement, picking up the car at the airport for the duration of their stay. Food tends to be cheap although, within the attractions, price and quality do tend to vary. Many visitors prepay for the attractions by buying passes that cover a set number of days, although the cost of visiting the many attractions can add a considerable amount to the cost of a holiday to Florida.

The East Coast cities

The next area we will consider is also on the East Coast of the USA and includes the city destinations of New York, Boston and Washington, DC. Because of the East Coast

Washington, DC. This remarkable city is made for tourists with wonderful sights like the Washington Monument and its reflecting lake.

location of these cities and the frequency of flights from the UK, these destinations are all offered as short-break as well as longer-duration holidays. Visitors tend to be couples or individuals taking this as their second holiday of the year. There are also large numbers of people who visit these cities for business purposes and, very often, a tourist stay will be tagged on to the end of such a trip. The weather in all three destinations tends to be similar to that in the UK, although there are extremes in both winter and summer that can cause very cold or very hot conditions.

New York has many attractions, including the Statue of Liberty, the Empire State Building, museums and Central Park. It is also well known for shopping, particularly the fashionable shops on Fifth Avenue. Broadway offers entertainment in the evening, and the range of nightlife, bars and restaurants New York offers should suit most people's interests.

Boston is much more restrained in both its entertainment and atmosphere. The first European settlers arrived here in 1620 in *The Mayflower* and there is a museum commemorating this event. The Boston Tea Party and the Freedom Trail are located in Boston, as are the universities of Yale and Harvard.

Washington, DC (being the capital of the USA) has many attractions connected with government, including the White House, Arlington Cemetery and memorials to Lincoln, Jefferson and Washington. There are also considerable numbers of museums, all located conveniently close to each other and easily accessible by public transport.

The West Coast

The West Coast of America has three main cities that attract visitors: Los Angeles, San Francisco and Las Vegas. A popular tour combines all three destinations with a visit to the Grand Canyon. The West Coast traditionally attracts young people (including couples), although with the numbers of people who now have links with American computer companies growing, the type of visitor to the region now varies considerably. The climate tends to be very hot in the summer and pleasant throughout the autumn and spring. San Francisco is famous for its sea mists or fog that comes rolling in from the Pacific Ocean in the late afternoon. Evening temperatures can be very cool in these resorts.

Los Angeles has many attractions to do with its strong links to the cinema, including Hollywood and Universal Studios. Beverly Hills is probably best seen through one of the many 'home of the stars' type tours rather than driving around the area. Disneyland is located close to Los Angeles and, although much smaller than the ones in Florida and Paris, it is still a major attraction. The beaches of Malibu, Long Beach and Muscle Beach (where people work out on the beach) are all popular with tourists.

San Francisco is much more relaxed than Los Angeles, and the trams make an interesting way of getting around this hilly city. The Golden Gate Bridge over San Francisco Bay is a well-known landmark, as is the notorious prison of Alcatraz, which can be reached easily by boat. Fisherman's Wharf is an attractive shopping region on the seafront close to the main attractions.

Las Vegas (in the middle of the Nevada Desert) is the gambling centre of the world with its 24-hour casinos. It is also the location of some of the most exciting themed hotel developments, including hotels and nightclubs that attract international performers and shows.

Travelling in the USA

Travelling around the USA can be done a number of ways, depending on the time and money available. Because of the vast distances that often need to be travelled, air travel is often the best option, and many airlines offer very cheap deals or air passes that cover a certain number of flights on one specific airline. It is possible to hire camper vans or motor-homes so your source of transport also becomes your temporary home. Car hire is cheap and readily available, but the driver must be adequately insured to cover all eventualities (including being sued for any damages he or she may inflict). Rail travel is good between some destinations using the AMTRAK rail system and can be an interesting way of seeing the scenery along the way. Greyhound buses offer a range of very cheap alternative ways of travelling, including the Ameripass scheme that offers unlimited Greyhound bus travel for a month at a time. However, for most visitors, the time factor makes the last two modes of travel unfeasible.

Canada

Canada, on the other hand, tends to be a destination in which visitors make use of coach and rail services. ViaRail offers a number of scenic journeys across the country. Canada is very large, covering 3,000 miles from coast to coast, and it encompasses six time zones. The main cultural influences in Canada are French and British and, indeed, many Canadians speak French as their first language. Traditionally, Canada has attracted VFR (visiting friends and relatives) traffic but there is now an

Toronto, with its distinctive skyline, is a very popular Canadian destination.

increasing number of visitors who go to Canada primarily for the scenery, which includes forests, lakes, mountains and rivers.

The main attractions in Canada are in Toronto (the largest city of Canada), with the Niagara Falls being visited either on the *Maid of the Mist* boat or by cable car. Toronto is also the home of the CN Tower, one of the tallest free-standing structures in the world. In the state of Alberta, the annual event of the Calgary stampede attracts many visitors to its rodeo and Wild West Show. The state is also home to the Rockies and the summer and winter resorts of Banff and Jasper. Many visitors will also include a trip to Montreal, Quebec (both very French) and

Ottawa on their itineraries, as well as a visit to the North West Territories and the diamond mines at Yellowknife.

Activity	Draw an outline map of Canada. On your map, mark the following places:
	• Toronto • Calgary • Banff • Jasper • Montreal • Ottawa • Yellowknife. Find out what the different time zones are across North America and mark them on your map with the difference from British (GMT) time.

The Caribbean

The Caribbean has seen considerable growth in UK tourists recently, mainly sparked off by a rise in the number of charter flights provided by tour operators to the main islands. The result has been a reduction in the price of holidays and the opening up of the Caribbean to mass-market travellers. However, many of these packages were originally offered on a room-only basis, and the cost of eating and drinking on many of the islands was very expensive, which added greatly to the cost of a holiday. The operators have now seen the necessity of including all-inclusive packages in their brochures which, although increasing the price of a package, have brought better value to the product. The majority of Caribbean accommodation is now on an all-inclusive basis, which does, however, reduce the amount of contact tourists have with the local culture and people (see Unit 2). There are still, though, room-only packages

available at both the cheapest and most expensive ends of the accommodation range.

The Caribbean is popular all year round (due to its good sunshine record), but there is a hurricane and rainy season between July and October. However, this season varies with the island or group of islands and so it is always best to check this. The islands tend to have excellent beaches, and there is a wide range of cruise products for customers who want either to cruise around the islands or to combine a cruise with a single stay on one of the more popular islands such as Barbados or Puerto Rico or with Florida on the mainland USA.

Activity	Draw an outline map of the Caribbean. On your map, mark the following islands:
	• Barbados • St Lucia • Trinidad and Tobago • Puerto Rico • British and US Virgin Islands • Dominican Republic • Jamaica • Cayman Islands • The Bahamas.

Each island (or group of islands) has its own history that is dependent on the country that colonised it, such as Spain, Britain, the USA, The Netherlands and France. This influence is also reflected in the buildings, food and languages of the islands.

The Dominican Republic is one of the most popular islands (particularly with the younger British traveller), mainly because of the low-cost, all-inclusive product that is offered. However, as a destination the Dominican Republic does not have as many established attractions as some of its more developed competitors. For example, Barbados has extensive beaches and watersports, along with lively nightlife areas close to the capital, Bridgetown. Jamaica has the famous Dunnes River Falls at Ochos Rios and the well-known resort of Montego Bay.

Australia and New Zealand

While *Australia* is roughly the same size as Europe, it has considerably fewer inhabitants. The majority of the population lives in the major cities on the east and west coasts. Many people visit these cities to be reunited with friends and relatives who have gone to live there (VFR).

Sydney is often the starting point for a trip to Australia, with its famous landmarks of the Opera House and Harbour Bridge. The Rocks Area (which is acknowledged to be the birthplace of the modern state of Australia) retains cobbled streets and many old buildings. Close to the city are the beaches of Bondi and Manley. The state best known for its beaches is probably Queensland, especially the Gold Coast, just south of Brisbane, with the resort of Surfers Paradise. The coastline between Brisbane and Cairns is packed with islands and island resorts on the Great Barrier Reef. Cairns allows easy access to the national parks, rain forests and beautiful white sandy beaches. Australia's most famous landmark, Uluru (formerly known as Ayers Rock), is not easily accessible for tourists, the closest town being Alice Springs in the Northern Territory. However, many travellers feel a visit to Australia is not complete without seeing Ayers Rock, especially at sunrise or sunset. The cities of Perth, Melbourne, Adelaide and Canberra do not tend to attract as many tourists as other regions of Australia, although Perth is very often visited because its location permits tours of the outback and to northern Australia.

Australia's unmistakable Uluru – formerly known as Ayers Rock.

Activity	Draw an outline map of Australia. Divide the country into its eight states. Find out which seas and oceans surround the country and mark these on your map. Now locate the following destinations and put these on the map: • Sydney • Brisbane • Canberra • Melbourne • Adelaide • Perth • Hobart • Darwin • Surfers Paradise • Cairns • Alice Springs • Uluru (Ayers Rock).

Most visitors to *New Zealand* are visiting friends and relatives. New Zealand comprises two islands (North and South), which are separated by the Cook Strait. Although the South Island is the larger of the two, the majority of the inhabitants and visitors are to be found in the North Island. Auckland tends to be the main destination for visitors, with a business centre, harbour and beaches close by. Boating is a popular activity, especially visiting the islands off the coastline. Wellington, the capital, is a good centre for shopping and entertainment but, because of its location, it has poorer weather than the rest of the island. Many tourists also visit the volcanic regions, especially Rotorua with its geysers, thermal springs and Maori culture. On the South Island the main city is Christchurch, which has a very British flavour and which is known as the 'garden city' because of its many parks and gardens.

Both Australia and New Zealand have very good access, with regular international flights either via the Far East or America and the Pacific islands. Many people planning a visit to Australia will want to stop over at a destination *en route* and, providing the airline is stopping at the destination the passenger wants to visit, there will generally be no extra charge for this. It usually costs more to fly to Australia via America, simply because of the distance involved. Perth generally costs less to fly to than Sydney, although passengers may want to fly home from a different point from the one they flew in to.

Australia, in particular, attracts young people on working visas who spend on average six months to a year working and travelling around the country. Travelling around the country can take a long time by road or rail, and so travellers who are short of time tend to use the good internal network of flights.

Be aware of the different climates both in and within Australia and New Zealand. Their summer months are our winter months, and vice versa. There are large variations between regions in New Zealand and Australia. Australian cities like Canberra, Melbourne, Adelaide and Sydney experience much higher temperatures than those in the UK. However, in Perth the climate is more like the Mediterranean, while the tropical conditions in Darwin and Cairns are very different from the rest of the country. These northern regions suffer from tropical storms and the rainy season should be avoided as roads to the more remote areas often become impassable.

The 'Prince of Wales' hot spring in Rotorua, New Zealand.

Chapter 3.4 The features of major destinations

Every destination has its own particular features which will appeal to different types of tourist. The features that give a destination its own particular 'flavour' include:

- climate
- topography
- natural attractions
- built attractions
- events
- food, drink and entertainment
- types of accommodation
- types of transport
- the accessibility of travel and tourism gateways.

As some of these features have already been covered in Unit 1, in this section they will be discussed purely in relation to destinations rather than to the travel and tourism industry in general.

Climate

Climate is a major factor when choosing a destination and will also influence the price of a visit (i.e. holidays may be more expensive when the weather is most attractive or reliable). There are, however, different aspects to climate, including sunshine hours, humidity, temperature and rainfall. Temperature alone is not a good indicator of how suitable a destination will be, as there could be a rainy season which still has high temperatures even though the days are overcast and rainy rather than sunny. Sunshine hours generally give a better indication of what the climate will really be like.

When making recommendations based on temperature, think carefully about what would be a sensible temperature for a particular customer. A family with young children or an elderly person might not want to spend their days basking in temperatures of 30°C. With growing concerns about skin cancer, people are generally more worried about the risk of sunburn, and some people will therefore select destinations that have a cooler temperature.

Activity	On a blank map of the world, mark the following:

On a blank map of the world, mark the following:

1 the Equator
2 the Tropics of Capricorn and Cancer
3 the major oceans
4 the areas prone to tropical storms.

Now, using a colour-coding system, illustrate the following climatic areas (use an atlas to help you identify these, if necessary):

- desert and steppe areas
- tropical areas
- continental or maritime climates
- mild or Mediterranean climates
- polar regions
- mountainous areas (where altitude affects the climate).

Using a world travel guide, write a brief description of what sort of weather can be expected by travellers to these six types of climatic region. Give an idea of the type of clothing that is recommended for visiting each of these regions.

> *Hint*: If you find this task difficult, choose a country within each climatic region and look up climate information for that country (for example, mountainous – Ecuador, tropical – Indonesia).

The activity you have just completed should help you to identify areas prone to tropical storms, but storms are seasonal. Therefore, when researching destinations prone to storms, check which months storms are likely to be a problem.

The climate of northern Europe (including the UK) has a strong influence on the number of visitors who go to a particular destination and the length of the tourist season in these places. If the weather is particularly rainy or cool in the summer, people are more likely to go further afield for their holiday. However, if the climate within their own country is good, late bookers may be tempted to stay at home.

Topography

By topography we mean the landscape (for example, mountains, lakes and coastline). Not all tourists are concerned about topography: those seeking an exciting nightlife or who want to do nothing more than stay in the hotel grounds all day might not be worried too much about what the destination looks like. However, for many visitors, topography is an important factor when deciding on their choice of destination.

Skiers, in particular, need to consider the suitability of a particular skiing region for their own abilities in the sport. If they are beginners, they will need nursery slopes with blue and/or green runs that are easily accessible. An advanced skier, on the other hand, needs to make sure there are sufficient black runs within the resort or, if the resorts are linked together, suitable runs he or she could use. The height of ski runs determines the likelihood of good snow conditions. However, high altitudes can be exceptionally cold, especially for inexperienced skiers.

Sometimes the aspect of the slope needs to be taken into account. South-facing slopes are the warmest and sunniest in the months of January and February but, towards the end of the season they can melt and become icy. North-facing slopes, alternatively, may have longer seasons. Not all skiers need mountains: cross-country or *langlauf* skiers are more likely to consider skiing in some of the flatter Scandinavian regions.

Many people prefer to select a destination that has hills and mountains, either purely from an aesthetic point of view or to ensure the resort is sheltered or protected from bad weather. If you have been to Tenerife, you are probably aware of the effect Mount Teide has on the two halves of the island. The southern resort of Playa de la Americas benefits from exceptionally sunny and reliably hot temperatures, whereas the northern resort of Puerto de la Cruz is much greener as a result of the wetter climate.

Some travellers (especially those who are older, less fit or asthmatic) have to be careful not to select a destination that has a high altitude as the air will be thinner and thus the risk of breathing problems will increase. Many of the brochures that feature destinations in South America will explain this in the descriptions that accompany the holidays on offer.

The type of lake or coastline is also an important consideration: whether the shore or beach has fine, coarse or pebbly sand or is rocky. One destination that has few or no

examples of beautiful beaches surrounded by such high and rocky cliffs that the only way of reaching these beaches is by sea.

Natural and built attractions

Natural and built attractions were discussed in Unit 1. If we look back at our original classification of travel and tourism destinations, we can probably add to this the type of attraction most likely associated with each destination grouping:

- towns and cities – built attractions
- seaside resorts – a combination of natural and built attractions
- purpose-built resorts – built attractions
- countryside areas – natural attractions
- historical/cultural areas – built attractions.

However, things are not as simple as this as the majority of destinations will have a balance of natural and built attractions (for example, towns and cities might also have rivers and parks, while countryside areas might also have ancient monuments and stately homes). Seaside resorts generally have both human-made and natural attractions, with cliffs and beaches often being next to funfairs and piers.

The following are examples of natural and built attractions that bring visitors to particular destinations.

Natural

Safari trips are often taken to such countries as Kenya and Zambia, where the main attraction is to see wild animals in their natural habitat. These safaris often accommodate visitors in tents so as to get closer to nature. On Himalayan treks, guides escort visitors on a range of tours through

beaches is the island of Malta, where holiday-makers sunbathe on the many rocky areas around the coastline. Families with young children and people who are not strong swimmers will need to consider how steeply the beach shelves into the sea and whether the area is safe for swimming. Several of the resorts in northern Spain, Portugal and southern France have railway lines running between the resort and the beach, while others have a major road running adjacent to the beach. Even for those people who are not interested in lying on the beach, a coastline or lakeside is somewhere they may wish to visit for its attractiveness.

The final point about topography is that, sometimes, the landscape itself can make a destination very inaccessible, and this will obviously affect how many visitors can go to that destination. There are these famous mountains. Sometimes it is one specific natural attraction that attracts visitors to a destination (e.g. the Victoria Falls, the Great Barrier Reef, the Sahara Desert or the Grand Canyon).

One of the most famous built attractions – the tower of Pisa.

Built

The most obvious examples of built attractions are the theme parks of Disneyland, Alton Towers and Busch Gardens. The university cities of Oxford and Cambridge attract many visitors, especially if there is an opportunity to tour the university buildings. Such buildings as the Palace of Versailles and the chateaux of France attract visitors to parts of that country that are off the main tourist trails. More recently, attractions have started to focus on the theme of people and work,

successful examples in the UK being Granada Studios, Cadbury's, Beamish and the Ironbridge museum.

Events

Many areas have annual carnivals and festivals that attract visitors to the region. In the UK there are a number of these events:

- the Notting Hill Carnival
- the Edinburgh Festival
- the Henley Royal Regatta
- the Eisteddfod
- the Oxford and Cambridge Boat Race
- various shows, such as the Motor Show, the Boat Show and Crufts.

Internationally, there are some very famous carnivals, such as the ones held in Rio de Janeiro, New Orleans and Venice. These carnivals are centred on music and colourful processions. To find out more about specific carnivals, either contact the local tourist board or look in the *World Travel Guide* in the social profile section for a specific country.

There are also events that are held on a regular basis (i.e. annually or every two or four years) but that take place in a different destination each time (e.g. the Olympic Games, the Winter Olympics, the Football and Rugby World Cups, the Ryder Cup and the Americas Cup). Most visitors to these events spend very little time exploring the country they are visiting and, generally, the only attractions they visit are connected with the event.

At all these events, an exceptionally high number of visitors will be attracted for a very short period of time. Hence there are always heavy demands on accommodation and catering over the days of the event. Transport (particularly on international flights) is also likely to be in high demand, especially on the dates immediately before and after the event. Prices are likely to increase, and there can be a low level of visitor satisfaction with the destination. Always advise travellers if an event is taking place during their stay as it is possible they may be making a reservation without knowing the full impact a major international event could have on their visit.

Food, drink and entertainment

The type of accommodation available in a resort greatly affects the range of food, drink and entertainment available to visitors. If there is a high number of all-inclusive hotels in a resort, there is unlikely to be the same number of catering and entertainment establishments you would normally find in a resort with a high number of self-catering apartments. However, most destinations still have a variety of restaurants, cafés, bars and nightclubs.

Often it is the local food and drink and the style of service that attract visitors to a specific destination (for example, Greece with its tavernas and very distinctive cuisine). Many people visit France for local French cooking and for the fine brandy and wines. However, many people will want to make sure they will have easy access to plenty of English food (for example, cooked breakfasts, burgers and steak and chips). Finding resorts that cater for such 'international tastes' is becoming much easier as many overseas destinations now have branches of very familiar international chains, such as McDonald's and Pizza Hut.

When considering nightlife, look at how many nightclubs there are and where they are located. While some resorts have deliberately concentrated all their nightclubs

within one area to cause minimum disturbance to tourists who want a quieter holiday, generally speaking, some resorts are much more lively than others. Some of the liveliest European resorts include San Antonio in Ibiza, Torremolinos on the Costa del Sol, Benitses in Corfu and Aghios Nikolaos in Crete. However, one resort does not paint the picture for the whole island: in Ibiza, Corfu and Crete it is possible to find exceptionally quiet, unspoilt resorts with only a handful of bars and small cafés.

Activity	What do you know about the traditional food and drink of different countries? Find out more about the food of the following countries: • Greece • Portugal • Spain • Turkey • Jamaica • Australia. Produce a poster or some other way to display the foods of one of these countries.

Types of accommodation

The accommodation in a destination will not only influence the types of catering establishments in the area but will also determine the types of visitor the destination will attract. Traditionally, families have selected either self-catering or three-star hotel accommodation, although current trends show that many families are now booking all-inclusive products, especially in the Mediterranean resorts. The more expensive four and five-star properties tend to attract couples and single visitors, who are more mature and who have a higher disposable income. Lower-grade and hostel accommodation very often appeals to young singles, groups or couples who might still spend a considerable amount of money in the destination but their priorities might be to spend this on entertainment rather than accommodation.

Obviously, an imbalance in the accommodation in a destination will affect the type of tourist who visits and what he or she might spend money on. Some of the islands in the Caribbean contain purely four-star or higher accommodation, and some of this is all-inclusive. In these destinations, the tourist community will be older and wealthier than on more traditional islands such as Jamaica and Barbados, where the larger amount of self-catering and three-star accommodation attracts families and younger couples.

The Algarve in Portugal and the south of France have traditionally had more self-catering accommodation than hotel accommodation, while the Balearic Islands and mainland Spain have a higher proportion of three-star, half and full-board hotels. This has resulted in the popularity of these destinations during the summer holiday months for families.

Types of transport

Many visitors to destinations do not make use of local transport. If they venture outside the hotel at all, this will usually be on foot, on an excursion or by booking car hire. However, there are visitors who rely on public transport to get around the destination, either because this meets their sense of adventure or because it is convenient and cheap.

Bus transport is found in most destinations and, in some places such as Turkey, there are exceptionally good long-distance as well as local bus services. Some destinations have special bus routes that are used by tourists only. These often link the hotels with the town centre or a tourist attraction (for example, the bus service that runs along the Costa del Sol to Gibraltar). In some destinations the bus transport might be a tourist attraction in itself, such as the old-fashioned buses that run around the island of Malta.

Internal train services are more evident in mainland Europe, especially northern Europe. Visitors to Switzerland often use the trains as their main way of sight-seeing, purchasing a rail pass in advance. Some destinations also rely on trains to transfer visitors between the airport and resort. Independent travellers touring Europe can use rail passes that allow a month's unlimited travel.

Train travel in Europe is well-developed; this is Stockholm, Sweden.

The Mediterranean islands are linked with the mainland by a network of ferry services, especially the Greek Islands, Corsica and the Italian islands of Elba, Sardinia and Capri. There are also many local ferries that service particular towns and beaches. For example, visitors staying in San Antonio, Ibiza (where the beach is small) can catch ferries to nearby larger beaches. There are also car ferries that link larger destinations, such as Barcelona with Majorca and Athens with Rhodes, Crete, Cyprus and Egypt.

Trams often provide a novel form of transport, but there are now very few places where a tram network still exists. In the UK the trams of Blackpool are an attraction in themselves, as are the cable cars of San Francisco. Amsterdam is probably the best example of a city that still makes extensive use of a tram service. Instead, most cities of Europe rely on an underground system which takes the traffic off the streets and speeds up travelling time (such as the London Underground and the Paris Metro).

Accessibility of travel and tourism gateways

Accessibility is one of the most important factors in a resort's popularity and development. The most popular mode of travel for tourists is by air, generally on a charter flight. Hence, most of the popular Mediterranean resorts are close to an airport. The island of Majorca demonstrates this well: the main resorts are on the south coast, running either side of Palma airport.

Transfer time is also an important consideration, and most tourists hope to be in their resorts within an hour or hour and a half of arriving at the airport. One country that has had problems with transfer times is Turkey. Transfer times could take up to four hours to some resorts from either Izmir or

Traffic jams are a potential problem with road travel.

Dalaman airports. As a result, a new airport was opened in Bodrum to service the popular resorts in this region of the country. Ski destinations can also suffer from very long transfer times, which are often hampered by bad weather. If you are recommending a ski destination, find out how long the transfer will take, particularly if you are dealing with a family with young children.

Some visitors arrive at their destinations through seaports, either as a result of catching a ferry, being on a cruise or there being no direct flight to the destination. Many mainland European ferry ports are linked to excellent road or rail networks to ensure ease of access, but such places as Paris are still a three or four hours' drive from the nearest ferry ports.

Travellers going overland either by coach, rail or self-drive may have to cross international borders to get to their destinations. These will generally be on main road and rail links but may require a detour in order to arrive at their chosen destination. The relaxing of immigration checks and border controls within Europe may make these routes easier for travellers in the future.

Chapter 3.5 Main travel and tourism gateways and routes

Travellers have a choice when deciding how they will get to their destination:

- road (motorways, major trunk routes, the Channel Tunnel)
- rail (high-speed trains and scenic railways)
- air (charter and scheduled flights)
- sea (ferry routes and cruises).

Activity	For each of the four methods of transport (road, rail, air and sea), make a list of each method's advantages and disadvantages. Compare your list with that of a fellow student.

When considering which mode of transport to use, you must consider cost, convenience, journey time and the services available. Sometimes, however, there are other factors that must be considered (e.g. people who have a fear of flying are more likely to travel by sea, road and/or rail). Similarly, families with young children may have a great deal of additional luggage, which makes the road option more favourable than air or rail. Some customers may not have a choice: for those booking a package holiday, charter air travel may be the only option offered.

Road

Every country has its own way of classifying its roads (just as in the UK, where we have motorways, A and B roads and local routes). While different names are used in different countries (in Germany a motorway is called an *Autobahn*), the general idea is the same. Many countries, however, charge tolls for using the motorways. This can add a considerable expense on to the journey, particularly if, say, driving from the north to the south of France.

One thing that *does* differ between different countries are the laws of the road, which include the following:

- speed limits
- the wearing of rear seat belts
- the carrying of equipment (such as warning triangles and fire extinguishers)
- the minimum driving age.

There are also regulations that affect British car owners (e.g. adjusting headlights and displaying a GB sticker). In some countries a UK driving licence is acceptable while others require an IDP (international driving permit) to be purchased in advance from one of the motoring organisations. Insurance should always be checked to find out if the cover (including breakdown cover) is valid for the countries being visited. If not, additional insurance must be purchased.

The Channel Tunnel offers a good alternative to the ferry routes for drivers, with its journey time of just over half an hour and the quicker loading time. Some people, however, find this route slightly claustrophobic, as drivers and passengers are required to stay in their cars for the whole journey.

Many people enjoy the freedom of having their own car overseas and, as some countries and accommodation chains offer hotel passes, the itinerary can be kept flexible. There are people who also take their caravan or motor-home with them, making use of the network of caravan sites available throughout Europe. Facilities have improved dramatically in recent times, and sites are usually fully serviced, with restaurants, cafés, bars, shops, swimming pools and other leisure facilities.

Rail

Rail travel between major European cities can now be exceptionally fast. When compared with air travel (which has a check-in time and time to unload baggage at the end of the flight), it is sometimes faster to travel by rail. The Eurostar service between London and Paris (using the Channel Tunnel) has become extremely popular with business travellers who not only appreciate that the

travelling time is the same as for the air journey but who have also started to see alternative benefits in this method of travelling. They can usually work on laptop computers for the whole journey, instead of having to switch these off for take-off and landing, and can use mobile phones to contact colleagues and customers. The other great advantage is that the train goes from the centre of London to the heart of Paris, without the need to travel to and from an airport.

High-speed train lines also link major cities and travel across borders. The most reliable way of finding out train information within Europe is by using the *Thomas Cook European Timetable*, which is accompanied by a rail map of Europe. This timetable will tell you what type of train operates between cities and towns and, in some cases, these trains will also have names. London has many different rail terminals, and other capital cities, such as Paris, also have more than one railway station. It is important to remember this as travellers coming into Paris on one of the boat trains from Calais may need to change stations to reach their final destinations.

Activity	Using a *Thomas Cook European Timetable*, on a map of Europe, plot rail journeys from London to Zurich, Frankfurt, Rome and Madrid. Look at the types of train that will be involved and where changes will be made.
	Identify where the border crossings will take place.
	How long does each journey take (approximately)?

There are also many scenic journeys that can be made on the railway networks, especially in countries such as Austria and Switzerland where the mountain and lakeside railways offer spectacular views. However, some of the other countries we have mentioned that are further afield also offer scenic routes, in particular railway journeys that cross Canada, Australia and the USA. These journeys take several days and the traveller will eat, sleep and drink on board the train. It allows them to see large sections of the country from the comfort of their own seats, without the worry of having to drive. This section would not be complete without mentioning the *Venice Simplon Orient Express*, the luxury train that travels between London and Venice. This offers a level of luxury, meals and service that is of an exceptional standard while travelling on this once infamous rail route.

Local rail services provide important links. The Docklands Light Railway feeds London City airport.

Air

As we have already seen, air travel is the most popular mode of transport and, as the number of air services and companies has increased, so has the competition – resulting in more reasonably priced fares. Many of the destinations you will be investigating have a mix of charter and schedule services (if you need to revise the difference between charter and scheduled flights, look back at Unit 1). Some of the more popular holiday destinations (such as Spain, Greece and Portugal) have a higher percentage of charter flights than such countries as France and Austria, where the majority of package holiday companies make use of scheduled services. If you look at Scandinavian destinations (i.e. Sweden, Norway and Finland) you will find there are no charter services, which shows rather dramatically the difference between the south and north of Europe.

In the UK, some airports (e.g. Luton and Gatwick) have high numbers of charter flights operating from them, whereas other airports (e.g. Heathrow) rarely have charter services. Regional airports (such as Manchester and Birmingham) have a combination of both types of flight. Where this happens, very often the scheduled flights are allocated departure times suited to the needs of business travellers, while charter carriers are allocated the less popular times.

Activity	On an outline map of the UK, locate all the airports that serve overseas destinations (i.e. the international airports).

Not only do some towns and cities often have more than one airport but also some airports have more than one terminal. At smaller airports there may be one terminal for domestic flights and another for international ones. However, at Heathrow and Gatwick this situation is less clear, and it is the airline (and, in some cases, the destination) that determines which terminal a traveller will use. The *ABC Guide to International Travel* and the *World Airways Guide* should be able to provide you with information about which terminal will be used for a particular journey.

It might also be necessary to consider which option is the better choice – a scheduled or charter service. Find out which airlines operate services to your particular destination (some are associated with a specific country. For example, on the Athens service both Olympic and British Airways offer frequent flights). There may be other airlines that also fly this route (such as Virgin) on a scheduled basis.

You then need to find out which companies offer charter services, and tour operators' brochures are a good starting point here. Do bear in mind, though, when looking at charter companies' services that the airline itself should be stated (e.g. Britannia rather than Thomson). You may find there are smaller tour operators who are also using the same Britannia flight. This is because they have booked a block of seats from Britannia on that flight to sell as part of their own holiday product.

Checking prices for flights can be difficult as prices are rarely published. British Airways still print scheduled air fares on a fortnightly basis, but travel agents usually use their computers first as there are likely to be special deals and offers on most routes. Charter operators also used to produce brochures quoting their rates but, again, this has now been put on to travel agencies' databases because of the constantly

changing fares. If you use a travel agent as a source of information for fares, ask him or her if he or she can print off the details so you have documentary proof of the prices to use with your work.

Sea

Sea travel from the UK can be undertaken from a wide range of ports and, as the routes can change annually, it is always best to check with the ferry operators or with the *ABC Shipping Guide* to obtain up-to-date information about who is operating which route. Generally speaking, Figure 3.2 should act as a guide to who operates where.

Route	Operator
Short routes, UK–France	P & O Stena Seafrance Hoverspeed
Longer routes UK–France	P & O Stena Britanny Ferries
UK–Spain	P & O Stena Brittany Ferries
UK–The Netherlands, Belgium and Germany	P & O Stena Hoverspeed Scandinavian Seaways
UK–Scandinavia	Scandinavian Seaways
UK–Ireland	P & O Stena Irish Ferries

Figure 3.2   The major UK ferry operators

Not all ports can be used to get to all destinations (the Scandinavian routes might operate from Newcastle only and the Spanish ports similarly from Plymouth and Portsmouth alone). When working out the journey time, the journey from the traveller's home to the port, the length of the ferry journey and the journey from the arrival port to the final destination must all be taken into account. Travellers also need to allow time for reporting to the ferry and for boarding. On longer routes it might also be necessary for a passenger to book overnight accommodation, which will add to the original cost of the journey.

A cruise ship visiting Glacier Bay, Alaska.

Activity	Obtain ferry brochures for the current year for the companies listed in Figure 3.2. On a map of northern Europe, identify where the departure and arrival ports are for each of these companies and link these together. (If you colour code each operator you will be able to tell more easily which ferry route is operated by which company.)

Cruise traffic from the UK is very limited as most cruise operators commence their cruises outside the UK (so-called 'fly cruises'). The reason for this is that the waters surrounding western France and northern Spain (the Bay of Biscay) can be very rough and, generally, the weather here is very unreliable. There is also little opportunity to stop during the first and last three days of a cruise, which would make cruise itineraries less attractive and which would be costly for the cruise operators. There are, however, some companies that run cruises either on a regular or one-off basis from the UK (e.g. Cunard). The most popular departure port is Southampton, although other ports have the facilities to cater for cruise departures.

Chapter 3.6 The changing popularity of tourist destinations

Several things can affect the popularity of a tourist destination and, sometimes, it is a combination of factors that makes or breaks a destination's popularity. The three factors that are explored here are as follows.

Economic:

- cost (accommodation, transport and costs incurred at the destination)
- other economic considerations, both in the UK and at the destination (e.g. fluctuations in the exchange rate).

Social and political:

- sales promotion and publicity
- the exclusivity of the destination
- over-commercialisation
- crime levels
- political instability/unrest
- favourable and unfavourable media coverage about the destination
- tourism management in the destination
- the growing numbers of people taking independent holidays (i.e. no longer tied to where tour operators offer packages)
- the growth of short-break holidays (i.e. where once a destination was considered somewhere to take a week or fortnight's holiday, it is now considered more suitable for a weekend break).

Environmental and geographic:

- accessibility
- climatic conditions
- pollution
- natural disasters.

As these topics are also covered in Unit 1, they will be discussed only very briefly here.

Economic factors

The cost of the various components that go together to make a holiday will affect a visitor's decision about whether a destination is worth visiting. This costing decision will be done either through studying the tour operator's packages (where the prices advertised in the brochures have a big influence on the decision-making process) or through the customer pricing the individual components of a holiday him or herself. If pricing the holiday him or herself, the customer is likely to consider the transport element first (the cost of airline tickets or a ferry journey could stop the customer researching a holiday in a particular destination any further). Special offers or good-value transport deals might encourage the potential traveller to investigate the next stage (i.e. how much accommodation, entertainment and local costs are likely to be).

Currency fluctuations affect the prices customers will pay for items when they are abroad, and such fluctuations may determine the success of a country's tourism industry. Two other things that affect the price of items for overseas visitors to a country are that country's cost of living and the prices at which goods are sold within the country. Exchange rates affect how much a tourist will get for his or her money: when the pound is strong and other currencies are weak, British tourists benefit greatly from a good rate of exchange for the British pound.

Activity	Which of the following European countries are considered expensive by UK tourists and which are considered to offer good value for money? If you can, give reasons for your answers.
	• Austria • Portugal • Bulgaria • Spain • France • Sweden • Greece • Switzerland • Norway • Turkey

Social and political considerations

Sales promotion and publicity

A destination will be promoted either by a tour operator or the relevant local tourist board or, occasionally, by a joint initiative involving both organisations. A tour operator might promote a destination because it wants to introduce a new product on to the market that is based in that destination, in which case it would use traditional advertising media, such as newspapers and magazine features. Alternatively, it might organise familiarisation visits to the destination for the press or travel agents in the hope this

Figure 3.3   Publicity can be negative or positive.

might generate advertising in the form of recommendations, newspaper or magazine articles or features on holiday programmes on television. Tourist boards advertise their products in both the national and travel press to raise awareness of their destinations and also to dispel any negative publicity that may have arisen about one of their destinations.

Media coverage, generally, can be either positive or negative. Positive media coverage often arises as a result of successful events that have taken place in a particular destination or through glowing travel reports in newspapers and magazines or on TV programmes. Negative coverage results from unfavourable newsworthy events (e.g. attacks on British tourists in Miami) or as a result of unfavourable reports on such TV programmes as Watchdog.

Exclusivity

Some destinations maintain their popularity by having an air of exclusivity (Richard Branson's island in the Caribbean is an exclusive destination that can be rented on a weekly basis). Certain resorts have an 'upmarket label', such as Monte Carlo, the Seychelles and Mustique. These destinations are not actively marketed – their names will do this for them.

Over-commercialisation

At the other end of the scale are the over-commercialised resorts, which have declined in popularity over the years as they are overcrowded and full of high-rise buildings. Benidorm is an example of a destination that has lost business because of over-commercialisation. Despite being a beach resort, visitors can find themselves a long way from the sea with a long walk through concrete canyons before they arrive at the beach. In such places, where tourism was viewed as a quick source of income, the management and control of new buildings and licensing arrangements might have been less stringent. Other resorts have evolved more sensibly and have set limits on the tourist capacity they can realistically cope with. Such measures include restrictions on building new hotels and other types of accommodation, including the height of new buildings. Management like this rarely happens at the start of the development of a resort and it is often too late to do anything about it when the problems start to emerge.

Crime

Crime can drastically affect the popularity of destinations and is something that raises a great deal of public interest when reported by the press. Unfortunately, when there is a great deal of inequality between the tourists and the local population, crime will more than likely increase. As we have just seen, Florida has had considerable bad publicity following increases in robbery on new arrivals to the destination. Some countries (such as Italy and Russia) have problems with organised crime, which also deters visitors. In some places violence towards tourists is so common, guards are posted at hotel entrances and visitors are warned not to go out after dark.

Political instability and unrest

Political instability and unrest (including terrorist attacks) are the biggest deterrent for visitors. The former Yugoslavia is still suffering from the after-effects of political unrest even though some parts of the country are now safe to visit. Similarly, instability in Africa and the Far East has affected the tourism industry. Places that were once viewed as travel and tourism destinations (such as Sri Lanka and Sierra Leone) now have very few visitors. Details of countries considered risk areas appear on the Foreign Office's danger list.

Changes in holiday patterns

As tourists have become more seasoned travellers, they now want different destinations to visit and more independent ways of travelling. This desire takes them away from the more popular package holiday destination to places further afield or more inaccessible. Now most people have both higher disposable incomes and more holiday time, people often take more than one holiday a year. Very often these additional holidays will be short breaks, which is one sector of the industry that has seen considerable growth recently. Towns, cities, purpose-built resorts and cultural destinations have all seen increases in visitor numbers as a result of this trend.

Environmental and geographic factors

Access

Access is still one of the most important factors affecting a destination's popularity, and so the building of new airports, ferry ports and other new routes into the destination will have a positive effect on its number of visitors. Accessibility, however, is something that can change as a result, for example, of border changes or of aircraft being unable to fly over a specific country's airspace, which can affect the journey time.

Climate

We have already considered the effect of climate on the popularity of a destination and how climate can determine the length of the tourist season. Global warming is likely to have further effects on the climate. Always make sure, therefore, that you use current statistics when quoting weather conditions.

Pollution

Pollution can take many different forms, from disastrous oil spills from tankers to litter thoughtlessly left behind by tourists. When pollution reaches unacceptable levels, this can result in bad publicity that will affect the popularity of a destination, especially when beaches and sea water are involved. Initiatives such as the blue flag beaches scheme have gone some way to identify resorts that are free of pollution like this. Poor air quality (particularly in areas of the Far East such as Indonesia) has similarly reduced the number of tourists wanting to visit regions so affected.

Natural disasters

Natural disasters (e.g. avalanches, floods, earthquakes and hurricanes) can devastate the tourism industry in a destination. The extensive media coverage that follows such a disaster can remain in people's memories for some time to come.

While this chapter has given some examples of things that can influence the popularity of a destination, not all of them are applicable to every destination. When you research a destination, look at the economic, social and political and environmental and geographical factors that might have affected your chosen destination's popularity.

Marketing travel and tourism

In this unit we will be looking at marketing and how it is used to support the travel and tourism industry. Marketing is an important tool used by most organisations to enable them to achieve their objectives. This unit is very closely linked to Unit 5 ('Customer service in travel and tourism') as much of the marketing process relates to identifying customers' needs and supplying the products and services that meet these needs.

Market research plays a big part in the identification of these needs and so the different methods of conducting market research are explored here. We will also look at the main marketing communication tools that are used to raise awareness of travel and tourism products.

The information in this unit will be useful for Unit 6 ('Travel and tourism in action'), where you will have the opportunity to apply the marketing techniques and methods you learn about in this unit. (This unit is also a common unit with the Advanced VCE in Leisure and Recreation.)

This unit will be assessed through an external assessment only. The grade you achieve in this assessment will be your grade for the unit.

Chapter 4.1 How organisations grow through marketing

There are five ways an organisation can grow through marketing.

Consolidation

A company continues to sell (or increases its sales of) its existing products or services by promoting these heavily in the market and by fighting off the competition.

Market penetration

Market penetration means selling more of your products or services to your existing customers. This occurs as a result of repeat business or through encouraging customers to switch from buying competitors' products to your own. Similarly, when organisations buy out other companies, they are likely to achieve market penetration by taking on the customers of the companies they have acquired.

Market development

Market development occurs when existing products or services are sold to new customers. This could result from increased promotional activities, through general advertising or by targeting advertising at specific groups of people. Market development also happens as a result of natural evolution (for example, through 'word of mouth' advertising).

Product development

Product development involves creating new products or services to sell to existing customers. Market research (see Chapter 4.4), for example, might have highlighted a gap in the products or services on offer to existing customers, resulting in a company introducing a new range of products or services. Examples of this include a travel agency that introduces a foreign exchange service for existing customers, or an overseas tour operator introducing new excursions to an established holiday product.

Diversification

Diversification is the most exciting way a company can develop but is also fraught with risk and expense. Diversification means developing new products or services to sell to new customers. This occurs quite often in the tour operations sector of the industry when a company introduces a totally new product to its existing portfolio of holidays. It also occurs when an organisation that has never operated in the travel and tourism industry before sets itself up in this market.

These ways an organisation can grow can be shown diagrammatically through Ansoff's product–market mix (see Figure 4.1). This matrix matches existing or new products and services with existing or new markets to demonstrate the strategies a company can

Product or service / Market	Existing product or service		New product or service
Existing market	Consolidation	Market penetration	Product development
New market	Market development		Diversification

Figure 4.1   Ansoff's product–market mix

use to maintain or expand its current market share.

To grow in this way, an organisation will devise a marketing plan. This plan will identify the actions the organisation must take, the dates when these must be completed, who has responsibility for implementing them and the costs involved in order that the organisation might grow and develop. The organisation's marketing plan will also link in to the organisation's overall objectives for its future operations.

Chapter 4.2 Marketing travel and tourism

So what is marketing all about? The simplest way of understanding marketing is to think of it as getting the right product to the right people in the right place at the right price and by using the right promotion. Hence marketing is a continuous process, and all aspects of an organisation will be involved in it.

Another definition of marketing (provided by Kotler) says that 'marketing is about putting the customer at the centre of the business'. In the travel and tourism industry, this definition is particularly important as a result of the competitive nature of the business. Customers (and their needs and

Marketing requires an understanding of customers and their needs. All of these people are potential customers!

expectations) are constantly changing, which is a challenge for anyone involved in the marketing of products and services.

Setting marketing objectives

Most organisations have a mission statement (a general statement about an organisation's overall aims). While a mission statement will very often be printed in the literature an organisation publishes, an organisation does not usually make public its marketing objectives. These objectives determine the marketing policies the organisation will pursue, and these objectives must be **SMART**:

- **S**pecific
- **M**easurable
- **A**chievable
- **R**ealistic
- **T**imed.

While public, private and voluntary sector organisations will have different objectives, some of these may be similar. For example, to:
- increase visitor numbers
- target a new client group
- diversify the methods used to promote the products
- increase awareness of the products
- improve customer satisfaction
- conduct market research using existing customers.

Marketing objectives might also be related to increasing profits or to keeping spending to within a budget, or might include forging closer links with the local community. A voluntary sector organisation might have as one of its objectives increasing its numbers of members or volunteers. Whatever the marketing objectives, these must link in to the organisation's overall business plan and be appropriate for the environment within which the organisation is operating.

Analysing internal influences

Before an organisation can start to look at the external things that will influence its operations, it must look within itself to see what is likely to work in its favour or what might be a problem in the future. Many organisations, for example, find they cannot develop at the same rate as the new products or services that are coming on to the market as they might not have the internal resources or capacity to cope with the increase in business such new products or services might bring. To investigate its Strengths, Weaknesses, Opportunities and Threats, an organisation carries out a SWOT analysis (see Figure 4.2).

Strengths	**W**eaknesses
Identify the key strengths of the organisation. For example: • well trained staff • good customer base • a reliable product • excellent accommodation.	Confront the weaknesses of the organisation. For example: • high turnover of staff • a lack of new business • high prices • limited market research.
Opportunities	**T**hreats
These could be external opportunities (for example, the development of a new business park or housing estate that could bring with it new business opportunities) or internal (for example, a newly established regional marketing team).	Threats might be internal (such as the resignation of a manager) or external (for example, new competition in the market).

Figure 4.2   SWOT analysis

However, SWOT analyses are useful only if they are used to develop plans that will address strengths and weaknesses and to identify strategies for dealing with the

opportunities and threats. Very often these issues can be resolved at a local level as a result of feedback from local staff who have identified a strength, weakness, opportunity or threat that might otherwise have been overlooked by senior management.

SWOT analyses can be used by any organisation, whether it is in the profit-making sector or not. They can also be used effectively by destinations to identify the current situation it is in and to highlight how that destination can move forward.

Activity	Select a city, town or region you are familiar with and that is regarded as a tourist destination. Complete a SWOT analysis for your chosen locality to assess its strengths, weaknesses, opportunities and threats.

Analysing external influences

The travel and tourism industry is particularly susceptible to external influences, some of which can be identified or even predicted. Other influences, however, are totally outside anyone's control (for example, weather conditions, outbreaks of war or illness and natural disasters). Because it is not possible to manage external influences outside anyone's control, this section focuses only on those factors that can be identified or predicted.

These influences can be divided into general and competitor-specific influences, and one of the tools used to identify general influences is PEST (or STEP) analysis. (Whilst this type of analysis has two names, the basic procedure is the same. It is just that the order of the steps involved can be changed.) This technique is used to consider the overall environment the organisation is operating in and what might affect the organisation's overall market (see Figure 4.3).

Environment	Possible influences
Political	For example, changes in government (in an overseas destination, this could greatly affect the tourism product. Changes in the governments of unstable destinations could result in coups or military intervention, which will reduce the number of tourists visiting the destination). Political issues could include changes in policy or legislation (for example, controls on foreign currency or strikes and civil unrest).
Economic	Economic factors can affect both visitors and destinations. For example, if taxes are reduced this could increase the disposable income people have to spend on holidays. Alternatively, if the cost of living rises at a destination, this will affect the destination's popularity with holiday-makers.
Social	Social factors include such things as demographic changes. For example, the UK is currently experiencing an increase in the age of its population and a decrease in the number of people having children at a young age. It also includes changes in lifestyles or cultures. The fashionability of destinations is also an important influence in the social environment.
Technological	These include changes in technology and the way these affect people's buying habits (for example, the increasing use of the Internet, particularly for buying last-minute bargains). Similarly, in the future, the introduction of a super-jumbo carrying 1,000 passengers could affect people's choice of long-haul destinations.

Figure 4.3 PEST (or STEP) analysis

Competitor-specific analysis is less scientific and often involves someone taking on the responsibility for monitoring the services and products offered by competitors. Very often, a great deal of this information can come only through people who are working directly with customers or in a particular destination. For example, a local tour operator's representatives might receive inside information from hotel managers about tour companies who have approached them for contracts or who might be aware of new developments being built locally and that are being supported by overseas companies. Similarly, people recruiting staff for a new agency that is opening locally might approach people who are already working in travel agencies in the area. Much of this information relies on good, open communication systems within the organisation, so that the appropriate people are informed about competitors' plans.

Identifying and analysing customers' needs and expectations

There are two parts to identifying and analysing customers' needs and expectations: the market research that gives you your initial information about your customers, and market segmentation, which allows you to consider your customers as individual groups of people to target.

First of all, however, when identifying customers' needs and expectations, it is worth while looking at Maslow's 'hierarchy of needs' (see Figure 4.4) and how this relates to the travel and tourism industry. Generally speaking, as people get older and become more financially secure, so their identification of need moves up the hierarchy. The width of each band in the hierarchy is also proportionate to the number of people who are likely to be within that category. So, for example, very few people travel for self-fulfilment purposes.

Market research aimed at identifying customers' wants and needs will help to locate people on this hierarchy of needs (we look in more detail at market research later in this unit). Once customers have been positioned on the hierarchy, we might be

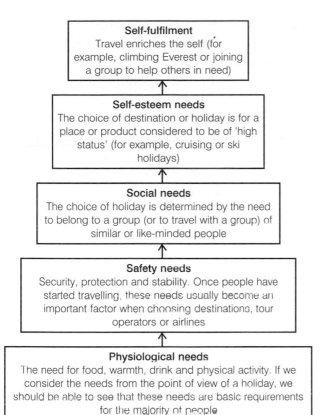

Figure 4.4   Maslow's hierarchy of needs

able to make some assumptions about what their expectations are of a travel or tourism product. For example, people travelling for physiological needs could be seeking a break for health reasons and might be looking for a product such as a short stay in a health club. At the top of the hierarchy might be people who travel for religious reasons or to find themselves. Independent travel arrangements would be more appropriate for people like this.

The way we split people into groups like this for marketing purposes is called 'segmenting' the market. Market research identifies things about customers so it is possible to link specific customer types to products. The characteristics of these segments (people's needs and wants from products, the way in which they buy and their hobbies and interests) will affect the

way marketing takes place. And because there are very few companies who have a product they can sell to all customers, by segmenting the market a company can focus its promotional activities accordingly and, it is hoped, target the right people.

Activity	Think about where you are on this hierarchy in relation to the travel and tourism industry. Now select five other people of different ages and question them about their needs from a holiday. Identify where these people fit into the hierarchy.

Developing a 'marketing mix'

Earlier we noted that marketing involves getting the right product, at the right price, in the right place and using an effective means of product promotion. The technical term for this is the 'marketing mix'. The marketing mix is all about ensuring the different factors involved in marketing are mixed together effectively to achieve the organisation's marketing goals of meeting customers' needs and expectations (see Figure 4.5).

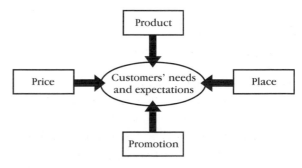

Figure 4.5   The marketing mix

The four Ps of product, price, place and promotion all work together, and it is necessary for an organisation to attend to all four if the organisation is to be successful.

For example, if the product is not right for the market, it will not matter how good the price is or how much the product is promoted, people will still not buy it.

Evaluating progress

Because the travel and tourism industry is in a constant state of evolution and because customers' needs and expectations are always changing, organisations must continuously evaluate their progress to determine if all aspects of their marketing mixes are appropriate for the current situation and the prevailing business environment. What all organisations must remember is that the customer is at the centre of the marketing mix and that the customer is an integral part of the marketing and development of products and services. The individual components of the marketing mix are considered in the next chapter.

Chapter 4.3 The marketing mix

This chapter describes in detail the four Ps of the marketing mix. Although you need to be able to evaluate each element separately, it is also important to look at how the four Ps interact with each other and relate to the organisation's overall mission and objectives.

As we have already noted, it is important that companies combine these elements of this mix successfully because, if they do not, the consequences could be disastrous. Consider the following case studies. The possible outcomes of getting the marketing mix wrong are given for the first two case studies; it is up to you to work out the possible outcomes for the third.

CASE STUDIES: The marketing mix

Scenario 1
A tour operator prices an exclusive round-the-world trip (staying in deluxe hotels with first-class travel arrangements and tours to remote and undeveloped tourist attractions) too low.

Possible outcomes
It is unlikely the target market the operator had in mind would book this holiday, as people might consider the low price to be an indication the holiday would not be of a suitable quality. The people who might book might not be interested in the types of tours organised by the guides, preferring instead to visit more well-known sights. Hence customer dissatisfaction could result in complaints, and it is unlikely the tour would be run again.

Scenario 2
A tour operator runs an advertising campaign for Ibiza night-club weekends in magazines such as *The Radio Times*.

Possible outcomes
It is unlikely any of the target market would see these adverts and, as a result, there would be few, if any, bookings. It is unlikely the weekends would go ahead due to a lack of bookings.

Scenario 3
A new theme park advertises its opening offers for prebooked college and school groups too early, before arrangements are in place for bookings to be made.

At the same theme park, companies are invited to tender for the catering units. Despite the many fast-food outlets that apply, the management of the theme park thinks they can make more money by having sit-down restaurants with a minimum price of £7.50 per person.

Possible outcomes: questions

1 What effect would the lack of booking arrangements have on people who are investigating different options for a school or college trip?

2 How would most visitors to the theme park react to the sit-down restaurants?

3 For both the booking arrangements and the eating facilities, what might be the long-term outcomes for the theme park?

Product

The product itself might be a mix of different products and services. For example, a holiday to a specific destination is likely to include:

- flights
- accommodation
- food
- coach transfers from the airport to the hotel
- sight-seeing
- the services of an overseas representative and airline crew
- entertainment
- the amenities and facilities available at the destination.

These individual products and services are intangible: you are not able to see them before you buy them. The overall product is also perishable – it cannot be stored and sold at a later date: once the date for the holiday's commencement has passed, it cannot still be sold. Staff are similarly a major part of the overall product as they play a key role in the customer's experience.

The travel and tourism product is yet even more difficult to control because it is readily affected by external influences and is subject to change. This creates particular challenges for the people who work in marketing because the image the company has portrayed about the product in advertisements and brochures might not live up to everyone's expectations. For example, the sky might not be as blue and the beaches might be more overcrowded than they appear in the brochure. Similarly, hotels might change considerably in the time between taking photographs and these photographs appearing in the final brochure. What is, therefore, important is to ensure the holidays offered by a company have a good mix of quality individual products and services.

A product will be much easier to define if you are aiming at a specific market (for example, the youth market or the 18-30 years age range). In such an example, market segment is likely to be determined not only by people's ages but also by their interests, disposable income, lifestyles and needs (look back at Maslow's hierarchy of needs to see where such a group of people might be positioned on the scale).

Activity	Use a brochure to choose a tourist destination. For your chosen destination, list all those things that are likely to form the *product* part of the marketing mix for this destination.

Products also go through different stages of development, which is known as the product life-cycle. This means that as a product ages, so it goes through periods of growth, maturity and, finally, decline. Decline can be delayed if the product is looked after and given new leases of life. In the example of a theme park, this delay in a product's decline can be demonstrated through rides that are

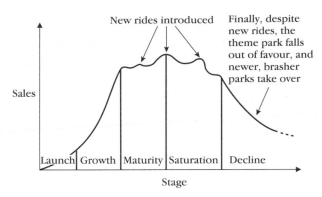

Figure 4.6   The stages in the life-cycle of a theme park

changed to meet new trends or to become more frightening or faster. If the rides are *not* changed, the theme park may still continue to be successful but what is more likely to happen is that competitors will develop new products and rides and so the theme park will go into a steady state of decline. Visitor numbers will gradually start to drop and it will probably be too late at this stage for the management to rectify the situation (see Figure 4.6).

As we have already seen, an organisation's mission and objectives will influence the products the organisation sells and how these products are developed. The mission and objectives outline the way the organisation will want to promote itself and how it sees itself developing in the future. Very often, to fulfil those things outlined in the mission and objectives, companies develop specific brands to enhance the products they currently sell and, for similar reasons, they concentrate their efforts on distinct segments of the market. This tactic can influence the product life-cycle as the effective *branding* of these products may prevent product saturation and decline.

CASE STUDY: Branding

Thomson has developed the products within the Thomson brand to meet the requirements of specific market segments. In so doing, the company hopes to extend the life-cycles of the products they sell.

- The main Thomson product features a summer sun, winter sun, cruise and ski product along with specific brochures for different types of accommodation (such as villas and apartments) and for specific destinations worldwide (such as Florida).
- Skytours is the budget product segmented towards families with limited disposable incomes.
- Portland Direct sell products people can book by telephone or using the Internet. This product offers discounted and last-minute rates.
- Club Freestyle is the fun holiday product targeted at young adults.
- Just is a no-frills brand that has recently been introduced and that is segmented towards couples.

Thomson has also segmented the products within its main brand. To promote the idea of up-market, high-quality accommodation, the company has introduced a gold and platinum award classification scheme for hotels and apartments.

Thomson also has products aimed at niche markets (for example, its Crystal ski product, its holiday cottages group – with cottages in the UK and France – and Austravel with its flexible travel arrangements to Australia).

The Thomson Group has also redesigned its Lunn Poly shops into 'new concept stores'. These stores have brightly coloured decor and the staff wear more informal uniforms to give the impression of discounted prices and good value for money. Lunn Poly opened their first holiday superstore in June 2000 in Fosse Park, Leicester. This shop is open seven days a week, has 70 staff and specialist areas for late deals, families, short breaks, sun seekers and dream escapes, as well as Internet desks, information areas, a café, toilets and a children's play area.

Question
Collect a range of brochures for the Thomson products described above. How have these brochures been designed to emphasise the different brand images of these products? (Consider such things as which age groups would find them appealing, the style of the language used, those things emphasised in the photographs, etc.)

Place

Place means two things in relation to the marketing mix: first and foremost it means the holiday destination. Secondly, however, it means the place where customers enquire about or purchase their holiday – i.e. the travel agent, ticket office or tourist information centre that makes the sale or provides the information and advice.

The location of travel and tourism organisations

Location is a key issue for organisations that sell leisure products, particularly retail travel agencies. As you will already be well aware, most retail travel agencies are located in the main shopping centres of towns and cities, but there is more to location than just the street the agency is situated in. Consider some of the following issues.

Access

How do people get to the shopping centre? If by public transport, how do people reach the central shopping area from the bus and train stations? Are there bus stops in the high street? (If the answer to this is 'yes', just think about how much free advertising a travel agency could have while people are waiting for buses and looking into the travel agency's window.) How about the car parks – where are the pedestrian exits?

Shopping patterns

Where do people shop? Big department stores and well-known chain stores often attract high volumes of customers, and so a location near one of these shops could guarantee a great deal of passing trade, as long as potential customers actually walk past the branch or office without having to cross over the road.

Type of customer

You would also need to consider whether or not the shops in the area attract the same types of customer you want to attract and whether or not people are likely to be considering buying a holiday when on a shopping expedition to this particular area. For example, are people likely to book a holiday when buying the weekly groceries in a busy supermarket? While some travel agencies have set up branches in supermarkets, this has met with mixed success, and the more traditional types of agency have tended to avoid such locations.

The economic well-being of the area

What is happening in the area? Are shops closing down because a new development is taking business away from the town centre? Many of the new out-of-town shopping centres are having a big impact on the shops that have remained in town centres.

Advertising space

How much window space is there for advertising material? Corner locations are particularly good sites, especially if there are windows on both exterior walls.

Even with a good location, however, you will still need to attract people into your agency to make a booking and, hence, as we have noted many times before, the appearance of the agency will greatly influence whether or not customers actually walk in through the door.

The Internet

As the Internet is becoming more and more widely used both in the home as well as at work, this method of marketing travel and

tourism products perhaps deserves a mention here. However, the travel industry has been rather slow in developing this marketing tool and in making its products readily available this way. The products that have sold well so far have been those that have been targeted at the independent traveller (for example, flight-seat and accommodation only deals).

Activity	Obtain a map of the centre of your local town or city. Now visit the centre of your local town or city and, on the map, mark the location of travel agencies. Next plot other factors on to the map that could influence the success of these agencies. For example:

- the major department stores
- the major chain stores
- popular fast-food restaurants
- bus stops
- train and bus stations
- car parks (plus their pedestrian exits)
- attractions or facilities that bring people into a specific area
- whether or not the town or city has a prime central area.

For each travel agency, assess the suitability of its location. Which are in the best locations? Are there any vacant lots where you would locate a travel agency (give your reasons)?

Finally, prepare a report that discusses the location of each agency and that makes a recommendation (based on your findings) for the ideal location of a travel agency within your town or city.

Companies such as lastminute.com act as the middle person between the airline and the customer. They market the fares of many different airlines and sell these on to customers, generally at exceptionally good prices. When there is a great deal of excess capacity on certain flights and routes, Internet companies are able to change their prices much more quickly than traditional travel agencies, which gives Internet company customers instant access to these discounts. Some customers still have concerns about the security of paying for their bookings over the Internet, and this might be one of the main reasons why more travel bookings are not made this way.

The location of destinations

The other meaning of place, of course, is the destination itself. A place could be a country (e.g. France), an area (e.g. the Costa del Sol), a resort (e.g. Brighton) or a purpose-built destination (such as Disneyland Paris). The place could also be the accommodation itself (e.g. Center Parcs), an attraction (e.g. the Cheddar Gorge) or an event (such as Wimbledon). (Place as a tourist destination is discussed in more detail in Unit 3.)

Price

Price is still very much an important factor to be taken into account in many people's decision-making when purchasing a travel or tourism product. Prices vary considerably for similar products, and no two products are likely to be identical. For example, two similar holidays might have two different prices because they have different flight times or room types.

The pricing of products is usually based on the following factors:

- What are customers prepared to pay?
- What are the competitors charging?
- What do the individual components of the product cost when added together?
- Will the product make a profit?

Travel and tourism organisations also employ different pricing techniques.
- *The going rate*. Organisations look at what their competitors are charging and offer similar prices for their own products and services.
- *Promotional prices*. For example, special offers (two for the price of one) or money-off vouchers.
- *Discounting*. Companies will reduce prices (discount) when, for example, the departure date is getting nearer but there are still many seats or holidays left to sell. Tour operators usually reduce the price to try to attract more customers and so to reduce potential losses.
- *Market skimming*. This is where new products (that have little or no competition) are offered at a high price because people are not concerned about paying more for the privilege of being one of the first people to experience the product.
- *Prestige pricing*. An image of exclusivity is maintained for high-quality products by keeping their prices high (for example,

on the Blue Train and on certain cruise holidays).

Travel and tourism products are also subject to seasonal and peak/off-peak pricing. In such cases, differently priced bands will apply to the same product.

- *Package holiday* rates vary according to the season. During the school holidays it is much easier to attract families to the Costa Brava than, say, at the end of September. But there are still hotel beds to fill in September.
- *Airlines* charge different prices for fares in economy class, depending on the day and time of departure, whether or not a weekend stay is included and the amount of time before departure that payment is made in full.
- *Hotels* have different tariffs for business people, weekend stays and single customers. During the week, hotels can be full of business people who are more concerned about a convenient location than price. Over the weekends, however, these hotels might be half-empty and so they try to attract holiday-makers to stay on Fridays, Saturdays and Sundays by offering special discounted rates.
- *Attractions* may charge peak, off-peak and group rates.

Airline tickets, in particular, are becoming ever more complex. For example, some airline companies now recommend service charges to be added to ticket prices to make up for the lower rates of commission now paid to travel agents.

Check your understanding

We have looked at some examples of what affects price in the travel and tourism industry. Make a list of all these factors and any additional ideas you might have.

Promotion

If people are not aware of a product or service or that you sell it, they are unlikely to make a purchase. Hence products and services must be promoted. There are a number of promotional activities travel and tourism organisations can use:

- advertising
- direct marketing
- public relations
- personal selling
- promotions and stunts
- sponsorship.

These different methods are explored more fully later in the chapter 'Marketing communications'. However, for an organisation to maximise people's awareness of its products and services, it must have a balance of different promotional activities.

Products and services are promoted in different ways depending on the type of travel and tourism organisation and the sector it is in. Companies whose main objective is to make a profit will have much larger budgets for promotional activities than those organisations in the not-for-profit sector. Organisations' objectives in undertaking promotional activities will also vary (e.g. a tourist destination with the objective of raising awareness of its region will use different promotional activities from a theme park that might want to increase visitor numbers). A major tourist region or specific country will be more likely to advertise overseas, whereas a resort such as Paignton might focus on the UK market. Some examples of how different sectors of the industry might use promotional activities are as follows.

- Small tourist attractions and hotels will make use of the tourist information service. They will advertise in the service's brochures and leaflets that are distributed to visitors and other tourist information centres in the network.

- Tour operators produce brochures, which are still regarded as their main promotional tool. These are distributed through travel agencies and by direct mail to customers.
- Travel agencies and tour operators concentrate their advertising and promotional activities on the last week of December and the month of January, with over 30% of all advertising spend being made during this period. A great deal of this spend goes on TV and press advertising.
- Major hotel chains place advertisements in the Saturday and Sunday newspapers throughout the year but particularly in the summer months when people are looking for last-minute places to stay.

As we noted above, the majority of travel and tourism organisations use a range of different promotional activities following the steps in the AIDA model. (Unit 5, page 189 has further points the AIDA model.)

CASE STUDY: The AIDA model

The following is an example of how AIDA might work for a theme park introducing a new ride at the start of the summer season.

A *Attention* may be attracted through a high-profile advertising campaign on television showing snippets of the ride but leaving customers wanting to find out more.

I *Interest* could be developed further through direct marketing (e.g. leaflets delivered to households in specific target areas of the country). These leaflets might contain a competition to do with the ride, which will help the company with its market research and will enable it to create a database of potential customers.

D The *desire* for the ride could be increased through a public relations initiative (for example, a well-known band could be invited as the first people to try the ride). This event might feature in either the national or local press, depending on how famous the group is.

A *Action* should ensue as a result of these activities but sales promotions during off-peak times (such as two for the price of one admission costs) would encourage people to visit the theme park during these times.

Some of these promotional activities will be very costly but, by ensuring all the steps in AIDA are followed, the success of the ride and promotional campaign will be maximised. It is important that, once you have gained the customers' attention and interest, this is converted into desire and action, thus turning a *potential* consumer into a *real* customer.

Questions
Think about your last visit to a theme park or other attraction.

1 What attracted your *attention* and gained your interest?
2 How were you persuaded to take *action* and make the visit?
3 What would you have done differently if you were promoting the attraction by following the AIDA steps?

Try it out	Select one example of a promotional activity that could be employed by the travel and tourism industry. Using a product of your own choosing, describe how the principles of the AIDA model could be applied to this activity.

A good marketeer will make use of all the components of the marketing mix to target the particular groups of customers who meet the organisation's marketing objectives. If we consider the example of the theme park given earlier, the marketing mix could be applied as follows:

- *Product*. Rides, attractions and catering geared towards a specific age group. (In the case of a theme park such as Legoland these would be targeted at very young children, in Thorpe Park at a slightly older age group and in Alton Towers at teenagers and adults.)
- *Place*. The physical appearance of the park must reflect the target group, and good access and parking facilities are essential.

Special arrangements for group and school bookings will enhance its popularity, as will flexible methods of making reservations, including the use of the Internet.

- *Price*. Family, group, multi-user and discounted off-peak admission rates are all appropriate strategies for the pricing of theme parks. However, pricing should be competitive with other, similar attractions.
- *Promotion*. As discussed in the AIDA model, a range of different promotional activities will be employed. However, the activities must be timed to create extra interest around reopening time in spring, to maintain interest throughout the summer and to attract people to make late summer bookings.

As you will appreciate by now, the marketing mix works differently for each company, sector and type of organisation. If you compared the example of the theme we have looked at throughout this section to a travel agency or tour operator, you would find significant differences in the way product, place, price and promotion are interpreted.

Chapter 4.4 Market research

Market research is concerned with finding out more about an organisation's customers and potential customers, including their needs, their reactions to products and services, their buying habits and their satisfaction or not with their travel and tourism experiences. There are times when it is best to conduct market research on the general public rather than on customers as this may give an insight into why some people are not customers of the organisation. Once information has been collected, it must be analysed so it can be used effectively by managers and marketeers. Good market research could provide the answers to the questions an organisation has about its customers.

The starting point for any market research project must be to identify the *objectives* for the research. Once the objectives have been decided, appropriate methods for collecting the information can be explored (for example, a questionnaire or interviews). The research can then be carried out, the results analysed and the findings reported back to the organisation.

Activity	As a group, discuss all the reasons you can think of for travel and tourism organisations to conduct market research.

Market segments

We have already looked briefly at market segmentation (the way the overall market can be split into groups so companies can focus their marketing activities on meeting the needs of a particular client group).

Customers can be segmented in many different ways, and it is important the way customers are divided is appropriate for a particular business's needs (for example, if you have a product that is aimed at people who enjoy horse riding, it might not be appropriate to segment these people by any other interest but horse riding).

The following are examples of the different ways the market might be segmented. By:

- age
- socioeconomic group (see below)
- lifestyle or family circumstances.

Sometimes groups might overlap (for example, both younger and older groups might enjoy skiing holidays, sun holidays, holiday centres and such tourist attractions as the National Parks). Family groups might comprise people across the whole socioeconomic scale (for example, in one family the grandparents could be retired, their children could be employed and their grandchildren could be at school or college). Similarly, holidays such as cruises are just as likely to attract mature single people and couples whose children have left home as young married couples on honeymoon. However, by segmenting markets in this way it is easier to identify and develop products to satisfy particular customers.

Segmenting by age

Age is the first way most organisations will segment the market as the majority of products target a specific age group. For some products, age is very obvious (for example, Twenties aimed at people in their 20s and Saga for the over 50s). Other products might be more subtly differentiated. For example, we noted above that different theme parks (such as Legoland, Thorpe Park and Alton Towers) target specific age ranges (the very young, teenagers or adults). For some products (e.g. flights and train journeys) age may not be relevant but specific marketing initiatives (such as off-peak or senior citizens discounts) might focus on a particular age range.

Activity	Working in small groups, list all the travel and tourism products you can think of that are aimed at a specific age group.

Segmenting by socioeconomic group

People have traditionally been divided into socioeconomic groups depending on their incomes and employment status. The most established way of doing this is through the classification system devised by the Institute of Practitioners in Advertising (see Figure 4.7).

Group	Definition
E	Retired people, people on low incomes, the unemployed, students and those receiving benefits
D	Unskilled manual workers or semi-skilled workers
C2	Skilled manual workers
C1	Office staff and junior managers or supervisors
B	Middle managers and professional people (e.g. teachers and accountants)
A	Senior managers, managing directors and professionals (e.g. lawyers and doctors)

Figure 4.7   Classification by socioeconomic group

This method of segmenting the market is generally used to group people together who have similar buying habits or to identify people who are likely to buy a specific product or service. Segmenting in this way also extends to the newspapers and magazines people read: the people considered likely to buy a product or service will be targeted by advertising placed in the newspapers and magazines these people most often read.

Activity	As a group, discuss the advantages and disadvantages of an organisation using socioeconomic groups as a method of segmenting people (for example, are there any drawbacks in grouping retired people with unemployed people?).

Segmenting by lifestyle or family circumstances

Because of the limitations of socioeconomic classifications, many organisations now use lifestyle as a way of segmenting people. There are many different ways this can be done. For example, many American systems have specific names for people at various stages in their lives: *empty nesters* are people whose children have now left home and so who are likely to have an increased level of disposable income; similarly, *dinkys* are double-income, no-kids couples who have no children and who are both earning so, again, might have very high disposable incomes. The stages in a person's life that might affect his or her purchasing decisions when considering buying travel and tourism products or services are shown below.

Children and teenagers.

Children and teenagers might not have any money to spend themselves but they have an enormous impact on the purchasing decisions made by their parents or guardians.

Students.

Students may not have much disposable income but might have the time available for travelling, very often taking a year out and travelling extensively during this period.

Single people.

These people often have high disposable incomes and a desire to buy as many travel and tourism products as possible each year.

Couples without children.

Again, these people may have high disposable incomes. Very often, these people want exotic or unusual products.

Families with children.

For such people, value will be paramount, alongside reliability and safety. Facilities for children will be a big factor in the decision-making process for many people in this group. Families will be restricted to travelling during the school holidays.

Couples whose children have left home.

These people will probably try different products from those they experienced as a family. A recent increase in disposable income might prompt them to travel further afield or to book up-market products. They will also be able to travel at off-peak times.

Elderly people.

Elderly people often go away for long periods of time, especially over the winter months. Money can be an issue for these people, but those who are experienced travellers will want to keep going on holiday.

Mature single people.

Such people will look forward to their holidays as an opportunity to meet new people. Hence they will often purchase products where there will be a high level of social interaction (including cruises, coach tours and special interest products).

Differentiating by lifestyle and family circumstances can identify those people who are buying specific products and services and helps with the development of new and existing products. It can also help organisations employ those marketing strategies likely to be the most effective for specific customer groups.

Other ways of segmenting

There are other ways an organisation might segment the market (for example, by geographical area, gender or hobbies and interests). These can be very powerful methods when the product or service the organisation is offering is specialist in nature. Examples include companies that arrange pilgrimage tours aimed at specific religious groups or an airline company introducing a new flight from a regional airport targeted at people who live within a 50-mile radius of the airport.

Check your understanding

For a specific travel and tourism product, explain how this has been segmented by:

- age
- socioeconomic group
- lifestyle and family circumstances
- other methods of differentiation.

Market research strategies

As with all areas of marketing, market research must be planned very carefully in advance. The starting point for all market research is to determine what it is you need to research or to find out and set out the objectives of your research. The sort of things you might need to find more about could relate to the 4 Ps and/or potential customers. If, however, you already have target customers in mind, you might want to find out the following about product, place, price or promotion.

Product. What key features would the customer expect (or like to see) in the product (for example, catering, mode of travel, accommodation type, entertainment, location, etc.)? You might also want to find out more about your customers' lifestyles to help you determine the days, times, months, etc., your product should be available. Your customers might have experienced similar products before, in which case you could ask them what they enjoyed or did not enjoy about their previous experience. If you already have an idea about the sort of product you want to offer, you might want to test some sample ideas on them to find out how important these would be to their enjoyment.

Place. You might need to find out more about your customers' buying habits (for example, *when* would you need to sell the product and *how*). How do your customers currently make their bookings: through travel agents, by telephone or over the Internet? How far would they be prepared to travel, and what would they expect to find when they get there?

Price. You need to establish an appropriate price people would be prepared to pay for your product. You might also want to find out about any special offers that would encourage your customers to buy your product, including discounts for early bookings and payment, off-peak pricing, family rates, group discounts and repeat purchase offers. You might also be interested in finding out if they would pay more for the addition of meals, drinks or other services (such as extra excursions or children's activities).

Promotion. Information about your customers' lifestyles, interests and hobbies will direct you to the most successful ways of advertising your product. For example, some researchers ask questions about what people remember about current promotional activities on TV or in the press in order to help them develop their own promotional materials.

Once you have identified what you need to find out, the next stage is to consider how you will conduct the research. This could include primary or secondary research (see Unit 3) or a combination of both. There are three important things to consider when choosing market research methods.

1 *Whether or not the methods you are contemplating using will give you the answers you need.* It is all very well deciding on what you think might be an exciting market research strategy but that method does not, in the end, help you in any way.

2 *The costs involved and whether or not you have the necessary budget.* You may need to change the strategy in some way once the finer details have been worked out to make allowances for cost.

3 *How quickly you need the information* and the amount of *time* each market research method will require to plan it, prepare it, carry it out, analyse it and evaluate it.

Cost is always a limiting factor in any market research strategy. Therefore a good starting point for any research is to find out if any of the information already exists. In most organisations, research will probably have been carried out before, and this could have some relevance to the research being planned. However, it is important to consider how relevant and up to date this information is. It may also be worth

investigating what information is already held within certain regions and localities (for example, by regional tourist boards or by county or borough councils). Your own school or college may similarly hold information about your local community as a result of research it has done itself or that has been done by an outside company. This might also have been analysed in some way that could be useful to you.

However, it is unlikely any existing information will provide you with exactly the information you need to meet all your market research objectives, so you would probably still need to undertake further research to complete the picture. The different methods of market research you could select include:

- primary research (e.g. questionnaires, observations and focus groups)
- secondary research (both internal and external to the organisation).

(See the following pages for more details about both these types of research.)

Once you have reached this stage in deciding your marketing strategy, it is a good idea to go back to your original objectives and to what it is you need to find out. It may then be necessary to refine and amend your plans. Now set key dates for the stages in your market research strategy and how these fit in with the overall marketing plan. For example, there are likely to be promotional activities or stages in the development of the product that will rely on the results of the market research. Review how these dates match up and make sure there is sufficient time to analyse and evaluate the results of the market research.

The final stage before starting the actual market research is to conduct a trial run to see whether any amendments are necessary.

This should be done by selecting a small sample of people who are representative of the group likely to be involved in the research. A trial run enables you to try out the questions in a questionnaire or to conduct a mini-observation or short focus group session (see below). The question that must always be asked at this stage is: do the results supply us with the information we need?

Next you should undertake a short analysis of the results in order to review what has been achieved. As a result of this, you might want, for example, to change the order of questions, refine the wording, change a banding for answers (see opposite) or take out or add questions. The way the results are to be recorded might also need changing or the location or time of day when the questions are asked. An observation might need to have its criteria changed or the method for recording the results adjusted. A facilitator in a focus group (see page 148) might find the ambience is not conducive to free discussion. The facilitator would then need to look at some of the stimuli being used to promote answers. It is important these changes are made now as a result of the findings from the small sample so the main research project will be a success.

Primary research

You have already come across primary sources of information in Unit 3. As you will remember, primary research means obtaining information directly from the source, which will generally be through an appropriate individual person or group of people. Such information is gathered through questionnaires (surveys), observations or focus groups. In some industries, experimentation or testing is also

Primary research through a focus group.

used as part of primary research but in travel and tourism these are not easy techniques to use. Primary research allows you to tailor your research to specific objectives and has the following advantages over secondary research (see pages 148–50):

- it is more up to date
- you have more control about the type of information that is collected
- the information sample will be appropriate to your specific objectives
- the information you required might not be available in published research.

Questionnaires

The most common method for conducting primary research is the questionnaire or survey, which can either be conducted face to face, by post or over the telephone. A questionnaire should be able to supply you with information about a person's age, socioeconomic group and lifestyle. However, we must always bear in mind that, for some people, this type of information is very personal and, therefore, sensitive. Banding (e.g. grouping people by age or income, etc.) can help alleviate this problem and will also assist when it comes to collating the information. For example, a question about income might be banded as shown in Figure 4.8.

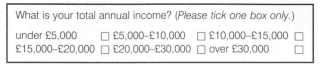

Figure 4.8 Banding incomes in a questionnaire

Note also that, by adding a box after each band for the respondent to tick, you are making the questionnaire simpler to complete and the questions easier to answer. If you are posting the questionnaire or expect people to complete it themselves, this is particularly important: if people think the questionnaire might involve a great deal of writing and time to fill in, they are less likely to complete it.

As well as collecting general information about people, you need to ask specific questions linked to your market research objectives. Therefore at all stages when designing a questionnaire, ask yourself the following two questions:

1   How does this question relate to my objectives? (In other words, will the response you are likely to obtain address your objectives?)
2   How am I going to make use of this information?

The second question is particularly pertinent when looking at the type of question that is being asked. If you ask closed questions (see Unit 5, page 186 for details about open and closed questions), especially those that have a yes or no answer, consider how you will be able to make use of these replies. Such replies might enable you to find out about a customer's current buying habits, but will they enable you to make recommendations for the future? It may be

that a no answer will require a further question to give you more information about why a customer has given a negative response.

Attitude scales are frequently used to obtain a customer's opinion on something or to gauge a customer's satisfaction with a particular product or service (an example of an attitude scale is given in Figure 4.9).

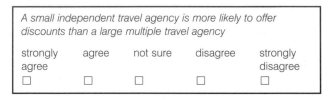

Figure 4.9 An attitude scale

Open questions tend to be used when very little information is available about a particular topic. However, care needs to be taken with open questions in surveys as you might receive a different response from everyone who is surveyed, which proves a nightmare when collating or using the information. Try to give the respondents some possible responses to the question, and have an 'other' section to cover all eventualities.

Questionnaires seek to find information that is either *qualitative* or *quantitative* (or a combination of both types of information). Which type of information is needed will very much depend on the market research objectives and the strategy, including the types of research that will be used.

Qualitative information concerns people's beliefs, personal reactions and feelings. Although the questionnaire will employ set questions, the wording of these questions might enable the respondents to talk freely. Qualitative information is particularly helpful when developing parts of the marketing mix and for finding out what influences people to buy certain products. This information should give the organisation an insight into how people feel about a new concept or idea, and should also tell you about what they dislike or would want changed. Devising questions to obtain qualitative information requires skill, particularly in ensuring the respondent is not prompted into giving 'set' responses. As we have already noted, analysing such information can be particularly challenging, especially if many different answers are given to the same question.

Quantitative information is collected to generate statistics and will generally be expressed as percentages, fractions or specific numbers. Very often we see customer satisfaction statistics expressed as quantitative data (for example, 75% of customers rated the food at this hotel as excellent, or 20% of customers have complained about the late arrival times of flights).

In market research, quantitative data also includes information about the product or service's target market (including people's ages, lifestyles, income, leisure and travel habits, spend, etc.). These types of data are particularly useful when segmenting the market and for specific parts of the marketing mix (such as price). Analysing this type of information can be done quite quickly and the data can be input into a computer by people unskilled in analysing the results of questionnaires. Once the data have been produced, marketeers can use and analyse this information themselves.

When putting together a questionnaire, make sure you follow these guidelines:

- keep the language simple and never use jargon
- start off with easy questions
- do not make the questionnaire too long

Direct interviews often produce good results.

- do not ask leading questions (questions that beg a certain response or a particular answer).

Once the questionnaire has been produced, it is important it is piloted. To do this, try out the questionnaire on a small number of people to see how it works. There may be changes you will need to make (for example, if there is a question people cannot or are unwilling to answer or if most answers to a certain question come under the 'other' category as opposed to one of your suggested answers). You might also find the questionnaire is difficult to administer. This could be due to its length or to the way in which data are to be recorded. It might also be as a result of the sequence of the questions, which could be resolved easily by changing the order.

Activity	Collect a range of different questionnaires and identify the different techniques they use to ask questions.

Next, identify a travel or tourism topic you could research and which you could research using a questionnaire. (You are going to distribute your questionnaire to your fellow students, to students around your school or college and/or to friends and relatives, so make sure the topic you choose is something these people might have/could feasibly experience.) Now devise a questionnaire you could use for this research, following these stages in its development:

- identify your market research objectives
- design the questionnaire
- conduct a pilot survey
- make changes to your questionnaire
- conduct the actual survey
- record the results.

Present your findings to the rest of your group.

Note: As mentioned above, you will have to use fellow students and/or friends and relatives to conduct your survey. Ask your tutor if you are unsure how many people you will need to include in your pilot survey and in your actual survey.

The way you record your results will depend on the data you have collected (e.g. is it qualitative or quantitative, etc.?). You may have to experiment to find the best way to record your results. Use all the facilities you have available for this (e.g. a suitable computer program, overhead project transparencies, posters, etc.). Again, if you need help to record your results, ask your tutor.

Observation

You may find that a questionnaire does not provide you with all the information needed for your market research objectives. If this is the case, it would be appropriate to look at other primary research methods. Observation can be used to collect both quantitative and qualitative information. However, this method can be rather time-consuming and some thought needs to be given to how the results will be recorded and analysed.

Observation can be done simply by watching people either at work or leisure. Research into sales procedures or customer service standards is often undertaken by observing staff and recording the outcomes of their interactions with customers. It might also be necessary to find out how telesales staff are responding to customer queries by listening into their calls. This latter method is used frequently as it is relatively unobtrusive. However, if this is being undertaken, the organisation is required to advise customers this is the case, especially if the information is being recorded.

Observation on a face-to-face basis is slightly more difficult as it tends to be more obtrusive. You also need to make sure a member of staff does not deliberately change his or her attitude when carrying out a particular task or procedure as a result of being observed.

The observation of customers can be done more easily. For example, a travel agency might monitor such activities as:

- which sections of the brochure racks customers go to first

- which sales position in the agency most customers head towards
- whether customers take any notice of signs
- customers' reactions during busy times or in queuing situations.

Observation can also be useful in theme parks to establish the routes customers take to move between different rides and attractions or between different areas of the park. This can be used to identify areas of the park that have very little customer exposure and to inform planning decisions.

While observation can tell you about current customer characteristics, it is unlikely to inform you about the future or about customers' reaction to new products or services. Focus groups tend to be used for this method of research.

Focus groups

The idea behind focus groups is that a facilitator encourages a group of people to participate in a discussion that might also be recorded. The facilitator will usually have been trained to put people at their ease and to allow conversation to take place but to bring the discussion back to the main points if it starts to go off at a tangent.

Various techniques have been used to ensure the 'ambience' is appropriate for a particular focus group. For example, if you are testing reactions to a new product that includes holidays to Greece, you might decorate the room appropriately, have Greek music playing in the background, provide Greek snacks and make sure the room is light and warm. For focus groups concerned with holidays, all the participants' dress would be casual and the layout of the room would need to be relaxed and informal.

Focus groups have been a popular market research tool for some time now but have fallen out of fashion a little in the travel and tourism industry. However, they can still provide some very useful results.

CASE STUDY: Focus groups

Focus groups have been used successfully by Cosmos Holidays who were concerned about their image, particularly with teenagers and young adults. They invited people in this age range to apply to join a panel that would meet to discuss children's activity clubs and what they liked and disliked about these. This panel identified a number of things they would change, including the names given to clubs for young people, the logos on T-shirts, the types of activities available and the need for young people to have somewhere to go away from the rest of their families.

As a result, Cosmos made changes to their product for the summer of 2000, incorporating most of the changes recommended by this panel. The panel members were then given a holiday with their families to try out the revised product, to evaluate it and then to give feedback to Cosmos. This particular focus group worked well, especially considering that the people who were designing the clubs aimed at teenagers and young adults were considerably older than the participants themselves.

Questions
Imagine that you were arranging the Cosmos Holidays focus groups.
1 What main points would you aim to have discussed?
2 How many people would you invite to each session?
3 How would you record and analyse the results?

Focus groups can be used to guide future research, and the outcomes of a focus group discussion can be used to identify whether you need to obtain qualitative or quantitative data. The information obtained from focus groups can also aid in the design of questionnaires and in establishing the sample group of people who will be needed for the research.

For all the methods of primary research we have looked at, the one thing that will influence the success of the research is the selection of an appropriate sample. To choose the best sample possible, you must consider the objectives of your research and how you are most likely to achieve a good cross-section of results. For example, if you are asking for people's opinions about flights they have taken, it is obvious you will need to select people who have actually flown and, similarly, if you want to find out about buying patterns, the people you research must be purchasers of the product. The following should help you when selecting an appropriate sample.

- How large is your sample going to be? If it is a postal questionnaire, you will need to select a high number as the response rate will be lower than a face-to-face survey.
- Are you covering an appropriate range of ages, jobs, incomes, cultural backgrounds, etc., to provide you with a reliable cross-section of the people within a region?
- Is the survey going to be local, regional or national?

- Have people been selected at random? (For example, every fifth person who walks past you.)

Finally, think carefully about *when* and *where* the survey will take place. If you pick a time when a town centre is particularly busy, you will probably have access to a good range of people. However, if people are rushing around on their lunch break they are unlikely to want to participate. If it is raining, people will not want to stand outside answering questions and you may find it difficult to record answers if your paper is wet.

Make sure you prepare yourself well and that you take along the resources needed to complete your survey (for example, clip board, pens and paper). Check whether or not you need permission to conduct your survey – some towns and cities will require you to apply for permission in advance and to wear identification. Always tell people why you are doing the research, and thank them afterwards for their help.

Secondary research

Secondary research (see also Unit 3) is often referred to as desk research. It involves gathering data that have been produced by someone else and that might not necessarily have been produced for the same purposes as the research you are conducting, but that still might be of use to you. For example, a tour operator's reservations department might have reports about occupancy rates in different accommodation types or about seats on flights, which they use to plan the contracts for the following year. This information could also be useful for marketing purposes to show trends in travel and the peaks and troughs in the year when various marketing techniques should be employed.

Internal information

As we have already noted, secondary research can be either internal or external to the organisation. Most organisations make extensive use of internal data, which include:

- results of customer service questionnaires
- financial and budget information
- information about bookings
- sales records
- customer information
- existing customers' buying habits
- membership lists
- group booking details
- results of previous promotional activities
- minutes of staff, team or management meetings (see Unit 6)
- results of staff surveys.

In large organisations, most of this information will be held centrally at a head office and should therefore be relatively easy to access. In smaller organisations, this type of information might still be available but it might not have been organised into a format that is useful for your own research. However, it could still be very useful as a starting point for further research.

The questions you need to ask yourself before using any secondary sources of information are as follows:

- How old is the information?
- Does it represent the whole organisation or just the results from one region or sector of operations?
- How reliable was the data collection method?
- Has this information already been used and, therefore, are there people who could help me with my own research?

External information

There is now a wealth of information that can be accessed as secondary information, particularly through the Internet. External secondary information such as this can be useful when looking at travel and tourism trends both in the UK and overseas. Travel and tourism organisations that can provide this type of secondary information include:

- the British Tourist Authority (http://www.visitbritain.com/)
- English Tourism (http://www.englishtourism.org.uk) and the Scottish, Welsh and Northern Ireland Tourist Boards (http://www.visitscotland.com/ http://www.visitwales.com/ http://www.ni-tourism.com/)
- the World Tourism Organisation (http://www.world-tourism.org/)
- regional tourist boards
- overseas tourist organisations.

There are also organisations that conduct specific surveys containing details of travelling patterns. For example, the International Passenger Survey (http://www.mdst.co.uk/index.html) is produced by the Department of Employment. This survey is conducted annually at airports and ferry ports to ascertain the destinations and reasons for travel by the British travelling public. Details about the world economy in general are published by the OECD (Organisation for Economic Co-operation and Development).

Census figures will give you more general information about UK residents, although remember the census is conducted every ten years only so the information it contains could be slightly dated. Local authorities should be able to provide you with information about the residents in a particular area and details about the local population. Many local authorities also conduct their own research into the tourism facilities in their area and so might be able to help with details about attractions, accommodation and catering. Specialist market research organisations (such as Mintel – **http://www.mintel.com**) produce reports of their findings. However, a fee is often charged for making use of these reports and so you might find information such as this is less easy to find in libraries or at your college.

If your research focuses on a specific sector of the industry, find out whether or not there is a trade organisation for that sector. For example, if you wanted to research travel agencies, ABTA (**http://www.abtanet.com**/) would be a good organisation to contact. Alternatively, for ferries or cruise holidays, try contacting PSARA (the Passenger Shipping Association for Retail Agents).

Organisations within a particular sector might also be able to help you with information (for example, tourist attractions, tour operators, travel agencies or airlines). Treat this information with a degree of scepticism, however, because if such organisations are prepared to publish and to make available this information to the general public, this is likely to be for publicity purposes. Few organisations will issue the results of their research if these results could help their competitors in any way.

The one publication that should be used for travel and tourism research is the *TTG* (*Travel Trade Gazette*). This journal publishes on a regular basis information that relates to specific topics or subjects (including popular destinations, the class of travel used by business travellers and the market share of different sectors of the industry). You might need to work through back issues to find the relevant information but this information will be a valuable supplement to your own research.

You might also find information in brochures. Thomson Holidays now print the results of some of the their customer service questionnaires in their brochures. This information could be useful if you were researching customer feelings about products, destinations and hotels.

Activity	As a group, brainstorm the strengths and weaknesses of primary and secondary research. Next, in report form, make recommendations about where and when it would be appropriate to use the different methods of market research discussed in this section.

Analysing the findings of market research

Once you have collected your findings, you need to organise these so they can be used for decision-making. You will probably find the most appropriate way of doing this is to use a computer program such as Excel. If you record your results on to a program like this, you will be able to produce pie charts and graphs and demonstrate your findings.

It is not, however, normally appropriate to use graphs and charts for qualitative findings. These results will need to be summarised and written up as prose.

As we noted in Unit 3, when writing up the findings of your secondary research, make sure you credit the author of any report or research findings you have used. Apart from the fact that you should always acknowledge your sources, this will also enable you to provide evidence of the sources you have used and to show how these have been integrated into your overall research.

Always make recommendations as a result of your research, and make sure these are linked in to your findings. You will need to identify any strengths, weaknesses and limitations that have arisen as a result of your research. If there are possibilities for future research, mention these in your report.

Chapter 4.5 Marketing communications

In such a competitive business as travel and tourism, a wide variety of marketing communications are used by all sectors of the industry. In this industry there is always a need to raise awareness of products and services. Because of the seasonal nature of the industry, much of the marketing takes place at specific times of the year (for example, tour operators and travel agents in December and January, and tourist attractions during the school holidays).

Advertising

The travel and tourism industries advertise their products in the press, on TV, on the radio, in magazines, over Internet and through leaflets. The amount of money spent by the industry on advertising is very large: the travel and transport sector spent close to £200 million on advertising during the first half of 1999, and this amount is increasing each year, being 15% up on the previous year. Needless to say, the highest amount is spent in January (approximately 30% of the industry's spend occurs during this month).

Not all sectors of the industry spend the same amount: tour operators tend to spend double the amount on advertising than do travel agencies. The biggest spenders in the first half of 1999 were Thomson, Thomas Cook, Lunn Poly and Kuoni.

The press

The press is used extensively by travel and tourism organisations, particularly the Sunday papers which are considered a good medium to use as people are usually relaxed when reading these and are therefore likely to be in a more receptive mood for considering holidays. However, organisations also use a range of other newspapers, including the national and local press, to advertise anything from discounts, special departures, new products and late offers. It is important customers' lifestyles are taken into account when using this medium, as advertising can be targeted towards specific client groups through the newspapers they are likely to read. Advertising in newspapers should be consistent and branded according to your organisation's style to ensure customers take notice of and recognise your organisation. Specialist newspapers are also used for advertising, including the travel trade press. Advertising in this type of newspaper will raise travel agents' awareness of your particular products, which could lead to increased sales.

TV

Advertising on television is expensive, especially during the peak viewing times in the evening. However, travel and tourism organisations who advertise on television still tend to use these peak times (especially during soaps, films and game shows) to target the adult viewers who are usually watching at this time. Because of the cost of TV advertising, though, many smaller companies do not use this way of advertising.

Radio

Radio advertising is cheaper than TV but the audience is smaller and there is always the danger that, if someone is driving or working, he or she may not be able to write down details about a product or service. For this reason the amount of detail in a radio advert tends to be kept to a minimum. Low-cost airlines have made good use of radio advertising and, at a more local level, some travel agencies broadcast regular weekly adverts giving details of special late offers.

Magazines

One of the most successful places to advertise travel and tourism products are the specialist magazines that enable organisations to target special interest products at particular segments of the market. For example, sailing holidays might be advertised in specialist boating magazines, and golf holidays in golfing publications. Particular products can also be targeted at specific age ranges or lifestyles, making use of customer information collected through market research.

The Internet

As we noted earlier, the Internet is rapidly developing as a useful marketing tool, particularly for those organisations who have set up products to be sold specifically this way. This form of advertising is likely to pose a threat to the more traditional tour operators and travel agents who have not embraced this new technology.

Leaflets

Most travel and tourism organisations produce leaflets of some description, either to advertise promotional events, special offers or specific products. However, the tourism sector probably makes greater use of leaflets as a form of advertising, in particular, tourist attractions, guided tours, accommodation and catering. These organisations are reliant on tourist information centres, shops, hotels, libraries, etc., displaying their leaflets to encourage customers to use their products and services.

Activity	Select one *travel* and one *tourism* product. Research the advertising media used to promote both products and, where possible, collect examples of these or, in the case of TV and radio advertisements, describe as clearly as you can what the ads said or contained. Produce a display showing how advertising was used to sell both products.

Holiday brochures

Advertising creates awareness or curiosity about a product or service. A potential customer so aroused might take the next step in purchasing the product or service (i.e. finding out more information about it). If such information is not available, this could greatly affect whether or not a customer includes a particular company's product or service in his or her evaluation of the choices on offer. A brochure is particularly important at this stage: all the hard work that has gone into advertising the product or service might be lost if the customer is not able to find out more about it. If other companies offer a similar product and if their brochures are available in the travel agency or tourist information centre, the customer might make his or her decision based on those companies' brochures (look back at the section on the AIDA model earlier in this unit).

The holiday brochure is the main tool a tour operator and travel agent uses to sell a product. It is not possible to show the customer what his or her holiday will look like, but the brochure can give details about the flight, the resort, accommodation and transfers to encourage sales. The thing to remember is that the holiday brochure is a marketing tool and that tourist brochures are promoting a product rather than giving an impartial view.

Many of the major travel agencies have agreements with the tour operators guaranteeing the way the tour operators' brochures will be displayed on the racks. While in some cases this will not be a very specific agreement, some companies will want guarantees about how many brochures will be displayed and where they will be positioned on the racks.

Activity	Visit travel agencies in your local area to look at the brochures on display. Study how the brochure racks are set up and the types of customers these brochures are aimed at. Consider the range of tour operators that appear on the brochure racks and the size of these companies. Discuss your findings with the rest of your group.

Direct marketing

Direct marketing means selling a product directly to the public rather than going through such intermediaries as travel agencies or tourist information centres. A number of different methods are used for direct marketing.

Brochures and leaflets

Brochures and leaflets can be sent directly to customers. Organisations often maintain databases containing information about customers who have travelled with them previously or who have made requests for information. As new products and services are introduced, customers can be informed about these developments. This system can be costly, and the take-up of products and services by customers is often very low.

Direct mail

Direct mail allows organisations to mailshot potential or existing customers. Using this method, organisations can target specific people, professions, clubs, societies or regions of the country, etc. Special offers and competitions often accompany mailshots.

Telemarketing

Telemarketing is very similar to direct mail but telephone communication is more personal and the organisation receives an immediate response from the customer. This form of marketing has not been used extensively in the travel and tourism industry, although it has occasionally been used in the accommodation and time-share sectors.

Door-to-door distribution

The door-to-door distribution of flyers (brief advertising leaflets) is often undertaken on a local basis making use of the free newspapers that are delivered regularly or through the postal system. Flyers can be produced at a relatively low cost and can be included with a range of other organisations' advertisements. The problem with door-to-door distribution is that, because a great deal of junk mail comes through our letterboxes, many of us throw it away rather than reading it.

Direct response advertising

Direct response advertising is often used in conjunction with a competition or other promotional event. When people enter the competition or respond to the event, their details are sent on to the travel and tourism organisation that has funded the activity, who will then contact the potential customers directly.

The importance of direct marketing or personal selling to the travel and tourism industry should never be overlooked. With the emphasis on *place* in the marketing mix, the travel agent, tourist information staff, overseas representatives and reservations agents are the people who deal with the majority of customers. The way in which they promote and sell an organisation's products will affect sales and visitor numbers (selling skills are discussed more fully in Unit 5).

Activity	In small groups, discuss the advantages and disadvantages to a travel and tourism organisation of using direct marketing communications.

Public relations

Public relations covers a very wide area but, broadly, concerns the image an organisation would like to project about itself. The way an organisation achieves this is usually through press releases and activities the organisation is involved in (e.g. sponsoring charitable events, donating money to worthwhile causes or subsidising sports or arts activities, etc. – see below).

Press releases tend to be used for the following reasons. To:

- promote awareness of new products and services
- inform people about changes in the organisation, including new staff members or changes in ownership
- dispel bad publicity that might have arisen about a particular organisation or country, etc.
- publicise events or promotions that are to take place
- tell people about any awards or prizes the organisation has won.

Press releases are different from advertisements in that they inform people rather than simply advertise a product or service. The wording will, hence, be different from an ad, and there will be contact details should a newspaper require further information. No charge is made for using press releases, but there is also no guarantee a newspaper will run the story or when. As newspapers receive many hundreds of press releases each day, the key is to make sure your press release attracts attention and is newsworthy.

Many large organisations have their own internal newspapers designed to raise awareness of the organisation's aims and activities amongst the staff and to encourage teamwork within the organisation. Of course these newspapers are aimed primarily at an organisation's own employees, but they can be used to promote public relations activities the organisation is involved in.

Destinations frequently use high-profile events as public relations activities, which often involve celebrities and well-known companies. Events such as the Cannes Film Festival, the Edinburgh Festival, Expo and the Olympics bring considerable publicity to a destination and increase visitor numbers, not just during the event itself but for some time afterwards. More specifically, events such as the switching-on of the Blackpool illuminations by a celebrity will feature in many national and regional newspapers as well as on television programmes.

Cinema can also be a very powerful medium for tourist destinations. Several years ago there was a rise in overseas visitors to Scotland as a result of such films as *Rob Roy* and *Braveheart*. A similar increase in tourist numbers took place in London following the release of the film *Notting Hill*.

Tour operators, airlines, hotels and destinations all hold press events ranging from meetings to launch a new product to invitations to members of the press to join them on a trip to sample the product for themselves. It is hoped such events result in a feature in a newspaper or on radio that,

although about a particular destination or hotel, will refer readers to a specific airline or tour operator for reservations. On a grander scale, there are many TV holiday programmes that will give ten minutes of prime television time to a product if the programme team has been invited to try out a holiday, hotel or mode of transport.

Charitable deeds are high-profile public relations activities, especially if they involve sponsorship. Such activities often involve giving local charities prizes or gifts such as free holidays, flights or accommodation. Organisations often make donations out of their profits, and some have even set up their own charities (for example, British Airways have set up a charity to enable children with disabilities or illness to travel to such destinations as Disneyland). The industry also holds sporting events such as golf, go-karting and skiing to raise money for specific charities, thus raising the profile of the (often famous) participants and organisers alike. These events are often covered in the travel press, such as the *Travel Trade Gazette*.

Sales promotion

Sales promotions are targeted at either the public or the trade and both forms of sales promotion are used extensively in the travel and tourism industry.

Sales promotions made to the public include the following.

- Discount vouchers and coupons (for example, two for the price of one at an attraction, or money-off vouchers for airlines).
- Competitions to win free holidays or admission to attractions, many of which will generate ideas for future promotional campaigns by asking entrants to suggest slogans or tie-breakers.

- Promotional gifts (e.g. free pens, key rings, posters and balloons) that incorporate the organisation's name.
- Incentives and loyalty discounts (including air miles schemes and reductions for visiting an attraction several times). Hotels and airlines make good use of loyalty schemes, especially for business travellers.
- Shows and events for the public (including travel exhibitions and stands at such events as caravanning and camping shows).

These promotions increase the organisation's exposure and are an important way of raising awareness about a company, product or service. Competitions can be particularly effective if they require entrants to call in to the organisation to register or to collect the results.

Sales promotions are also offered extensively to the trade and include the following.

- Discounts on flights, holidays, hotels and attractions. These are usually valid at off-peak times only and many such schemes are now managed by specialist companies that book for the travel trade only.
- Educational or familiarisation trips. These are organised by tour operators, airlines, hotels and tourism organisations to raise awareness of products, destinations and services.
- Trade exhibitions. For example, the World Travel Market (held at Earls Court in London) runs for three days in November and attracts many exhibitors and visitors from across the whole of the travel and tourism industry.
- Free products. These include a whole range of branded bags, T-shirts, beach towels, mugs and gifts. The trade is

constantly looking for new ideas about how to use such things to advertise their products.

Most of these promotions are regarded as being one of the perks of the trade. The opportunity to take advantage of educational visits and discounted products is one of the good points about working in the travel and tourism industry.

Activity	If you have the opportunity, visit the World Travel Market. This should give you an idea of the size and extent of the industry you are entering. Make notes during your visit. Include organisations and areas of the industry where you would like to work in future.

Sponsorship

As we have already noted, some of the sponsorship activities undertaken by the travel and tourism industry are very local in nature and focus on specific community activities, whilst others are much more high profile. For example, travel companies have started to sponsor television programmes, particularly travel shows and game shows. These companies provide competition prizes in exchange for reduced-price advertising prior to the programme being broadcast.

Travel companies also sponsor events, with airlines and hotels taking an active lead in this type of sponsorship. Some travel companies have sponsored individual teams at sports events.

Some companies also sponsor their employees to obtain additional qualifications. This can either be done as an in-house activity or can attract external applicants.

The communications mix

In the same way that an organisation will consider its marketing mix, it will also want to use a range of marketing communications. The balance between the different communications will be directed by the product, the target market – and, probably, the budget!

Marketing communication and the law

Advertising of all kinds is regulated by the Advertising Standards Authority, which ensures advertising is legal, honest, decent and truthful. There are, however, specific issues that relate to the travel and tourism industry (for example, special offers and late deals might no longer be available by the time a potential customer reads a newspaper advertisement). Each sector of the industry also has a *regulatory body* (an organisation that issues guidelines as to how each company within a particular sector should behave). For example, the Association of British Travel Agents (ABTA) issues a code of conduct recommending the way tour operators and travel agents should present the information that appears in their brochures and advertisements.

All marketing communications are affected by legislation, in particular:

- the Trades Descriptions Act 1968
- the Package Travel, Package Holidays and Package Tours Regulations 1992
- the Consumer Protection Act 1987
- the Data Protection Act 1984.

The Trades Descriptions Act 1968 was set up to ensure that statements made by traders to consumers are fair and accurate. Section

14 of this Act is particularly relevant to the travel and tourism industry. This section applies to the brochures, advertisements and promotional activities a travel or tourism organisation produces or organises along with what a sales person tells a customer about a product or service. Under the terms of this section, even if a company or representative of that company has no knowledge of the statement being false at the time a brochure was published or an advertisement made, the company and its agent can still be liable for issuing false information under the terms of the Trades Descriptions Act. This means that it is of paramount importance that tour operators, for example, inform both customers and travel agents of changes and updates to ensure they do not break the law when they find the products and services they are offering are different from what is specified in the brochure.

The Package Travel, Package Holidays and Package Tours Regulations 1992 also cover the accuracy of information given to customers. These regulations apply to any package holiday that involves an overnight stay or is over 24 hours long and includes two of i) accommodation, ii) flights or iii) ancillary services like excursions or car hire. The regulations confer responsibility to the tour operator for any aspect of a holiday they have sold, including those parts of the product they have no direct control over. This includes car hire, excursions, transfers from the airport to the hotel, accommodation and the amenities and facilities in the resort. These regulations mean that, for a tour operator, the responsibility for checking the accuracy of information now extends further than merely hotel and flight arrangements: the regulations cover brochure descriptions, price revisions and altering or cancelling arrangements.

The Consumer Protection Act 1987 protects people against products or goods that prove to be defective or cause damage. In relation to the travel and tourism industry, this Act also includes misleading prices and the way the industry promotes discounts and special offers. The Act covers such things as special offers that contain specific restrictions, such as the purchase of the travel agent's own insurance policy to receive a discount on a holiday, or restricted products, dates or companies.

The Data Protection Act 1984 covers data held by organisations about potential or actual customers. Such information might have been collected through market research, competitions or from customer service feedback forms. Under the Act, a company cannot pass on information to another company without the permission of the individual concerned. This includes very specialist mailing houses who hold general information about people and who often send out promotion material on behalf of specific client companies.

The Act also contains restrictions on how much information an organisation can legitimately request from people and can hold about them. However, the more personal data a marketing department can collect, the more useful this is likely to be for its future activities. To overcome this problem, if personal information is held by a company, the company is required to register this with the Data Protection Authority, and individuals have been given the right to know what information is held about them.

Customer service is very important in the travel and tourism industry because many organisations provide similar or identical products and services. There is also a high level of customer contact (particularly on tours and sight-seeing excursions when the guide will spend a great deal of time with the customers). The quality of customer service is often the only thing that distinguishes one organisation from another in this highly competitive sector.

This unit deals with all the reasons why excellent customer service is so important in travel and tourism and how it helps organisations keep existing customers and attract new ones. The part personal presentation and communication skills play in dealing with customers is also explored, as is dealing with customers who have different needs. Handling complaints is an essential part of customer service, and this must be dealt with properly. You will also learn how to measure, monitor and evaluate customer service procedures and practice.

The unit gives you the chance to gain practical skills, knowledge and understanding you can put to good use in many other units in your Advanced VCE. It links well with Unit 6 ('Travel and tourism in action') and is also a common unit with the Advanced VCE in Leisure and Recreation.

The unit is assessed through your portfolio work only. The grade on that assessment will be your grade for the unit.

Chapter 5.1 Why excellent customer service is important

Why are customers so important? Because the industry is dependent on customers and because without them there would be no business. If a customer is not happy with the service he or she receives, the customer will either go elsewhere or will look for an alternative product or service. When a customer is happy with the service he or she has received, the customer will more than likely come back to the same organisation and may also tell friends and family about the good service he or she has been given.

Activity	Divide a sheet of paper into two columns and label these A and B. In column A, list all the commercial benefits there are for travel and tourism organisations that offer excellent customer service. In column B, list all the negative effects on a business should its customer service be of a poor standard.

In column A you should have included some of the following:

- increased sales
- more customers
- a better public image
- an edge over the competition
- a happier and more efficient workforce
- satisfied customers
- customer loyalty and repeat business.

Each of these will now be considered in more detail, including the effects of what happens when the service is poor.

Increased sales

At its most basic, a customer will only make that initial purchase if he or she has received good service from the person making the sale. Consider the customer who wants to book a holiday. This person might have the choice of several travel agencies or, alternatively, could book directly with the tour operator. The service the customer receives on the initial contact with the travel agency is what will either inspire him or her to book or turn away to a competitor.

First impressions are paramount, and that includes not just the way the customer is greeted but the whole experience from walking through the door to closing the sale. A customer expects a travel agency to be clean, tidy, uncluttered and the sort of environment where it is safe to hand over large sums of money. Brochure racks should look attractive, interesting and be well stocked, as many customers might not want to deal with an agent on their first visit. Even if you do not have the brochure that is wanted in stock, the customer may still return if your organisation has made a favourable impression. Treat each enquiry as though it is a potential booking. If a customer feels he or she is not being given good service, he or she will leave and go elsewhere.

Once a customer has made a booking, he or she is likely to want additional services, which will result in extra sales. For example, a customer booking a holiday will also need insurance and foreign currency. He or she may also be thinking about car hire, overnight accommodation or travel to the airport. If you can provide an excellent level of customer service, you can maximise the sales on an individual booking. If the customer is dissatisfied with the service received, there is nothing to stop the customer making these additional purchases through a competitor.

Increased sales do not just apply to travel agencies. Once customers are using a travel or tourism product, the same principle will apply. For example, customers who have had an enjoyable flight are more likely to buy duty free items on board than those who feel they have been ignored until the moment to buy these goods arises. Similarly, if customers staying in a hotel are happy with the hotel, they will probably also use the bar and restaurant facilities rather than going outside the hotel. Holiday-makers who have just arrived at their hotel in an overseas resort will be unlikely to buy excursions at the welcome party if they are armed with a list of complaints about their journey, transfer or accommodation.

More customers

Word of mouth is the best recommendation anyone can give you about a product or service. If a customer has had an excellent experience, this customer will probably tell friends and relatives about it, which could result in more customers for your organisation. The best thing about this form of advertising is that it does not cost money and is under the direct influence of the person delivering the customer service. On the other hand, if someone had a bad experience, that person is likely to tell a similar number of people – if not more – about it.

With some sectors of the industry, if customers have had a really good time, they might arrange for a group of friends to

come with them the next time. This is particularly true of attractions or accommodation, but might also apply to transport and tour operations as well.

So far we have focused on commercial benefits: how does the non-commercial sector fit into this? If a tourist information centre has a good local reputation for the service it provides, local hoteliers and businesses are more likely to recommend their guests or customers to visit it. This should in turn increase the visitors' use of local attractions and amenities rather than losing the visitors to alternative destinations.

A better public image

The public image an organisation has is likely to come about as a result of what the media say about that organisation. League tables about such things as airline and train delays inevitably lead to comparisons being made amongst competitor organisations. Similarly, newspaper reports compare different attractions in terms of both value for money of the attractions themselves as well as the catering outlets inside the attractions. Tour operators have started to do price comparisons to show how their products compare with other companies'. Customers are now not only more experienced about travel and tourism products but also about their rights. Bad publicity on a television programme such as 'Watchdog' can give an organisation a very poor public image. The main problem, however, is that, as your business grows and your customer numbers increase, the higher the likelihood is that things will go wrong.

Activity	Some organisations have managed to maintain a good public image. Discuss which travel and tourism organisations you feel have a good public image.
	Make a list of the reasons why you feel these organisations have managed to retain their favourable public image.

So, how does an organisation maintain or improve its public image?

- By ensuring the customers do not have cause to complain – by providing excellent customer service.
- By building on its strong points, those things that created a positive public image in the first place.
- By making sure its after-sales service is as good, if not better, than the initial sales.
- By being involved in, and supporting, local events.

- If a customer does complain, by ensuring he or she is kept informed and updated about progress.

An edge over the competition

Before an organisation can gain a competitive edge over its competitors, it must find out what the competition is offering. This means being aware of any new initiatives, products or services the competition has developed and, at least, keeping up with these. Then, by offering that little bit extra, you can make sure you are better than the competition. There are many ways this can be done, but the concept of caring for the customer is a good starting point.

Caring for customers is all about anticipating the customers' needs and meeting these. When an organisation has regular customers, this can be done fairly easily, especially in business travel where records of each customer's details and requirements will be held within the agency. However, with new customers this is more difficult and requires good listening and observation skills. For example, a customer may feel uneasy about a particular situation. If the customer has never flown before, say, your job as a check-in clerk might involve reassuring the customer or explaining the process to him or her in more detail. You could then alert the staff at the boarding gate and on board the plane so they have been forewarned about this customer and are able to make the flight more enjoyable. Similarly, if you worked at a theme park, you might have a customer who is confused and who is asking too many questions at once. You would need to listen carefully to this customer and help him or her to plan his or her day so as to see as many shows and to go on as many rides as he or she wants.

The financial advantages of having an edge over the competition can be lucrative, both for the general and business travel sectors. In both sectors, if a company can increase its business with some of its suppliers it will achieve increased levels of commission. Also, suppliers are more likely to participate in joint marketing ventures and discounting initiatives if your organisation is the number one agency selling their products in your town or city. Under schemes such as Thomson Preferred Agency system, the top sales companies are rewarded for their efforts.

A happier and more efficient workforce

Satisfied customers, increased sales and a better public image have a very positive effect on the morale of the staff who work for an organisation. There is a great deal of job satisfaction to be had from knowing you have helped customers and provided the best service possible. When customers write in letters of commendation or come in to tell you about what a good time they had, this can make up for the long hours you might have been working.

On the other hand, if you have to deal with a stream of complaints about the products you sell or your services, this may make you feel very negative about both your job and the organisation you work for. Members of staff in such situations cannot work efficiently as they are constantly dealing with problems which, thus, reduces the amount of time they have available to do their normal jobs. This will lead to staff who are unhappy and who will eventually leave the organisation.

Finally, if the workforce is happy and efficient, there are likely to be fewer complaints from the customers. An enthusiastic person delivering the service will make the whole experience for the customer much more enjoyable. Also, an efficient team will make far fewer errors which could occur if the team is under stress and pressure due to the large numbers of dissatisfied customers it has to deal with.

Satisfied customers

Achieving customer satisfaction is the result of meeting or exceeding the customer's expectations. Customer expectations tend to be high: they might be based on a dream that has been sold to them through an advertisement, brochure or leaflet. Also, customers are not able to see the travel and tourism product in advance – it is what is known as an 'intangible product'. The product could similarly have been enhanced in the customer's mind by previous experiences or recommendations from friends and family. In the case of a holiday, this dream is probably what they have spent 48 weeks of the year working towards – and they expect it to be excellent! This is why customer satisfaction is not always easy to achieve.

Many organisations have mission statements so as to encourage a coherent view about customer service across the entire organisation – and this includes customer satisfaction. There may also be charters that set out what customers can expect from the organisation providing the service.

Activity	Think of an occasion when you were a satisfied customer (this can be for any product or service – something bought in a shop, bought over the telephone or booked through an agency or company, etc.). Write

down any preconceived ideas you had *before* you went to or contacted a company or organisation to buy this product or service. Now make a note of how these expectations were met through the experience you had with the company or organisation.

Organise your ideas into a bullet point list of why customer service was so good in the example you have chosen. Now swap your ideas as a group so you can see if your peers have similar views to your own.

Through completing this activity you should now have some ideas about what makes customers satisfied with the service offered. However, all customers are different, and not every dissatisfied customer will complain – many just won't come back. It is these customers who are the most worrying because, unlike a complaint, you do not have any feedback from the customer about what it is he or she is dissatisfied with. As a result, you will not be able to make changes to the product or service you offered. Therefore, always try to get the views of dissatisfied customers because, if it is a problem that can be readily resolved, this will reduce the number of problems you will encounter in the future.

Customer loyalty and repeat business

Customers who are happy with the service they receive will sometimes stay loyal to the organisation they usually deal with. However, in such a competitive environment as travel and tourism, regrettably, this does not always happen. Customers will shop around for the best deal (whether it is for a holiday, flight, insurance deal or hotel). There are very few customers who are not swayed by price!

Customers may continue to use one company because of the service it offers or because of the edge that organisation has over the competition. Where repeat business does happen, customer satisfaction will probably be higher because the likelihood is you know what the customer's needs and expectations are and will be more likely to meet these.

Computers have made this task much easier, as details of a customer's previous bookings, preferences and likes will be easily retrievable. *Customer relationship marketing* is a powerful tool when seeking to do better than one's competitors. Customers need to know they matter to you, and small details about personal preferences show you do know your customers. It is also useful for customers if they do not have to go through the business of giving their details to you each time they make a booking! And a loyal customer who is not satisfied may still return – providing the complaint is handled properly.

Loyal customers may still decide to go elsewhere if, for example, the level of service drops. This can also be a problem in travel agencies when staff leave to work elsewhere as, sometimes, customers feel more loyal to a person than an organisation and may hence take their business away when their favourite member of staff leaves.

Chapter 5.2 Personal presentation

We have already mentioned the importance of first impressions. In this chapter we consider the ways in which you can present yourself to the customer, and how the ways you present yourself will affect your employability, job satisfaction and the future success of the organisation that employs you. The importance of the following are explored:

- dress
- personal hygiene
- personality
- attitude.

Dress

Staff working face to face with customers need to be appropriately dressed. Dress code will obviously differ with different job roles and between companies. The majority of organisations in travel and tourism now have uniforms staff in customer service roles must wear. For example, at a major theme park there will be different uniforms for different job roles. Someone working on an information desk might be wearing a suit whilst, on rides and attractions, clothing is likely to be trousers and a sweatshirt. Entertainment staff will probably wear character outfits. In such organisations as travel agencies, tour operators and airlines, the uniform worn by all staff could be the same. Some staff working for tour operators that supply differently branded products might wear similar uniforms but there may be a different colour scheme for each individual brand. Other operators might try to keep each brand as distinct as possible.

Uniforms benefit an organisation in that they ensure the company's desired image is conveyed to customers. The company's brand image will then be recognised through the colour, pattern, emblems or style of the uniform the staff are wearing. We are now starting to see examples of large organisations who are using the same uniform throughout all their subsidiary companies to reinforce the product name during the whole purchasing experience. This works most effectively when the travel agency staff, airline crew and overseas representatives all have identical uniforms or style of uniform. From the point of view of the staff, a uniform can bring about considerable savings in buying work clothes and can also take away the worry about what to wear each day.

Where an organisation does not have a uniform, it is important staff think carefully about what is appropriate dress. If you are dealing with the public face to face, you must ensure your clothing suits your organisation's image and does not offend customers. Below is a list of items of clothing that would not be acceptable dress for many organisations:

- skirts that are either very short or very long
- jeans or leggings
- training shoes
- T-shirts or sweatshirts
- clothing that exposes a section of the waist.

Many organisations have policies on the amount and type of jewellery that can be worn. A good guide is 'keep it to the minimum' – wedding, engagement or signet rings, sleeper ear-rings, simple chains, etc., only. Although you may find body piercing attractive, many of your potential customers may not. Dangling ear-rings can be a positive hazard in theme parks.

Whatever you wear to work, it should be clean and pressed. And don't forget your shoes – clean these too!

Activity	Think now about your own clothing: do you have anything suitable for wearing in your first job? If you are to do work experience as part of your course, discuss with your group what would be suitable to wear for different work experience placements.

There is one area where dress is not so important and that is where most of the business is conducted over the telephone or in writing. This would include jobs with tour operators based in the UK, or in tele-sales

for an airline company, travel agency or tour operator. Dress tends to be much more casual in these situations because the staff do not have to work face to face with the customers. Some organisations, however, might still set strict dress codes when others might be very much more relaxed in their approach to this part of their operations.

Personal hygiene

Personal hygiene is just as important as dress. It is, however, a very wide area to cover here but some things you *must* consider include the following:

- wash and bathe frequently to reduce unpleasant body odours. This includes both yourself and your clothing
- have a well groomed appearance, with hair that doesn't look dirty or untidy
- make sure your hands and nails are clean. You will find your hands are on display to the public all the time if you are involved in a sales role, particularly when using a computer
- reduce the risk of bad breath by avoiding alcohol and by being careful of what you eat.

These are general pointers that apply to anyone who enters the world of work. Remember, your customers aren't just the external kind – they also include the colleagues and managers you will be working with.

Some jobs will have more stringent personal hygiene rules than others, usually as a result of these jobs involving the serving of food and drink. There may be rules about having long hair tied back or up, about not wearing nail varnish and about the wearing of rubber gloves provided. These rules are intended not only that a hygienic service is offered to the customers but also to minimise the risk of the organisation being prosecuted should a customer suffer food poisoning or other ill-effects as a result of the service.

Personal hygiene may seem like common sense but, if it is not maintained, it can create a lot of bad feeling in the workplace. Discussing personal hygiene issues with a member of staff is one of the most difficult situations a manager can be faced with. However, if it is not tackled, the result could be the team dislikes working with that particular person and customers will similarly not want to deal with him or her. On a positive note, if you feel clean and well groomed, this will probably increase your confidence when speaking to customers and make you a more effective team member.

Think it over

Imagine you work with someone who is pleasant, easy going and a very good worker but who has a personal hygiene problem he or she does not seem to be aware of. How would you tackle this?

Personality

The travel and tourism industry has job roles that suit all types of personality, from those people who are lively to those who are fairly quiet. However, one thing you must do is think about whether or not the type of job you would like to do suits your own personality. If you are the sort of person who is happy to be in the background and enjoys a quiet life, an overseas representative would not be a good job to choose. However, there are many other job roles with tour operators (in administration, reservations or operations, for example) that would be perfectly suitable for you.

Personality is made up of many different things and so it does not necessarily follow, say, that a quiet person will be more sensible than a loud person. There are, however, some personal qualities that are desirable for most careers in travel and tourism:

- good communication skills
- friendliness
- enthusiasm
- an ability to use your own initiative
- a good team player
- good motivation
- honesty and trustworthiness
- dependability
- intelligence or common sense
- an ability to listen.

Some of these qualities can be developed (for example, communication skills and the ability to listen). Others, on the other hand, such as honesty, being a good team player and common sense, are not something you can study or practise. The qualities of dependability, good motivation and enthusiasm will result from how you feel about your job. If you do not possess these qualities, you have probably not chosen your job wisely.

Activity

Conduct a personality audit on yourself. Write down a list of what you feel your own personal qualities are. Now, for each quality, explain in one sentence how you could demonstrate to a potential employer you possess that particular quality. Make sure your sentences explain what you *do* rather than what you *have not* done.

For example, let us look at the qualities of honesty and trustworthiness. One of your sentences could be:

While I was a prefect I held a number of positions of trust.

> Or:
>
> *In my Saturday job I have responsibility for stock control and for running a till.*
>
> But **not**:
>
> *I have never broken the law and so I am an honest and trustworthy person.*

Some job roles will demand additional, specific qualities. For example, an overseas representative will in addition need to be a good organiser, to be confident and to enjoy change and challenges. To find out more about the personal qualities that are desirable for a specific career, you should contact either your careers library or an organisation that operates in the sector you are interested in joining. Alternatively, speak to people who are already doing the job – they will be able to tell you what types of personality they look for when recruiting new members of staff.

Activity	In pairs, discuss the following job roles and the sort of personal qualities people in these jobs must possess. Make a list of these qualities for each role: 1 a manager in a retail travel agency 2 a rides attendant in a large theme park 3 an entertainer on a cruise ship 4 a guide employed at a stately home 5 a member of an airline's cabin crew 6 an overseas children's representative with a tour operator. Compare your lists with those produced by a pair of fellow students.

Some jobs within travel and tourism require specific qualities, particularly in specialist areas like this crèche.

Attitude

Attitude is the way in which you think, act and speak. Your attitude can be changed, but only if you want to change it. 'Attitude' is a word that is used frequently in the workplace but it is used to mean a number of different things: attitude to work, to the organisation, to management, to colleagues and to customers.

When someone says you have a good or bad attitude to your work, this could mean one or many things. It could include the following.

Time-keeping
- Are you always early, on time or frequently late?
- Do you readily stay on at the end of the day or are you up and off at going home time?

- If you work shifts, do you have problems working nights or early mornings, or do you enjoy the variety?
- Do your lunchtimes over-run, resulting in your colleagues going late for their lunch?

Additional tasks
- Do you volunteer to help people out when they need it, or do you keep quiet and carry on with your own work?
- Are you looking for the next challenge or are you happy to become proficient in your own specific job role?
- Do you teach people things you know about or see this as something that could threaten your own position?

Accuracy
- Do you generally take time to complete work and check through tasks, or do you rush through it and pass on to the next stage?
- If you are not sure what to do, do you ask for advice or make a guess?
- Do others return your work to you because of errors, or can it be processed easily?

All these things have a big impact on the work of the team and the efficiency of the organisation. If you work for an organisation that has a staff appraisal system, you may find your attitude to your work is something that is commented on by line managers.

Think it over

Although the points in the lists above apply to the workplace, they could (with a few modifications) apply to students on a course like yours. What is *your* attitude to the work you must do for this course? Use the questions above to help you decide this.

Your attitude towards the *organisation* you work for can, initially, be spotted through your appearance and how proud you feel to be associated with the company. People who make the effort to look presentable will generally feel positive about the organisation they work for. This can also come across in the comments you make to colleagues and customers. Try not to speak in a negative way about either your own organisation or your suppliers. Such easily made comments as 'they're always doing that in accounts – we get these problems all the time' or 'your travel agent obviously hasn't booked that for you' can present both your own and other organisations in very bad light. Customers have chosen your organisation to process their travel or tourism requirements, and they are unlikely to make a reservation or to become regular customers if the staff have a bad attitude towards their own organisation.

Attitudes towards *management* are particularly important and can be a big problem in large organisations where the management is more remote and seemingly more distant from day-to-day dealings with the public and the organisation's employees. However, as an employee, you need to have a certain amount of respect for those who have been in the business longer than you, or who have developed skills and knowledge you do not possess. Remember that, if you stay in the travel and tourism industry long enough, one day you might also be a manager.

Your attitude towards your *colleagues* is important for there to be effective team-work. A team is a group of people working towards a collective goal and will always contain a mixture of personalities and abilities. The travel and tourism industry is quite distinct from other industries in that it is rare for customers to deal with one person only: they will generally come into contact with many of your colleagues. For this reason it is important good communication and teamwork skills ensure the customer's experience is excellent. The customer is likely to remember only the weak link in the chain, so positive attitudes towards your colleagues and respecting them as people are essential. If colleagues feel they are not valued or respected, they might decide they are not going to help you out, which will ultimately reflect badly on your delivery of customer service. For example, a hotel receptionist is usually the first point of contact for guests of the hotel. If the receptionist curtly dictates orders to other members of the hotel's staff he or she considers inferior in status, these staff members may be both reluctant and slow to follow his or her orders. Consequently, the services these staff members provide the guests might be done grudgingly and tardily, which will result in the guests complaining to the receptionist. A vicious circle results: the receptionist will reprimand the staff, who will consequently feel even more hostile towards the guests.

The final point is your attitude towards the *customers* themselves. Always treat customers as though they are the only people you are dealing with. Give them the help, advice and time they deserve, and do all in your power to make sure they become repeat customers. Most importantly, however, respect them as people and try to empathise with their situation.

Chapter 5.3 Types of customers

The travel and tourism industry has a wide range of customers. Therefore to provide excellent customer service you need to be able to consider what the needs of different customers are and how to meet these needs. The customers you are likely to come across are:

- individuals
- groups
- people of different ages
- people from different cultures
- non-English speaking people
- people with specific needs.

Activity	In small groups, discuss the different types of customer you might encounter in the travel and tourism industry. What are these customers' specific needs? How will these needs differ from one customer to the next?

Obviously, individuals and groups are likely to comprise people of different ages and from different cultural backgrounds, as well as non-English speakers and people with specific needs. More skill is needed to deal with these different combinations of needs, and that is something which comes with experience, knowledge and practice.

Individuals

By individuals we mean:

- people by themselves
- couples
- families
- friends.

There are no specific guidelines as to when a certain number of individuals becomes a group but, as a general rule, once numbers exceed 8–10 this would be classified as a group. Individuals are likely to be the most frequent type of customer you will deal with, and this will usually happen on a one-to-one basis (either face to face, in writing or over the telephone). You need to concentrate on their individual needs, asking questions to establish what it is they require. Because you are focusing on an individual, there are likely to be fewer disruptions than when dealing with customers in a group. You should, therefore, be able to maintain eye contact with the customer.

Individual customers, however, are likely to expect more or to be more demanding than a group, and the transaction will often last longer than it would if you were dealing with a group. When you deal with individuals you might be able to remember the customers' names and so will be able to acknowledge them in future visits. If you deal with high volumes of individuals (for example, on an airline or at a tourist attraction) this is far less likely.

Groups

Groups can be exceptionally valuable to an organisation and, providing they are managed well, do not necessarily create extra work. The group's common goal could be what brought this group to your organisation in the first place (e.g. a love of architecture, skiing enthusiasts or delegates to a convention). You may also find you are competing with other companies and so will have to provide quotes and details of the service you can offer. Not all organisations offer the same benefits to groups making bookings, but the following are examples of the types of things that can be expected when making a group booking.

Discounts. These are often 5–10%, but can be higher. There may also be special group rates (for example, in the hotel industry, a group room and meals rate will probably be negotiated).

Free places to group leaders. These are the people organising the trip and are likely to be the main decision-makers. With coach travel there will also usually be free places for drivers, and ferry and tourist attractions usually offer free meals and special lounges for coach drivers. Some tour operators also offer group leaders the opportunity to take a free (or very much reduced-rate) familiarisation trip to help them plan the arrangements.

Special group travel arrangements. These might include special check-in arrangements or seating on the transport.

Welcome parties or cocktail parties. These are organised to get the trip or holiday off to a good start.

Excursions or special visits. These might be arranged to suit the group's needs. Sometimes these are an extra or could be included in the overall price.

A guide or representative from the company. This person will make sure the group is looked after for the duration of the visit.

Group bookings tend to differ from individual arrangements in that the numbers are very often fluid and can change on a regular basis. This means names are rarely confirmed until close to the date, although some tour operators ask for names to be confirmed at the time of booking. If you are making group arrangements, make sure you find out the key booking dates and communicate these to the organiser.

Sometimes selling to groups will require presentations or talks to be given. These are useful as they give you the opportunity to get a great deal of information over to the whole group quickly, and you can also bring your own personality into play. Always make sure everyone can hear, and allow time at the end to speak to individuals who have specific questions. Generally, this is best done on an informal, mingling basis rather than asking people to voice their concerns in front of the whole group.

People of different ages

You will find differing ages in both individual customers and in groups. As a general rule, the very young and the very old need more time and care than the middle age ranges. Examples of different age ranges you are likely to come across are as follows.

Children (2–12 years) and infants (under the age of 2 years)

These customers have quite a lot of say in the purchase of travel and tourism products, especially children. The majority of families will focus their decision-making on such things as children's facilities, clubs and the suitability of destinations. The tour operators have now realised that, by offering children's clubs, they can also offer children's excursions, thus giving the parents some time to themselves and thus maximising the profit made in the resort.

Teenagers and young adults (12–18 years)

These people are too young to book their own travel arrangements (unless approved by a parent or guardian) and have needs that vary from adults and children but, nevertheless, there are very few products that cater for them. Some tour operators organise clubs for this age range, but the interests of a 12-year-old are very different from a 14-, 16- or 18-year old, and vice versa. This tends to be the forgotten or ignored group in travel and tourism products.

Adults

Adults are the people who pay for the product but who do not necessarily make the decisions. The adults will be the customers you have most contact with. Make sure you keep any discussions you have with adults on a professional and respectful basis. Take into account people's status and name. For example, a man and woman might not be married and, if they have children, their children's surnames could differ. Do not make assumptions. Two men travelling together asking for a double room might not be partners – they might simply be confused about the definition of room type. If they are partners, this is none of your business.

Elderly customers

Age is an issue, even though many customers see age as a state of mind rather than something that applies to them. Many elderly customers are exceptionally active and will participate in more hazardous activities than people half their age. Again, the golden rule is don't assume that, because a customer is elderly, he or she will need assistance – but do make that offer. Some elderly customers will need help with explanations about what is happening or with actual assistance in getting from point A to B. Make sure you treat their requests with dignity: you might

find that elderly gentleman travelling to Canada for the first time to see his daughter becoming a regular traveller. This type of customer is more likely to stay loyal to your organisation than any other – providing a high level of service is given.

Every customer you deal with is likely to be of a different age but all customers have individual needs that need to be met or exceeded as part of your delivery of customer service.

Activity	We have just been discussing customers of different ages. Look at one sector of the travel and tourism industry and identify what products are on offer to cater for these different clients. Produce a poster to show your findings.

People from different cultures

While the UK has become increasingly multicultural in recent times, there is still, regrettably, a lack of expertise in the travel and tourism industry about how to deal with customers from cultural backgrounds different from their own. Under no circumstances should we treat people differently simply because of their cultural background. However, we may need to establish whether or not certain customers have specific dietary requirements that need catering for (for example, vegetarian meals and not being served food that goes against certain religious beliefs).

Non-English speakers

When you come into contact with non-English speakers and do not speak their language yourself, first of all find out if one of your colleagues speaks their language. You will probably have noticed the flags worn by airline staff to denote which languages they are proficient in and, in tourist information centres, there is usually a list of the languages spoken by the staff. However, in many organisations there is usually little language proficiency on site, which means you will have to consider contingency plans. Find out if there is a common language in which you can pass on general information (e.g. French or German). This might start off the conversation and clarify a few points.

The other strategy is to consider whether diagrams, maps or written information can be used. Pictures can often be more informative than anything else at this stage, particularly if the customer actually requires information.

You will find that some jobs require you to speak a second language (for example, air stewarding and overseas representation). However, in this country our language ability tends to be limited and, in the majority of travel agencies, tour operators, accommodation and tourist attractions, little else is spoken other than English. A second or third language is exceptionally useful and

will increase your chances of entering your chosen profession.

Customers with specific needs

This is potentially a vast area, as anyone can have a specific need determined by any aspect of his or her life. This section will try to identify some of the main specific needs you are likely to come across.

Wheelchair customers

The needs of these people could range from ensuring they have adequately adapted facilities to assistance in getting on and off airplanes or rides at an attraction. When dealing with these customers, always make sure you communicate with the customer rather than the helper accompanying him or her. Get down to their level, and do not assume they do not want to take part in what is going on.

Blind people

You may need to explain things to blind people rather than expecting them to follow what is happening on, say, a computer screen. Many attractions and hotels have instructions in Braille to help these customers.

Deaf customers

You need to take special care forming your words clearly so a deaf person can follow what you are telling him or her by reading your lips. You may have people in your organisation who have learnt sign language and who can help deaf people. For those who are hard of hearing, some organisations have installed special hearing loops.

Customers with learning difficulties

Very often these people are harder to identify but if you do realise a customer has learning difficulties, allow him or her more time to take in what you are saying and be prepared to explain things clearly and patiently. If you are finding it difficult to communicate, do not keep repeating the same message but think how you could rephrase or explain something in a different way.

Other needs

There are also customers who have specific needs because of the situation they are in (for example, people travelling with young children or expectant mothers). It is always best to find out what regulations apply to people in such situations (for example, can a single person travel with twins under the age of 2 years on a plane, and up to what stage in the pregnancy can a woman be allowed to travel without a doctor's certificate?). Once you have found the answers, try to give the maximum help you can.

While you must not discriminate against any of these customers, you must be honest with them and, if your facilities are unlikely to be sufficient or adequate enough for their needs, explain this and let them make their own decision. And make sure that any other suppliers whom these people might have contact with (for example, tour operators, transport companies and hotels) are informed of their precise needs.

Activity	In small groups, and for each different category of specific need, draw up a set of guidelines for one sector of the industry explaining how this sector could cater for all these customers' needs.

Chapter 5.4 Dealing with customers

People who work in the travel and tourism industry deal with customers on a regular basis and there will be times when you will deal with your own customers. The following methods of communication are used:

- face to face (either on a one-to-one basis or when dealing with a group)
- on the telephone (making and receiving calls)
- in writing (receiving and replying to letters).

In some job roles, you might deal with one form of communication only but many sectors of the industry rely on their staff being able to use all three methods of communication.

Face-to-face communication

Face-to-face communication is the easiest way to create an impression on your customer and, it is hoped, this will be a favourable impression. Remember, first impressions are important, and first impressions are usually made within 30 seconds.

Activity	In groups of three or four, discuss any first impressions you have had in your dealings with the travel and tourism industry as a customer or potential customer (think about as many experiences as you can – things that have happened on your holidays, on day trips, on visits to theme parks, etc.).

How would these impressions have been different if the member of staff had given more thought to his or her own delivery of customer service? Compare your group's findings with those of the rest of your class.

So, how can we create a good impression when dealing with customers face to face? Figure 5.1 contains guidelines about what you should do every time a customer approaches you.

- Smile, and make sure your smile looks genuine rather than forced.
- Put what you are working on to one side so it looks as though you are ready to deal with the new customer and so your work area looks tidy.
- Look at the customer in the eye and maintain this eye contact.
- Offer assistance. In the case of a travel agency or tourist information centre, this might require you to come out from behind your counter and approach the customer. Shouting 'Can I help you?' from behind the counter is unlikely to endear you to that customer.
- Speak clearly and make sure you adopt an appropriate tone and volume for what you are saying.
- Listen to what the customer is saying and do not interrupt – let the customer tell you what it is he or she is interested in doing.
- Show interest. Making notes of important points (e.g. dates, duration, destinations or interests). This will not only remind you of what the customer has said but shows you are treating that person seriously as a customer.
- Always thank the customer at the end of the transaction and make sure he or she knows who you are and what he or she needs to do next.

Figure 5.1   What we should do every time a customer approaches us

If you are making a formal presentation to a group (for example, at a welcome meeting for the customers of a tour operator) there are different strategies you will need to adopt (see Figure 5.2).

- You will need to set up the room or area, so always obtain an approximate idea of numbers and have some extra places should they be needed.
- Make sure everyone can see you clearly and that your voice will carry to the back of the room (if not, it might be necessary to use a microphone).
- Use visual displays – maps, posters, photos or short videos (not more than 10 minutes) and give out handouts.
- Always stand near the entrance to greet people individually and to direct them, but make sure you arrange separate appointments to see customers with problems afterwards.
- Introduce yourself and start your presentation, making sure you pace what you are saying so it isn't too fast or slow (don't worry about nerves; these often spark off that extra bit of adrenaline that makes your talk more interesting).
- Allow time at the end to speak to individuals and to provide extra help and advice.

Figure 5.2 Making a formal presentation

During your Advanced VCE programme you should have the opportunity to develop your presentation skills as part of Key Skills. Make the most of that opportunity (see the activity below) because it will really help you in your face-to-face contact with customers once you are at work.

Activity	It is very difficult to know what the strengths and weaknesses of your own face-to-face communication skills are. The objective of this activity is for you to be self-critical about how you communicate and to draw up an action plan to improve on your weak areas and to build on your strong ones. Prepare a short presentation for your group. This could take one of the following scenarios: - a welcome party - an introduction to a group prior to them being guided around a tourist attraction - a sales presentation to a group of people planning a holiday.

You will need to set up the room before you make your presentation, and your presentation should be recorded on a video camera so you can assess your performance.

Following the presentation, watch the video with your tutor and agree on what you did well and what you could improve. Discuss activities you could include in your action plan that will help you meet your overall objective of improving how you communicate face to face.

Non-verbal communication (also known as 'body language') is just as important as the words we use when communicating with a customer. Giving the right message through our body language has already been covered in some of the things discussed here, such as smiling and maintaining eye contact. However, there are other ways our body language can show we are interested in what a customer is saying.

Standing or sitting upright with your hands at your side or behind your back will give an open or welcoming message to a customer, whereas slouching or crossing your arms in front of you gives a closed or hostile impression. Try to avoid fidgeting, playing with your hair or items of jewellery, or the excessive use of gestures for no apparent reason, as these will only interrupt the customer's concentration.

Activity	Produce two lists, one listing ways in which body language (or non-verbal communication) can help you when dealing with customers and the other listing ways it could hinder you in your interactions with customers.

When dealing with a customer face to face, you must balance the verbal and the non-verbal so you communicate effectively and positively. Start to think now about the techniques you could adopt that would help you with the different types of customers we identified earlier.

On the telephone

Most companies now rely very heavily on the telephone for their delivery of customer service and, although computers tend to be used to make reservations, there are still some products that are sold mostly by telephone. Some of the same principles we discussed for face-to-face communications also apply to the telephone, but there are additional things we need to consider to ensure the call is effective (see Figure 5.3).

- Make notes in advance. Are there key points you will need to communicate (for example, reference numbers, dates and names)?
- Smile. You will sound enthusiastic and friendly if you are smiling when you speak on the telephone.
- Have all the documentation close to hand so you can look up any information you need quickly.
- Speak clearly and make sure you adopt an appropriate tone and volume for what you are saying.
- Listen to what the person is saying on the other end and do not interrupt. Check at the end you have understood. Unlike face-to-face communication, you do not have non-verbal signals to confirm your understanding.
- Show interest. Making notes of important points (such as dates, duration, destinations or interests) will remind you of what the customer has said afterwards.
- Ask for clarification of anything you do not understand, especially the spelling of names – this will reduce the need to phone back later for further information or clarification.
- Make use of the phonetic alphabet (see below) when spelling out names or giving reference numbers.
- Always thank the customer at the end of the transaction and make sure he or she knows who you are and what he or she needs to do next.

Figure 5.3   Communicating by telephone

The phonetic alphabet mentioned in Figure 5.3 is an internationally recognised way of spelling things out over the telephone (Figure 5.4). You will find that, as your proficiency improves with this alphabet, it becomes much easier to use and decode what other people are telling you.

A alpha	H hotel	O oscar	U uniform
B bravo	I india	P papa	V victor
C charlie	J juliet	Q quebec	W whiskey
D delta	K kilo	R romeo	X x-ray
E echo	L lima	S sierra	Y yankee
F foxtrot	M mike	T tango	Z zulu
G golf	N november		

Figure 5.4   The phonetic alphabet

Activity	Try spelling out your own name using the phonetic alphabet.

In some job roles, the majority of the business is done over the telephone in call centres. There is a great deal of pressure when working in a call centre, as targets will have been set by the management for a certain number of calls to be answered in a specified time and also, perhaps, for so many sales to be converted into bookings. Managers monitor the calls being made to ensure quality is consistent across the whole department. This might not sound like a good place to work but the work is usually more highly paid than face-to-face work and there are opportunities to work less conventional hours as call centres are often busy in the evenings and at weekends.

Activity	Make a test call either to a hotel, an attraction, a tour operator or tourist board to find out information about a particular product. Make a note of what the person on the other end of the line says. Now look at the conversation to see if there is anything you would change to improve the service that was provided.

> Role play a similar call, this time with you as the staff member and one of your peers as the caller. (This could be done using two-way telephones or by using different extension numbers.) After the call, ask your peer to assess how you dealt with his or her enquiry. Now swap parts and do the role play again.

You will probably have realised by now that you have to be very careful about what is said over the telephone. In particular, you must be careful about any conversations you have with colleagues or when talking to yourself whilst you are dealing with a customer. Always make sure you use the hold facility on the telephone if you need to check information, but tell the customer he or she will be put on hold. And never forget the customer: keep him or her updated with your progress so he or she does not think he or she has been cut off.

In writing

There are many ways written communication is used in travel and tourism apart from the standard way of writing letters. Some examples of written communications used in the industry are:

- letters
- advertisements
- displays (including window cards and foreign exchange rates)
- signs
- menus
- tariffs
- bills, invoices and accounts
- noticeboards
- faxes
- itineraries and timetables.

The main guidelines when using written communications are that your communication must make sense, must convey the message you intend it to convey and it must be correct. When you first start to write to customers, it is a good idea to ask an experienced colleague to check what you have written to see if he or she understands what you have said and so your colleague can give you advice about anything that might be missing. There are times when it will be necessary to consider the layout to see if the message could be conveyed more easily (for example, an itinerary for a flight will look much better if it is set out in columns rather than in prose). Figure 5.5 gives an example of such an itinerary.

Itinerary – Mrs T Last		
Wednesday 10th May	Check in London Heathrow terminal 1	09:30
	BA 644 departs London	11:00
	Arrives Paris Charles de Gaulle airport	13:00
2 nights reserved at the Hotel Ibis, Charles de Gaulle airport, in a single room on bed-and-breakfast basis. Telephone number 37 578570.		
Friday 12th May	Check in Paris Charles de Gaulle airport	14:00
	BA 653 departs Paris	16:00
	Arrives London Heathrow airport	16:00
*Please note all times quoted are local		

Figure 5.5   Specimen itinerary

When using times, always use the 24-hour clock and, if there is a time difference, quote times in local rather than UK time and annotate the written work to show this (see Figure 5.5).

You will also need to check there are no spelling or grammatical mistakes in the communication. This is reasonably easy to do on a computer but people's names and place-names often are rejected by spellcheck and so you will have to check these yourself. When producing posters, displays or window cards using your own hand-writing, make sure the writing is clear and accurate. Do not use jargon in these communications: it is very easy to abbreviate 7 nights to 7 nts, London Gatwick to LGW or half board to HB, but not all your customers will understand what these mean.

Chapter 5.5 Selling skills

The majority of travel and tourism organisations are dependent on sales and the ability of their staff to make these sales. All members of the team are responsible for sales, whether or not they have direct contact with the customers. However, the people who have face-to-face customer service roles will probably be selling their products, company and themselves throughout their working day. Many will be visible to passers-by, and the impression created by a travel agency or tourist information centre may be the deciding factor in starting or stopping a selling situation.

Others might have more control over when they make sales (for example, in business travel or telesales). Here, you might have time to collect yourself before answering each call, and there may be times of the day when you can be more relaxed. In other situations selling will be very intensive as a result of the condensed, intensified time you are with the customers (for example, airline cabin crews and overseas representatives at a welcome meeting).

You may feel some roles are not sales orientated (for example, in administration or operations support for a tour operator) but these roles are just as important in achieving sales targets. The support these roles lend the organisation will free up people so they can deal purely with selling either face to face or over the telephone. A speedy reply to a request for information or a well produced quotation are just as important to a sale as the way in which the product is described and sold.

You will probably have gathered by now that selling is heavily dependent on teamwork.

Think it over

You have been dealing with one employee at a travel agency who has been very helpful in supplying you with information and advice about a group holiday you wish to book. You decide to go ahead to book the holiday and return to the travel agency only to be told the employee you have been dealing with is away for a week and to come back on his or her return as no one else knows anything about the holiday. What would you do?

Teamwork is not just about how different people's roles can support each other but also about how people genuinely work as a team to reach the company's sales objectives.

The company's or organisation's sales objectives will greatly affect the techniques used by its sales people. A privately owned travel agency or tour operator will have totally different sales objectives from a tourist information centre or National Trust shop. The following are examples of the different types of sales objectives you might come across in both the commercial and non-commercial sectors of the industry.

Commercial sector (e.g. retail travel agency)

- A specific overall sales target for the company, split into regional, branch and individual targets.

- Sales targets for high-earning products, such as insurance, car hire and ancillary services.
- Sales targets for company-owned products (for example, package holidays, charter airline seats, foreign exchange or cruises).
- Competition will be encouraged; league tables showing sales achieved might be published, both within and between different branches.
- Sales targets will be monitored by the manager and are likely to feature in staff appraisals.
- Product knowledge and sales skills are the main focus of staff training.

Non-commercial sector (e.g. a tourist information centre)

- Few sales targets are set. The focus is more on providing information and advice and supporting local tourist functions. Sales of products for profit are very much regarded as a secondary or support function.
- The majority of sales are on a referral basis, with little or no money being collected at the centre. For example, when recommending a hotel, the tourist information centre will earn 10% of the hotel's charge to the visitor should the recommendation be taken up. When recommending attractions, it will not receive anything.
- Competition among staff and branches and target setting for sales are rare.

Whatever situation you work in, you will need to learn the selling skills that are used by the industry to:

- raise customer awareness
- establish rapport with customers
- investigate customer needs
- present the product or service
- close the sale
- deliver after-sales service.

Raising the customer's awareness

It is important you have the customer's attention before you start selling anything to him or her. Very often, what attracts a customer to a particular product or idea is an advertising or publicity campaign, but it could also be something impulsive on the part of the customer that starts the sales conversation. For example:

- window cards advertising cheap flights or late availability
- the appearance of the travel agency itself (e.g. warm and inviting on a cold, wet winter's day)
- events or activities the customer has heard about
- promotional activities undertaken by a destination, a chain of hotels, an attraction, etc.

Once the customer has made this initial contact it is important you do not lose him or her. We have already mentioned how important first impressions are, but there are also techniques you can develop that will ensure you keep the customer's attention. These are discussed in more detail below.

Activity	Think about sales people you have met whilst buying, or trying to buy, various goods. What did you like or dislike about these people? Make two lists, one for likes and the other for dislikes.

As a result of doing this activity you will have started to identify what makes a successful sales person. Personality is the key to this. It is your personal way of dealing with a customer that will keep his or her attention or make him or her disinterested in either making a booking or using your company.

Establishing rapport with the customer

'Rapport' simply means having a good relationship with a customer, and one of the key points in establishing rapport with a customer is making sure he or she feels important and minimising any distractions. Use an appropriate tone of voice and the type of language suitable for that particular customer, and make him or her feel relaxed and comfortable. If possible, sit the customer down and start to engage him or her in conversation. Maintain eye contact, smile and give out positive body language signals.

There are a couple of 'do nots' at this stage: do not answer the phone or chat with colleagues unless this is relevant to the customer. Do not allow the customer to pick up a load of brochures and leaflets without first having contact with a member of staff. If the customer is allowed so to do, he or she is unlikely to remember what the staff are like (or even where he or she picked up the brochures) and will probably not return.

By now, it is hoped, you will have started to establish a rapport with the customer, and will be holding a conversation with him or her. What you must now do is maintain this rapport throughout the sales situation. Because the customer is buying a high-value product, it is important you gain his or her trust at an early stage. This is quite easy to achieve, providing you are honest throughout the entire transaction. You've probably heard people refer to good sales people as able to 'sell snow to the Eskimos' or other similar expressions. This is not what selling is about, and if you do sell products the customer neither wants nor needs he or she is unlikely to return. By being open with the customer, he or she will probably tell you things that are very useful to you, so pick up on these. If necessary, find out about previous holidays or experiences to identify what the customer enjoyed or disliked. Make sure you do not give your own opinions here – it is essential you find something that suits the customer, not something *you* would want to do.

Activity	Choose a travel and tourism product you would be interested in buying (make sure this is something you might feasibly buy and do not make it too complicated. Check with your tutor if you are unsure what to choose). Visit a suitable local organisation and role play being a customer interested in buying this

product. Make sure you give the sales person the opportunity to raise your awareness and establish rapport with you.

Prepare a short presentation for your group about what you have learnt – good or bad – from this experience. Close your presentation with ideas about how you would make initial contact with customers if you worked for this organisation.

Investigating customer needs

There is only one way you will find out what a customer needs, and that is through asking questions, listening to responses and considering available options. The really important point is to *listen*. Research has shown that we listen to only about 30% of what we are told. The reason for this is that we are usually working out our response whilst the other person is speaking. Pause after the customer has finished and repeat back a couple of key points. *Never* make assumptions about a customer, his or her needs, likes or situation. Ask open questions rather than closed ones to find out more about what the customer needs and wants. (*Closed* questions are ones where the reply will usually be either 'yes' or 'no': will you be travelling alone? Will you want us to book your accommodation? *Open* questions demand more fuller replies (see the activity below).)

At this stage, keep the questions focused and relevant. Find out the customer's name, but don't ask for unnecessary details, such as the names of everyone who is travelling, until later in the process. Make sure you either write down what he or she says or key it into the computer so the customer does not have to repeat things.

Activity Select a sector of the travel and tourism industry and make a list of *open* questions that could be used in this sector to investigate a customer's needs. Try starting the questions with

- *Where* (e.g. *where* have you considered visiting?)
- *When* (e.g. *when* would you like to travel?)
- *How* (e.g. *how* would you like to get there?)
- *Why* (e.g. *why* did you enjoy Ibiza?)
- *Who or whom* (e.g. *who* will be travelling with you?)
- *What* (e.g. *what* type of accommodation would you like to stay in?)

(The suggested questions above might apply to a travel agency; other sectors you could try this activity for are tourist information centres.)

Once you have an idea of what your customer's needs are, you could then ask more specific closed questions to help you with the finer details. This will, it is hoped, point you in the direction of a couple of suitable products or services you could recommend to the customer.

Presenting the product or service

You should now start to focus on giving the customer information about specific products and on telling him or her about the options that are available. Consider what selling tools your organisation has that might help you here. For example:

- brochures and leaflets
- tourist board information
- maps and atlases

- videos
- personal recommendations from members of staff
- Viewdata.

Use these tools selectively and carefully to provide *relevant* information for the customer, and be aware of any time limitations the customer may have (e.g. someone who has popped out in his or her lunch hour may have other things to do before returning to work!). It is best not to overload customers with too much information at this stage. Do not tell them about every available product; select the ones most appropriate for their needs.

Activity	You have started work in a very busy retail travel agency and have been handed a number of customer requests that came in over the weekend. For each request, find two suitable products and list the selling points for each one. • A package holiday at a three-star hotel in Majorca for a family in a fairly quiet resort. The hotel must have children's facilities and be either half or full board. • A four-star hotel close to Heathrow airport that offers car parking for two weeks and transfers to the airport. The hotel must be available either on a room-only or bed and breakfast basis. This booking is for a young couple with no children who are going to Mexico for two weeks' holiday. • A short ferry crossing to France for a two-day trip for two adults taking a car. They will find their own accommodation in France. Now role play selling one of the products to a fellow student.

Once rapport starts to develop, you may find the customer raises objections to certain parts of the product (for example, a night flight or a shingle beach at the resort). One of the keys to successful selling is to point out *benefits* of these features. For example, the night flight mentioned above could have several advantages, including:

- you (i.e. the customer) could work on the day of departure
- you get 7 or 15 full days in the resort rather than losing days through travelling
- the hotel room will be ready when you arrive
- the flight is likely to be cheaper than a daytime one.

The shingle beach is a bit more difficult, but there may be ways of selling benefits depending on facilities available in the resort. For example:

- the hotel pool is excellent, with free sun loungers and a bar
- there is a lido on the seafront, which most people use for sun bathing.

Activity	In the previous activity you identified the *positive* selling points about a product. Now consider critically what a customer might point out as being *negative*. Try turning these around into benefits.

Being aware of products and features customers might raise objections to is an invaluable selling skill. By finding ways and means of selling these as *benefits*, you will be able to rise to meet any objections a customer might have.

Closing the sale

'Closing the sale' means bringing your discussions with the customer to a successful conclusion – i.e. you successfully *sell* a product and the customer is happy to *buy* that product. Start to close the sale when you spot positive buying signals from the customer. These signals include the customer:

- asking an increased number of questions
- starting to picture him or herself and the product as one (i.e. talking about this product as something he or she is going to have or take part in)
- checking dates in his or her diary
- contacting a partner who will be travelling with him or her
- making a great deal more positive comments
- displaying increased positive body language (e.g. leaning forward, looking pleased and enthusiastic).

At this point it is important to obtain a firm commitment rather than letting the customer go away to think about it. Try to hold any booking while you confirm the customer's commitment: it would be a shame if the last two seats on a flight went while you were explaining ticket conditions to the customer.

Closing the sale usually involves money. Make sure you are aware of how much you need to collect from the customer to cover any cancellation charges if he or she should change his or her mind and decide not to use the product or service. Explain cancellation and refund details to ensure the customer is aware of the conditions that will apply once he or she decides to proceed.

There may be agreements, booking forms or paperwork that now need to be completed. Always help the customer with anything he or she needs to complete, and do not rush the customer at this stage: he or she may still have questions or need to know information about visas or health requirements for a particular destination.

Check through the details you have recorded carefully, including the spelling of names, titles, ages and contact information. Find out if the customer has any special requests or requirements. Always look for sales opportunities at this stage. Does the customer need help with transport to the point of departure, car parking, foreign currency, insurance or overnight accommodation?

Activity	Collect a package holiday brochure and look at the booking conditions. Summarise the main points you would need to point out to a customer and list these. Compare this list with a fellow student's to see if there is anything you have missed or that is different for a different product.

Delivering after-sales service

There may be a whole range of services that take place after the sale has been made, including:

- invoices and confirmations
- further information about the product or service
- changes and amendments
- picking up the tickets.

These must be given with the same level of customer service as the sales procedure. Customers need to receive information promptly, and anything that is unclear will need to be explained. For example, when a ticket is handed over to a customer, you should always read through the details with the customer and check they are accurate. Point out where the flight number, airport, terminal and check-in details and departure and arrival times are on the itinerary and ticket. If there is a time difference, tell the customer about this; otherwise he or she might ring you up later asking why the flight takes less time on the way out than it does on the return.

Many companies also have additional after-sales services, such as welcome home cards and letters. This is a nice touch to remind the customer of who you are and also to pass on your best wishes.

Think it over

Why do you think it is important to deliver after-sales services with the same ease and attention as the sales procedure?

Activity	Select a tourism and travel product that is available locally and which you can research thoroughly. You are going to role play being a sales person trying to sell this product to a customer. As this role play will be video-taped, make sure you prepare yourself for this activity well in advance.
	When it is your turn to play the role of the sales person, make sure you use all the techniques discussed in this chapter, including:

- raising the customer's awareness
- establishing rapport with the customer
- investigating the customer's needs

- presenting the product or service
- closing the sale
- explaining any after-sales service.

With your tutor, evaluate your performance by watching the video, and agree on an action plan for your future development.

One of the tools often used in sales techniques is AIDA. We have adapted this sales technique to selling tourism and travel products below:

A (**a**ttention) – raise the customer's awareness

I (**i**nterest) – establish rapport with the customer and investigate his or her needs

D (**d**esire) – present the product or service

A (**a**ction) – close the sale and explain after-sales service.

Activity	Think back to the last time you bought a major product or service – did the sales person apply the AIDA technique? Make notes of those things the sales person did/did not do in using this technique. Now take an example of a product from travel and tourism and work out how you could use the same technique. (You may need to practise on a fellow student to see if you have got the technique right!)

Chapter 5.6 Customer service situations

We have identified many examples of how communication takes place in the travel and tourism industry, but communication is not just about sales (vitally important though sales might be). The following are examples of how communication is used in other areas of work in the travel and tourism industry:

- providing information
- giving advice
- taking and relaying messages
- keeping records
- providing assistance
- dealing with problems
- handling complaints.

Some of these happen on a routine basis (for example, providing information about late availability or what there is to do in a destination, and keeping records of customer requirements and sales). Others will be less routine and may require you ask for help and advice from colleagues or managers (for example, dealing with problems and handling complaints). Whether it is a routine or non-routine enquiry, always remain calm and polite and learn to recognise when you need to refer a customer to a more senior member of staff.

Providing information

Many customers will contact you for more information about products, services and destinations, and you must remember that a great deal of the work that happens in travel and tourism organisations is about providing *relevant* information. Therefore, do not *overload* customers with information. If a customer wants brochures that cover holidays in the Algarve, you could provide him or her with 40 or 50 brochures. Hence you must use questions to find out more about the type of holiday the customer wants. Your questioning could go along the following lines:

- Would you like self-catering, hotel or all-inclusive accommodation?
- Is there a specific resort you want to visit? (If not, does the customer want a lively or quiet resort?)
- Which airport would you like to fly from?
- Do you have a budget for your holiday?
- Are you looking for children's clubs or specific types of activities?

Once you are armed with this information, you can make use of your product knowledge, your organisation's preferred tour operators and travel directories to identify suitable products. (Remember, as when making a sale, take the time to go through the product with the customer and identify any additional sales opportunities that might arise, such as insurance, foreign currency and car hire.) You could also use this as an opportunity to check availability on the computer, particularly if it is over the school holidays.

You will also be asked for information that will not lead to a sale (for example, someone wanting directions or advice for a project he or she is doing). Always treat these people as though they are potential customers. The 14-year-old completing an assignment could remember the service he or she received from your company when he or she comes to make his or her first holiday booking in the years to come.

Activity	Role play working in a tourist information centre where you would provide a range of local information and advice to people calling into the centre. This could include some of the following requests: • good local restaurants • somewhere cheap and cheerful to stay • where to visit if the weather is poor • outdoor or indoor sports facilities • directions to the nearest chemist • how to get to the railway station. (While you might not have all this information available at your finger tips, the important thing to remember is the way you deal with the customers.)

Giving advice

You will often be asked for your advice about which product or service is best for a customer. (Remember, you are not being asked which one you would choose for yourself, but which would be the most appropriate choice for the customer.) This is always a difficult part of the job: you are working with very little knowledge about that customer and his or her likes and dislikes so, until you know the customer better, it is often a good idea to offer two choices and explain the benefits of each one. Try not to make these choices almost identical as this is likely to confuse the customer. All products are different so it should be possible to find two feasible alternatives (for example, two different four-star hotels, one large and one smaller, or two quiet resorts, one very remote, while the other just lacks loud discos).

When you have found a product or service that meets the customer's needs, jot down in bulleted list form the good points (or selling points) for each choice so you can make comparisons.

Some products or services are quite easy to give advice about (for example, which currency to take to Brazil or train times from London to York). This is because the information will be set out in a guide or timetable. However, always make sure the information you give is accurate and based on the most up-to-date publication.

Taking and relaying messages

Message taking is an important part of your job as colleagues might already be dealing with a customer or may be away from the office but will want to be informed about the customer's call. Whether the customer calls in in person or telephones, still offer assistance as it might be something you can deal with yourself.

When you take messages, your organisation might have message pads that have been designed especially for this task or you might have to jot down the information on scrap paper. There are certain, essential items of information your colleagues will need to deal with the message efficiently and effectively. These include:

• the date and time of the message
• whether the customer called in or telephoned
• the customer's and, if appropriate, the customer's company name
• what action was agreed (e.g. the customer would like to be called back or will come in again on Saturday)
• the customer's telephone number

- a brief idea of what the message is about (e.g. the flight to New York on 13 December or about client Anderson, reference H8KH65).

Always agree the action with the caller and pass on the message as soon as possible. It is a good idea to repeat back the details to ensure you have written down, for example, the correct telephone number or name.

Keeping records

Records are kept for a number of different reasons, some of which include:

- details about the customer and the booking or reservation he or she has made
- availability for accommodation or transport
- contract details and information about rates and what is included in a package
- customer accounts and financial information
- sales report and records of transactions
- booking forms
- staff records.

The record systems used could be manual, computerised or a combination of both but must be fit for the purpose originally intended. There may also be a need to keep paper backup records of some of the information held on computers.

As most records are now kept on computer, you have a duty of care to ensure the information that is recorded is accurate and up to date. You will also need to make sure the Data Protection Act is adhered to and that you use data for the agreed purpose only. The Data Protection Act was set up to protect the rights of individuals and to ensure individuals can gain access to any information an organisation holds on computer about them.

Some organisations still make manual records and, if this applies to your organisation, you will need to ensure your handwriting is clear and can be easily read by others. Take care when completing records to reduce the number of errors you make and always cross out mistakes and rewrite the information rather than writing over the top of existing writing. You will also find that some records (such as financial or audit documents) will require signatures to confirm they have been agreed by someone in authority or checked by a supervisor.

Activity	There are pros and cons to both manual and computerised record-keeping systems. Spend some time thinking about these and then produce a list of pros and cons for manual record-keeping systems and another for computerised record-keeping systems. Share your findings with a fellow student.

Providing assistance

There will be times when customers need assistance that does not require you to have any specific knowledge about the travel and tourism industry. A great many times this is a matter of simple common courtesy, but if you don't assess a situation quickly you might not identify that a customer needs your help and you could easily overlook that person. The following are examples of when such assistance would be needed.

- Helping with access to a building. This could mean helping someone who is having difficulty opening a door because he or she has a pushchair and heavy shopping, or it could mean assisting a wheelchair user by holding a door open and ensuring that person can get up any ramps.

- Providing assistance from check-in to boarding the plane. Again, this could mean helping someone with a disability or elderly passengers who might need assistance if there are long distances to walk or steps to climb. It could also involve escorting an unaccompanied minor (or child aged 12 years or under travelling by him or herself) on to the plane.
- Helping customers get on and off rides at a theme park. This would include giving them a hand if the surface is likely to be unsteady, or checking their harnesses have been fastened correctly.
- Getting a glass of water or cup of coffee for customers who have had to wait to see one of your colleagues.
- Organising a porter to help guests, who have just checked in at a hotel, to take their luggage to their rooms, or directing them to the nearest lifts or to their rooms.

Think it over

How would you feel if, laden with shopping or heavy suitcases, you were trying to open the door to get out of an office where you had just made enquiries about purchasing an expensive tourism product and not one member of staff came to help you to open the door?

It is always polite to check that assistance is required rather than just assuming the customer needs help. Some customers (especially the elderly and the disabled) can be very self-sufficient and find it very demeaning if you rush over to them and immediately start to make a fuss. However, this is quite rare and the majority of customers are appreciative of any help they are given.

Dealing with problems

The key to dealing with problems is tackling the problems in an efficient way and resolving them before they escalate into complaints. Your own knowledge about the organisation and its procedures or where to find the solution should be invaluable in dealing with problems.

Activity	In small groups, brainstorm all the possible problems that could happen to a customer either while he or she is on a holiday or when visiting a destination for a day.

Your list is likely to be huge and there will probably never come a time in your career when you will have encountered every single problem that can arise. However, there are some problems that happen more often than others and, as a result, these are discussed below.

Overbooking transport and accommodation

It is a sad fact that, because people cancel arrangements, the majority of transport and accommodation is overbooked by the people taking the reservations. Providing this is identified prior to the customer leaving for the trip, contingency arrangements can be made to offer alternatives. This is always the best option because, although the customer may be angry, it is better he or she knows now rather than when he or she arrives at the airport or destination.

Lost luggage

A customer arriving in Ibiza but his or her suitcase turning up in Crete is probably one of the most common problems. Fortunately, with bar codes on luggage tags these days, this problem is becoming less frequent. Most companies, however, can retrieve the luggage and get it to the customer within three or four days of the start of the holiday. If, on the other hand, the luggage is in a destination that has one flight only a week, this can be more tricky. If the customer has taken out holiday insurance, this should contain provisions to enable the customer to make emergency purchases.

Stolen belongings

In some tourism areas, theft is more of a problem than in others. The general rule is that the customer must report the theft to the police and obtain a copy of the police report. As it is highly unlikely the stolen belongings will show up, it is best to assume the customer will need to claim under the insurance he or she has taken out for the trip.

Illness

Most people might be slightly unwell at some time during their holiday due to excesses (of food and drink), the different climate, changes in diet, or too long in the sun. However, for some people, illness can be a major problem and may result in hospitalisation. If you are an overseas representative, you might find you are the person visiting an ill customer in hospital and translating what the doctors say. You might also have to make special arrangements for the customer's journey home or make arrangements for the customer's party to stay longer in the resort.

Lost children

This is a big problem for busy tourist attractions, as children see something that excites them and run off, often without any idea of where they are going. Staff should be on the look-out for children who look distressed or who appear separated from the rest of their party, and must make arrangements for them to be returned or looked after in the mean time.

Make sure you recognise your limitations when dealing with problems: *never* agree to do something you are unqualified to or not trained in. If problems are tackled well, this can bring job satisfaction and will also provide you with an opportunity to offer an exceptional level of customer service.

Handling complaints

By its very unpredictable nature, the travel and tourism industry tends to attract a high number of complaints. A complaint is more serious than a problem as a complaint is something you probably haven't been able to resolve. Some examples of complaints include:

- delays with trains, ferries or planes
- the cancellation of services (transport, sight-seeing or accommodation)

- dissatisfaction with an aspect of a holiday
- long waiting times at attractions
- poor meals
- complaints about members of staff
- prices that change between the time the quote was given and the actual day of booking.

However, in the travel industry a complaint could also include factors that are totally outside your area of responsibility. In the following examples there is probably nothing anyone could have done to prevent the problem from happening:

- poor weather conditions (including rain in sun destinations and no snow in ski resorts)
- an outbreak of disease in either a destination or a hotel
- beaches that are dirty or littered with hazards such as broken bottles
- people in neighbouring rooms or apartments who are loud and who hold noisy parties
- hurricanes or tornadoes
- local unrest (including strikes or civil war).

There is an added problem in that many of the services customers complain about are not your own services but are supplied by someone else. If this happens, you will probably have to take responsibility for all aspects of the product, regardless of whether or not the aspect being complained about was supplied by your company. Examples of this include:

- a bus driver transferring the customers from the point of arrival to the accommodation loses luggage or accidentally reverses over a suitcase that has not been loaded on to the coach
- ski guides who cancel or do not turn up for agreed sessions
- on an evening excursion, a group suffers food poisoning as a result of barbecued food that has not been cooked properly.

Most organisations now publish their customer complaints procedure, which should appear as part of the customer service charter. Always give the customer advice about how he or she should complain and to whom. And a customer will not thank you if you neglect to tell him or her that the complaint about the holiday must be made in writing to the tour operator within 28 days of his or her return to the UK.

Activity	Collect copies of customer charters or complaints procedures for travel and tourism organisations. Look for any common themes and for examples of good and poor practice in these policies from a customer's perspective. Draw up your own customer charter to include a section on how customer complaints will be handled.

Chapter 5.7 Handling complaints

There will be times when you will have to deal with customer complaints yourself, either in writing, over the telephone or face to face. Sometimes, however, when you are dealing with a complaint yourself, you might think the situation is deteriorating or is rapidly becoming something outside your level of competence. If so, refer the matter on to someone who is either higher up in the organisation or is more knowledgeable about the issue. There are, on the other hand, certain steps you should always follow when handling a complaint (see Figure 5.6).

- Listen to the customer carefully.
- Apologise in general terms for any inconvenience caused.
- Let the customer know the matter will be investigated fully and will be put right.
- Try to see the problem from the customer's point of view.
- Keep calm and don't argue with the customer.
- Find a solution to the problem or refer the issue to a supervisor or manager.
- Agree the solution with the customer.
- Make sure what you have promised to do gets done.
- Make sure you record details of the complaint and of any actions taken.

Figure 5.6   The steps involved in handling a complaint

The first point mentioned in Figure 5.6 about listening to the customer carefully we have already met when discussing face-to-face and telephone conversations. Again, it is useful to take notes during the conversation and, in the case of a complaint, you really do *not* want to ask the customer to repeat the complaint again: the customer will only become more irate as a result of this.

Let the customer shout, rant and rave to his or her heart's content but do *not*, under any circumstances, interrupt him or her. Some people need the opportunity to let off steam, and it's amazing how many people apologise at the end for getting so angry. Watch your body language at this stage: smiling is definitely *not* appropriate. Try to look concerned and interested, whilst not agreeing with what the customer is saying. When the customer has finished, you might need to recall his or her records on the computer or go to get the file or a copy of a brochure. At this stage it might be wise to clarify a few of the details and to summarise the nature of the complaint with the customer. This will confirm you have been listening and will also ensure there is nothing more the customer wants to add.

Apologies can be very dangerous but, if a customer has complained, he or she will expect *some sort* of apology. The best apologies are exceptionally general and do not admit responsibility for the product or service. For example:

- 'I'm sorry you have had cause to complain.'
- 'I'm sorry you were disappointed with your holiday.'
- 'I'm sorry the service you received did not live up to your expectations.'

This is clearly very different from saying something like:

- 'I'm sorry the food was bad on your flight.'
- 'I'm sorry the tour operator overbooked your hotel.'
- 'I'm sorry my colleague was rude to you.'

It is often very difficult at first not to fall into the trap of the second set of responses and, hence, to give the customer the impression you are agreeing with him or her. This could then be used against you at a later stage if the matter is not resolved.

You do need to explain that the matter will be investigated fully and try to be specific *now* about what you will do (for example, ringing the airline or faxing the details through to the hotel). You may, however, feel the matter is best dealt with in writing. If this is the case, advise the customer what is happening so he or she does not expect an immediate response.

Unless it is your own product, it is difficult to give any assurances about timescales, but the customer must feel you are acting efficiently and effectively. If there are published guidelines about response times (such as the ABTA *Code of Conduct*, which states set deadlines for the initial response and detailed investigation, or the tour operator's booking conditions, which list their complaints procedures) then, by all means, explain this to the customer. If there are no published guidelines, agree dates when you will chase the matter up and will report back to the customer. In all cases, make sure you record the matter in a diary to follow up at a later date as you do not want the customer to feel your level of service is poor as well.

Try to see the complaint from the customer's point of view - what might seem quite trivial to you was obviously important to this particular person. People have their own perceptions and standards about what they expect from products and services. There may have been other members of the party (perhaps who are elderly or very young) who were affected more by the impact of the complaint. Empathise but don't sympathise - how would you have felt if this had happened on your only holiday of the year?

Keeping calm is difficult under a barrage of criticism, especially when it concerns colleagues or something you have said to a customer. However, if you start to argue back or become defensive, this is likely to antagonise the customer even more. Things can then get out of hand. Other people might decide to contribute their bit, and the situation could become either emotional or violent. It is far better to listen and to take in the points being made rather than try to disagree. Even if you know what the customer is telling you is untrue or biased, now is probably not the best time to tell him or her, and this is unlikely to resolve anything.

You might already be formulating a solution to the problem and if, this is the case, see if the solution is acceptable to the customer. If you can see no solution, there are two ways to handle the situation. First, ask the customer what would rectify things. Sometimes a customer does not actually expect much to be done whereas, on other occasions, customers will demand a full refund, a free flight or an upgrade on his or her next journey. You will probably not be in a position to agree to this immediately, so explain this to the customer. If no solution is proffered, you will have to refer the issue on either to a manager or supervisor or to the supplier of the goods or service.

Once a solution has been agreed, make sure the customer is happy with it. In the past, companies made low offers of compensation or of discounts and, if the customer refused this, they were forced to offer a higher rate. It is always a good idea to telephone the customer to explain what has been offered, but do not offer advice at this stage as you might recommend something that goes against both your company's or supplier's interest. If the customer is happy with the solution, that is fine – you can now go on to the next stage in the process. If the customer is not happy, refer the matter back until an acceptable compromise is reached.

The complaint has been resolved, the customer is happy and feels you have handled the problem efficiently and promptly – and then nothing happens. What you must do is make sure that what you have promised does, in fact, happen. There could be a delay or problem (for example, if a cheque needs to be raised by a different department). What you need to do is to ensure that things keep moving and that the customer does not come back in a month's time complaining again.

The final part to handling a complaint is to record the details of the complaint and any actions that have been taken. Most travel and tourism organisations have reporting procedures so that management is kept up to date about levels of service and the number of complaints. You will probably also find that management monitors certain aspects of services and products to look for areas that need improving or for things that are not successful. If management is not informed about complaints, it is difficult to make informed decisions. It is also important you cover yourself in case the customer decides at a later date the complaint has not been resolved effectively.

Handling complaints is not always a negative experience. If a complaint is handled well, this will remain in the customer's memory. You will probably not lose this customer as a result of the complaint, and he or she will probably consider you as being very professional as a result of the transaction. Complaints can lead to additional sales, especially if you are

working overseas: your contact with the customer will build up a bond that encourages the customer to purchase excursions or car hire through you.

Activity	The first part of this activity requires you to write a letter of complaint about a problem (either real or fictitious) you have encountered in your dealings with the travel and tourism industry. This letter should be signed by you and checked by your tutor.
	In the second part of the activity you will receive a letter of complaint one of your fellow students has written. Read the letter carefully and identify what you believe to be the key issues of the complaint. Once you have identified these, decide what course of action you will follow and start your letter of reply.
	Once you are happy with the reply you have written, hand the original letter of complaint and your reply to your tutor for checking.
	You will next receive the reply to your original letter of complaint as written by another student. Discuss your reactions to the letter with the person who replied to you.

Chapter 5.8 Assessing the quality and effectiveness of customer service

Many travel and tourism organisations continuously monitor the quality of the services they provide to their customers. As a result of this, changes can be made in order that the organisation can ensure it is offering customers what they want, and so keep an edge on the competition. Customers often make comparisons with their previous experiences or their perceptions of what they originally expected from the product. Organisations also complete their own assessment of their customer service, which is based on what they expect different parts of the organisation to achieve. This system (which is known as benchmarking) assesses what is happening against set quality requirements and whether or not these are being achieved. The most common quality criteria used in travel and tourism are as follows:

- price/value for money
- consistency/accuracy
- reliability
- staffing levels/qualities
- enjoyment of the experience
- health and safety standards
- cleanliness/hygiene
- accessibility and availability
- provision for individual needs.

These apply to all aspects of the industry (e.g. health and safety is just as important in a tourist attraction as it is in a hotel or on an airplane). However, the methods used to identify the quality achieved will vary, depending on which sector of the industry is involved. It is important for organisations to look at a range of methods to obtain a balanced view about levels of service. These include:

- informal feedback
- surveys
- suggestions boxes
- focus groups
- 'mystery shoppers'
- observation.

Informal feedback

Informal feedback can come from a variety of sources, customers, staff, management and non-users (see below) being the most important ones. The main problem with informal feedback is that it can be unsystematic and, because the results are not formally recorded, they may not be an accurate reflection of what has happened.

Informal feedback from customers usually comes in the form of complaints or commendations. However, it is dangerous to assume that, because no one complains, everyone is perfectly happy with the service. A customer might be reluctant to complain or may think that the person whom he or she must complain to is inaccessible or unapproachable. It is always worth while passing on any informal feedback that comes from customers to line managers and colleagues. This often takes place at staff meetings or in training sessions.

Informal feedback from staff is useful, particularly if staff want to resolve issues at a local level and come up with new ideas. Again, team meetings to talk through different strategies and to obtain staff opinions on products and services can be

a good way of presenting a group opinion rather than individual members of staff giving their views. Sometimes this can make the discussion of customer service a lighter matter rather than more formal methods, and can encourage all staff to contribute.

Management feedback often comes informally as a result of a visit that might not have had as its objective the assessment of customer service. Managers might pick up on issues that have not been noticed by the staff, who are too closely involved in the service. They may also be able to make comparisons with other branches, offices or departments, which might be favourable or not. If management make comments informally, it is probably worth while acting on these observations as they might be an early warning of something that could be formalised at a later date.

Informal feedback from non-users of products and services is less common. It will possibly result from an enquiry that has not been converted into a sale and relies on contact being made with the customer. The problem with non-users is that, generally, you do not receive any informal feedback: they just go somewhere else or select an alternative product or service.

Surveys

Surveys are used extensively throughout the whole industry, especially to obtain feedback from customers about their rating of a product. The majority of surveys ask customers to rate something numerically or to use words (e.g. excellent, good and poor). These rating systems make surveys easier to analyse and permit comparisons to be made either with previous years or with other areas or products.

The most important thing with surveys is to obtain a good sample size. If a survey is completed by post, the likelihood is that, unless you offer some sort of prize, customers are not likely to return the survey. Overseas tour operators have an easy way of collecting feedback: the time spent on the coach on the return journey to the airport is an ideal time for customers to complete a survey. Some companies (such as Thomson Holidays) publish the results of surveys in their brochure so customers can look at how other guests have rated accommodation, food and the resort prior to making their booking.

Staff and management surveys tend to be used more for human resources issues than external customer service views, although views on products and services will be collected from staff. Staff views assist an organisation in refining what it offers to the public and demonstrate a company is interested in involving its staff.

External market research companies are usually employed to find out more about non-users and why they have chosen not to visit particular places or to use certain companies. They use a number of different methods, ranging from face-to-face interviews to telephone calling. Non-user surveys can identify what people's likes and dislikes are and they help to give ideas about what might encourage people to become users of the product. However, they are not a guarantee people will change their attitude if a product or service is changed.

Activity	Collect a variety of different surveys (these should include ones to do with travel and tourism products as well as with other products). Look at what works well in these surveys and identify whether they are targeted at customers, staff, management or non-users.
	Now devise your own survey to assess customer service in a local travel and tourism organisation. Identify which target group this would be aimed at, and whether it needs to be a postal, face-to-face or telephone survey.
	Try out your survey on one of your fellow students. You may need to make some changes, depending on the feedback you receive.

Surveys are something you will come across regularly once you are working in the travel and tourism industry. You will probably be assessed in your own appraisals against results from customer, staff and management surveys. The results of these surveys should be viewed as an opportunity to develop and improve on your delivery of customer service.

Suggestion boxes

Suggestion boxes will be either for staff or customers to use and are an anonymous way of assessing quality. They work especially well in large organisations where individuals might feel they cannot voice their opinions in any other way. Suggestion boxes must be easily recognisable and accessible. They will probably need to have paper or forms close by and pens so customers can complete them quickly. Suggestion boxes situated at the entrances and exits of hotels and attractions work well.

Focus groups

Focus groups are more commonly used as a market research tool (see page 148). The meeting will take place at a location that is not within the organisation and is often used to obtain the opinions of people who are new to a product or service that is being offered. The atmosphere needs to be relaxed and informal so people feel they are being involved in an enjoyable chat rather than being questioned. Various techniques are so used to give a focus group room the right ambience (e.g. pictures, attractive decor and/or food and drink). There will be a scribe who will record the proceedings so these can be analysed later.

Focus groups have been used in travel and tourism to obtain customers' views on new destinations and products.

'Mystery shoppers'

Mystery shoppers are used by all sectors of the industry to look at the information and advice provided and also at the level of service. A mystery shopper might be employed by either the organisation or through an independent company. They are also used by tour operators and airlines to see how their suppliers are making recommendations, and to check whether or not their products are being sold. The *Travel Trade Gazette* has its own 'top shop feature' which sends mystery shoppers into a range of shops in a town and city to assess each one independently. The shops are then graded and awards are given to the top shop each week (unless none provides a good service!).

Activity	Complete your own mystery shopper survey. Select one product from within travel and tourism and either visit or telephone an organisation for help and advice. Decide in advance what criteria you will use to base your assessment on. Present your findings to the rest of your group.

Observation

Your delivery of customer service will probably be observed as part of an appraisal. This could involve either your line manager or a trainer observing how you deal with different customers and looking at what you do well and which areas could be improved.

The other way observation is used is to analyse systems to try to improve the overall product offered to the customers. This could be done through a consultancy company or by using analysts from within the organisation. Such observers are unlikely to look at the specialist information you provide but will be more interested in how the customer's experience could be improved by changing systems, office layout or staffing levels.

Activity	Using the methods discussed in this chapter, devise a strategy for analysing customer service at a travel and tourism organisation in your local area. If you do not use some of these methods, explain why you did not select them for this activity. Consider what the implications of your research are for this organisation, and draw up a plan to implement any changes you would recommend as a result of your research.

This unit will give you the opportunity to work in a team on an activity that is relevant to travel and tourism. Although this unit is a very practical one, the success of your project will rely upon your group's ability to plan, carry out and evaluate your work together. You might be involved in organising an event or be involved in a business project, but the key thing to remember is it must be related to the travel and tourism industry.

Depending on the type of project you choose, this unit will link with many other advanced units, particularly Unit 4 ('Marketing travel and tourism') and Unit 5 ('Customer service in travel and tourism'). You will put the theory you learnt in these two units into practice and will be given the opportunity to develop those skills you will need when you come to work in the travel and tourism industry. This is also a common unit with the Advanced VCE in Leisure and Recreation.

Throughout this unit you will have the opportunity to collect evidence for all the Key Skills, particularly application of number. There will be many times when you will apply these skills to your activity.

This unit will be assessed through your portfolio work only. The grade awarded will be your grade for the unit.

Note: It is strongly recommended you read through this entire unit before you begin any work towards your project. You will then have an overview of *all* the issues involved when working on each stage of your project, and some of the things discussed later in the unit might be of even more help to you if you are aware of these from the outset.

Chapter 6.1 Feasibility of the project

Activity	As a group, brainstorm all the possible travel and tourism events or projects you could be involved in. It doesn't matter if some of the ideas seem a little ridiculous at this stage – you may find they develop into something more realistic!

The unit requires you to produce a business plan that will set out the full details of your chosen activity. This business plan will enable someone who has not been involved in your project to assess the likelihood of your project being a success, and it should also show how you have researched your project to ensure it is feasible. Although this outline plan will be developed by your team working as a group, you must also produce your own individual business plan.

Once your group starts its project, you must keep records of everything you are involved in, which includes both individual activities (such as telephone calls and producing posters) and group activities (such as meetings, helping others and participating in group activities).

On completion of the activity, you will need to evaluate it both on an individual and group basis. To do this you will need to consider what worked well and what was not so successful. This will help you, with hindsight, to identify how you could have done things differently.

Before you launch into a project, you must consider whether or not your project is feasible and therefore whether you should go ahead with it. While personal preferences or interests will inevitably influence your choices and your decisions, there are formal ways of determining whether your project will be a success. You must first carry out a feasibility study that will lead to an outline business plan. Your business plan must include the following:

- objectives and timescales for the project
- a description of the project
- your resource needs (this will include financial needs as well as physical resources and staffing)
- the legal aspects of the project
- the methods to be used to evaluate the project.

Approach your business plan as if it were a tool you would use if you were self-employed and were seeking the backing of a bank or sponsor to fund your project. Even if you were an employee you might go through a similar process when considering running a particular event or activity. Make sure you put in as much effort to this part of your project as you do to the rest of it as cutting corners at this stage will lead to problems later. For example, if you do not identify the resources accurately at this stage, this will impact on costs and, eventually, on the project's profit, break-even or, possibly, loss.

Much of the work at this stage will involve group discussions and, because this is a business venture, approach this work in a business-like way. Instead of having discussions, hold formal meetings with agendas and minutes.

Agendas

An agenda is a list of things to be discussed at a meeting (see Figure 6.1). Your agenda should be issued at least three days prior to the meeting and must state the following (see also Figure 6.2):

ABC Group
Agenda of the meeting to be held on 7 November 200X at 14:00 in the Travel and Tourism Office

1 Apologies for absence.
2 Minutes of previous meeting and matters arising.
3 Ideas for the activity:
   a presentation by A Group (talent show)
   b presentation by B Group (day trip to Alton Towers)
   c presentation by C Group (holiday destination exhibition).
4 Discussion of presentations.
5 Research tasks.
6 Resource issues for all three groups.
7 Any other business.
8 Date, time and place of next meeting.

Figure 6.1   An agenda

- name of your organisation or group
- date, time and place of the meeting
- apologies for absence from anyone who cannot attend the meeting
- a list of those things to be discussed
- AOB (i.e. any other business) – a set time at the end of the meeting when members can raise matters not included on the agenda
- date, time and place of the next meeting.

Keep the agenda items simple, and make sure you use headings rather than statements of fact (for example, 'Allocation of roles' rather than 'Roles will be allocated'). Ask members of the group to propose items so you can include these on the agenda. An agenda should be a way of stimulating discussion rather than informing the team of decisions that have already been made. Keep the order of items logical so you are not forced to switch between items.

Once you have held your first meeting, at the next meeting you will probably need to check the minutes (see below) of the previous (first) meeting to make sure any

issues/matters that arose from that meeting have been dealt with. You might also have what is called a 'standing agenda item', which is something that is discussed at each meeting (for example, 'Update on project timescales').

Activity

Draw up an agenda for your first meeting to include the points we have already discussed (e.g. date, time and place, items to be discussed, AOB, etc.).

Your agenda might look something like Figure 6.2.

Residential Group
Agenda of the meeting to be held on 2 November 200X at 11.30 in Room 14B

Apologies for absence
Items to be discussed

1. Allocation of roles
2. Aims and objectives of group
3. Research tasks
4. Resources

AOB
Date, time and place of next meeting

Figure 6.2   A possible agenda for a first meeting

Circulate the agenda to your team members and prepare for your meeting.

You will notice that the first item on the agenda in Figure 6.2 is the allocation of roles. This should be done early on in the first meeting because you will need to establish a chairperson and secretary for the meetings.

The chairperson is the person who will maintain order and focus throughout the meeting, and who will manage the meeting and the contributions made by the team. The secretary will be responsible for keeping the minutes of the meeting.

Minutes

Keeping the minutes (see Figure 6.3) means recording the key issues said at the meeting and ensuring these details are circulated to all the people in the group as soon as

ABC Group
Minutes of the meeting held on 7 November 200X at 14:00 in the Travel and Tourism Office

Present: David B, Helen, Jane, Suzy, Peter, Rahim, Zoe, Sarina, Sam, Liam and Tom
Apologies: David S and Kelly

Agenda item	Minutes	Action points
2	*Minutes of previous meeting and matters arising*	
	Minutes agreed as accurate. Allocation of duties in the last meeting has caused a few problems as Kelly, appointed as secretary, has been off sick since then. Team agreed to rotate minute taking, starting with Helen.	Helen to write minutes in Kelly's absence.
	Since previous meeting the group has been told it has to make objectives more measurable. All agreed any surplus would have a specific amount as a target which would be donated to charity.	Team leaders to rewrite objectives.
3	*Ideas for the activity*	
	a Presentation by A Group (talent show)	
	Presentation about proposed talent show to take place in college hall at the end of May. Participants will be from within and outside college. Prizes are likely to be donated by local companies. Small admission cost of 50p for spectators and participants. Main prize will come from this fund. Voting will be from audience.	David B to check availability of hall. Zoe to produce a budget.
	b Presentation by B Group (trip to Alton Towers)	
	Presentation about an end-of-year trip (open to all students and their friends) overnight to Alton Towers. Not sure how many will go or what it will cost. Could use minibus or hire a coach. Unlikely to make any money as costs need to be kept low. Aim is to have fun and celebrate finishing first year.	Helen to do market research on participation. Suzy to get rates for b & b, coach and entrance.
	c Presentation by C Group (holiday destination exhibition)	
	Exhibition in conjunction with Funways Travel. Our role will be to organise sponsors, market the event, run and organise the day and evaluate its success. This will bring in publicity for the course and develop links with local companies. We can have our own stall which will promote the course.	Jane to draw up list of sponsors. Liam to keep liaison going with manager of Funways Travel. Tom to get advertising rates.
	Event would be in March on a Sunday at the Holiday Inn.	
4	**Discussion of presentations**	
	Whole group discussed presentations and agreed it was too early to make a decision. All wanted to go to Alton Towers, but concerned about the cost. Tutors would have to accompany us. Talent show sounds a bit childish, but might work. Need to avoid unit test dates. Holiday exhibition might be too adventurous; we will need some money to advertise this.	Peter to check exam dates. Sam to discuss potential costs with tutors.
5	**Research tasks**	
	Market research team leaders agreed for each group to conduct primary research and assess feasibility of each plan.	Group A – Rahim Group B – Sam Group C – Sarina
6	**Resource issues for all three groups**	
	Ran out of time for discussion of resources. Each team to produce a resource list for discussion at next team meeting.	Team leaders to circulate list before next meeting.
7	**Any other business**	
	Agreed Sam would do minutes for next meeting.	
8	**Date, time and place of next meeting**	
	16 November 200X at 10:30 in the Travel and Tourism Office.	

Figure 6.3 Minutes of a meeting

possible after the meeting has closed. This particular role might be one no one is keen to take on and, if this is the case, you could consider rotating the responsibility for minute taking at each meeting.

The minutes of a meeting should include:

- the name of the meeting, the date, time and venue
- the names of the people present
- apologies for those who were absent
- if the minutes of previous meeting were agreed (i.e. everyone at this meeting agrees they are a true reflection of what was said or agreed at the previous meeting), any discussion of matters arising from the last meeting
- a record of the discussions held about any items on the agenda and a record of new business as per the agenda plus any actions agreed and by whom
- any other business
- date, time and venue of next meeting.

Activity	Hold your group's first meeting. At this meeting, allocate the roles of the chairperson and secretary. Keep minutes of this meeting and ensure they are circulated to all members of the team. Create a working file of your contribution to the meeting as well as filing away safely your copies of the agenda and minutes. You will add to this file as the project progresses.

Aims and objectives

The *aims* of your project should be a brief description of the what, how, when and where of your project. A well written aim should fit neatly into one paragraph and should give a broad outline of what you want to achieve, how you will achieve this, when, etc.

The *objectives* are the overall aims of your project (i.e. why you decided to do the project in the first place). If you think back to Unit 4, we noted (page 124) that marketing objectives should be *smart*. The same principle should apply to *your* team's

objectives. Therefore, these could include such things as:

- 'Raise awareness of a tourism project. Increase visitors by 10%.'
- 'Make a surplus of £200 that will be awarded to a charity or will be used to increase facilities for our course.'
- 'Boost morale and provide a social activity by encouraging all our year group to visit Bath for the weekend.'
- 'Develop marketing material for a local attraction to be implemented in time for its opening in April.'
- 'Generate business for a local travel and tourism industry. Increase travellers cheques sales by 2%.'
- 'Bring 100 visitors to a travel and tourism exhibition.'

Above all, you must ensure your objectives are realistic and achievable. An objective must be something the whole team is working towards; no one in the group must feel it will not happen. Therefore you must make sure there are set times when you are working on your project where you check whether or not you are on course towards achieving your objectives. At the end of the project, you will need to evaluate your team's performance against these objectives.

Your customers, their needs and how these will be met

Your project will involve customers (either internal – i.e. fellow students – or external – i.e. members of the public). For the project to be a success, you must identify who your customers are and what their needs are likely to be. The feasibility of your project will depend on you being able to identify your customers accurately (refer back to Units 4 and 5 if you need to remind yourself how important customers are).

The first thing is to establish who your customers are likely to be. You will need to discuss this as a group because, once you have established your client base, you will need to test this group of people to find out if they would participate in your project. Once you have established your customer base, this should also assist you in marketing your project. You may, for example, find there is more than one group of customers who would be interested in your project and, if you have internal as well as external customers, it might be appropriate to treat these groups separately when establishing their needs.

The easiest way to find out people's needs is to ask them. Therefore consider all the different methods of market research we considered in Unit 4 and select an appropriate method for your particular project. You might find there is secondary research you could make use of. However, be mindful that secondary research might be out of date or too generalised to apply to your own situation.

Activity	By now you should have a fairly clear idea about both your activity and your clients. Split your group into smaller groups (one to discuss each of the client groups you have identified and one to discuss competitor analysis). Now produce a questionnaire(s) that will: • confirm or reject these clients as your customer base • give you information to support the four Ps in the marketing mix • help you assess the feasibility of the project. Use this questionnaire with an appropriate sample of people and analyse your results.

The competitor analysis group will need to find out as much as possible about the competition's marketing mix. This could include some of the following activities:

• telephoning competitors for information about products and prices
• collecting samples of promotional material, including leaflets and brochures
• evaluating your competitors' trading locations.

You will now need to meet as a group to use your findings to consider whether or not your project is feasible. You could use a tool such as SWOT analysis to assist you in this (see page 125).

Present your findings verbally, if possible with the use of visual aids.

Now you know what your customers' needs are, you can develop a strategy to meet these needs. Add this to your business plan; it will be used later to assess the success of your project.

Marketing the project

You will have already done some work towards marketing your project in the previous activity, and may have looked at how your competitors are marketing their products and services. You may, however, have ideas of your own that are innovative and that are very different from the existing ways marketing is carried out in the travel and tourism industry. At this stage, it is important you keep an open mind and consider all the possibilities for the marketing your project.

As a quick recap on the marketing strategies we considered in Unit 4, consider if (and how) you could use the following to market your project:

- advertising
- direct marketing
- public relations
- personal selling
- promotions and stunts
- sponsorship.

You will need to be realistic about this and, if there is a limit to your budget, this needs to be considered at this stage.

Marketing strategies: some opportunities and examples

- If your project is a fund-raising event, it might be possible for you to advertise in local newspapers or on local radio for free.
- You might find you could produce brochures or leaflets in-house through the art department, or that your school or college has a reprographics section that could assist you with this.
- Direct marketing might be something you could undertake internally (i.e. with your fellow students).
- There should be plenty of opportunities for you to write press releases to send to your local radio stations and newspapers. You may also find there are opportunities to send these to specialist magazines or newspapers.
- Sales promotions are possible but could be too costly for the budget you have available.
- Local companies or organisations already connected with your school or college might be happy to sponsor you in your

venture. Do, however, make sure another department within your school or college has not already contacted them. If a company has already sponsored one event it may not feel too happy about being contacted again or, if several groups all write off to the same company, this might cause confusion about whom the company should sponsor.

Activity	Produce a marketing plan for your project that includes the following: <ul><li>your marketing objectives</li><li>the market research you will undertake</li><li>your target markets</li><li>the market segments</li><li>the promotional activities you will carry out</li><li>the types of media you will use</li><li>the times and dates of the activities</li><li>who will be responsible for each marketing activity</li><li>the factors that could affect your marketing campaign.</li></ul>

Physical resource needs

Physical resource needs should be considered early in the design of your project and could include:

- equipment (e.g. computers, overhead projectors, cameras, display stands, lighting rigs, etc.)
- venues/premises
- materials (e.g. stationery, photographic film, video tape, etc.).

Make a list of everything that will be needed for your project, and make sure you include everything. Do not assume you will be able to use school or college facilities for free: things like paper, minibuses, halls, refectories and telephone calls are all paid for by *someone, somewhere*. Include a list of the resources needed in your business plan.

If you are going to need resources you cannot obtain from your school or college, make enquiries about obtaining these now (see Figure 6.4). If you explain why you need the resource, many organisations will offer a discounted rate if they know it is for a fund-raising activity, and some might even agree to sponsoring your project in some way. This could include providing free prizes or loaning you equipment, providing the organisation is mentioned at the event or in your advertising material. Always investigate opportunities to buy in bulk, particularly with firms who may already have agreements with your school or college for the supply of stationery, etc.

The ABC Group
Tutor Group 56
Any College
Anytown
AT6 6PX

X August 200X

Mickey Mouse Balloons
Unit 424
Deptford Industrial Estate
London
SE12 7HH

Dear Mr Bang

Further to our telephone conversation earlier today, I am writing with details of the proposed exhibition we will be holding in conjunction with Funways Travel at the Holiday Inn.

We need to rent a machine for blowing up and tying balloons along with helium gas canisters. These will be needed between 08:30 and 12:30 on Sunday 13 March.

We will be giving all proceeds from the events to the local hospital trust, so any assistance you can give us with rates would be greatly appreciated. We would recognise your involvement in the advertising we would display at the travel exhibition.

I would appreciate it if you could send me your rates and confirm whether or not the equipment is available.

Yours sincerely

Tom Graham

Tom Graham

Figure 6.4   An enquiry concerning resources

Report
Resource needs for the ABC Group's project

To: Helen
From: David

1   *Introduction*

A Group are proposing to hold a talent show that will take place in the college hall on 21 May. Participants will be from within and outside college. Everyone will pay a small admission cost of 50p (spectators and participants). Local companies will donate runner-up prizes. There will be a main prize of £50, which will come from the proceeds of the talent show.

2   *Resources identified for the activity*

2.1   Physical resources

We have identified we will need the following resources for the activity:

- Main hall (already booked with reception)
- Sound equipment
- Lighting equipment
- Chairs
- Stage with microphones and stands
- Tables in entrance area
- Access to car park, reception, refectory and toilets
- Tickets
- Stationery (posters, pens and paper)
- Access to the travel office during lunchtimes the three weeks prior to talent show to sell tickets
- Prizes
- Cashbox

2.2   Human resources

- Compere
- Reception staff (5)
- Ushers (3)
- Cashier
- Backstage team (3)
- Lighting person
- Sound person
- Caretakers to set up hall and take down stage and put away chairs
- Refectory staff

2.3   Financial resources

Please find enclosed a cash flow forecast for the activity (Appendix 1) which shows the talent show is self-financing. We do not require any funding in advance of the activity.

The small profit we expect to make (£25.00) will be donated to cancer research.

3   (This part of the report will explain how these resources will be organised by the team.)

Figure 6.5   An example report about resource needs

If you need to find a suitable venue for your activity, consider the following.

- *Transport.* Will this be arranged or will people need to make their own way there? Investigate public transport facilities and car-parking arrangements.

- *Price.* Is the price competitive? Will the cost of hiring the venue mean you might make a loss? You will need to consider the numbers involved, and whether or not a minimum number of participants will be required to make it economic to hire the venue.
- *Date and time.* Is the venue available on the day and at the time you need it? The timing is important: it must be appropriate for your target group (for example, people who work may not be able to attend during the day on weekdays. If the venue cannot offer you a time to suit your target group, no matter how good you think the venue is, it is not suitable for your purposes).
- *Catering.* Does the venue offer appropriate catering and refreshments facilities for the project you are considering?

(An example report about resource needs is given in Figure 6.5).

Financial aspects

You must also consider what your budget for the project will be (i.e. the amount you are prepared to pay for the various aspects of the project). In business, management usually allocates a set budget to any new project the organisation is to become involved in. However, the budget for the project you are going to be involved in is likely to be zero, which means you must establish your budget yourselves by determining the costs involved in the project and, hence, the charge you must make to the participants to cover your costs.

Costs can be either fixed, variable or semi-variable. *Fixed costs* are the easiest costs to identify as they do not depend on the

number of tickets sold or the number of people participating in the event.

Fixed costs are likely to include:

- room rent or transport hire charges
- the costs of advertising
- equipment costs (either hire charges or purchase costs)
- prizes, etc.

Variable costs will increase as the number of people involved in your project increases. For example, the costs of raw materials, food and drink will increase the greater the number of people involved.

Semi-variable costs have both a fixed and a variable element. For example, printing costs might include an initial (fixed) charge for the artwork the printer produces for you and then a cost per copy of the poster, leaflet, etc., the printer runs off for you (the variable cost).

Activity	Make a list of the fixed, variable and semi-variable costs that are likely to be incurred in your project. Now choose who in your group will be responsible for deciding what these costs will be (i.e. delegate someone with the responsibility for managing your budget).

The other thing that needs to be considered is whether or not VAT is charged on items and if it is charged, are you able to claim this back through school or college. Some items are on what is called zero rated for VAT, i.e. no VAT is currently charged. Zero rated items include food (groceries not catered food), non-alcoholic drinks, international travel outside the EU and coach transport for 12 or more passengers. Standard rate of VAT @ 17.5 per cent is charged on the following items; hotel accommodation, meals in restaurants, alcoholic drinks, guides and courier services, commission and entrance fees, car parking and the majority of travel in the EU.

When working out the budget for your project, you will need to establish what is known as the *break-even point*. This means the number of sales, sponsors or participants you will need to make or attract to cover your costs. This should consider the costs, fixed, variable and semi variable and place them on a chart. Once you have done this, plot the price of the item or activity increasing in a line as numbers increase. The point at which these two points meet is the break-even point.

This is demonstrated in the following charts, which are based on a day trip to a theme park, which includes a fixed cost of transport, a semi variable cost of leaflets and variable cost of admission.

Suzy's group has decided that it will be too expensive to stay overnight, so have

decided to organise a day trip. She has now got the rates for transport (£460), admission costs (£6 per person), and local printing costs to advertise the day trip (£80 plus 80p per leaflet). Her market research shows that about 50 people could be expected if the price was between £10 and £15. She has decided to plot on a break even chart the costs and what would happen if the group charge £12 for the day trip (see Figure 6.6).

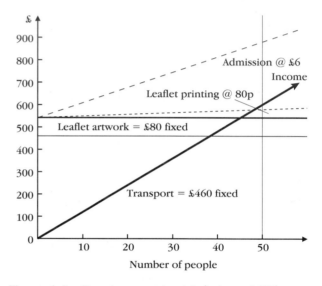

Figure 6.6   Break-even chart A (price of £12)

From this break-even chart you can identify the amount to be charged per person and the point at which you will not be in a loss-making situation.

Unfortunately, this will pay for leaflets and transport, but the admission price has not been covered. Her next idea was to try £20 per person see (Figure 6.7).

This has now ensured that all the admission costs have been covered, however £20 is considerably more than the market research told her people would probably pay. Her next step is to find out what happens if a compromise is sought and £18 is charged for the day (see Figure 6.8).

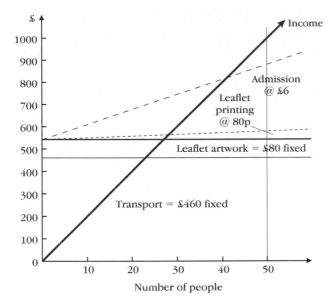

Figure 6.7   Break-even chart B (price of £20)

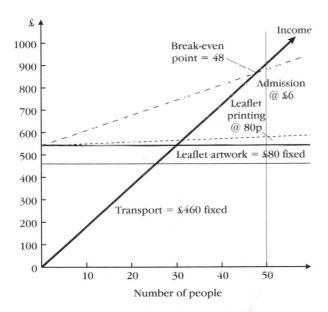

Figure 6.8   Break-even chart C (price of £18)

This particular price would rely on a minimum of 48 participants to make it pay. Suzy decides to propose this amount at the next team meeting.

There are of course alternative ways in which the price could be reduced through cutting some of the costs, including:

- Reducing the cost of the printing of the leaflets by seeking alternative forms of promoting the activity
- Shopping around for cheaper rates for the coach.

It is recommended that a contingency cost of approximately ten per cent is applied. This will cover you for any increase in costs or for if people drop out at the last minute. In some examples you might need to also consider the increase in raw material charges, particularly if you are including catering as part of the project.

Activity	Construct a break-even chart for your project. Identify what the costs will be and the number of people who need to be involved before you break even. How would a safety margin of 10% affect these figures?

From looking at the break-even charts you have probably also identified one big problem and that is that until you have collected money, it may be difficult to spend money. Some parts of your project will incorporate start-up costs, for example if you are organising an external event that requires advertising to generate interest it will be necessary to conduct the advertising first. If you have researched the feasibility of the event fully the business plan could be used to try and secure an advance to enable you to start off. It is essential that you speak to your tutor early on, as the college or school might not have the resources to enable this to happen.

What will happen to any profit you make? It is highly unlikely you will be able to keep this and split it evenly among you! You must give very careful consideration to how this money could be used to good effect. For example, the following could be acceptable uses of this money:

- for prizes to give out at the event
- donate the money to charity
- buy textbooks, a camcorder or equipment for your department
- use it to subsidise visits or trips
- put it towards an end-of-course prize-giving or awards evening.

Once money starts to come in, it is essential it is looked after both accountably and safely. Make sure you are clear about what forms of payment are acceptable (cheques and cash are generally fine, but do you have arrangements to take credit cards?). If payment is by cheque, to whom must the cheque be made payable? You will also need some system for banking cheques – will you have to make your own banking arrangements, or will your school or college arrange these for you?

You will need some system of recording the money you have collected. This could be a very simple system that records the date, the person's name, the amount and the signature of person who has accepted payment. This record could be kept in a book, on a sheet of paper or on a computer spreadsheet. You will also need to keep a running total of the number of people who have paid and of the total amount of money collected so you can keep people up to date with the likely success (or not!) of your project and so you will able to see at a glance whether there is enough money to make any payments (e.g. to suppliers, etc.). Keep *all* records separately from the money (for reasons of security).

Activity	Set up a spreadsheet to include all the costs involved in your project (if you are not yet at this stage, do this for the day trip to Alton Towers). See what happens to your financial forecasts if prices are increased by 5%, 10% and 20%. Then see what happens if prices are decreased by the same percentages. Print out your results and write a report explaining how the figures you have obtained will affect your planned activities. This activity will provide you with additional evidence you can use towards the information technology Key Skills.

You might also need to organise set times or days when money will be collected. Have somewhere safe and secure for this and make sure money collection is well supervised. Do not accept cash from people in corridors or in the refectory: apart from the safety aspect of this, you will more than likely forget who has paid you what! If you are required to pass any money you collect on to a tutor, keep the money in a locked money box and hand this over at the earliest opportunity. Do not take money home with you or leave it in a classroom or car.

When someone pays out money, he or she expects to receive something in return. However, travel and tourism products and services cannot be supplied immediately. The customer should be given instead, therefore, one of the following:

- a receipt
- tickets
- a note or letter of confirmation.

You will need to account for all receipts, tickets, etc., you issue and must make sure the amount of money you have taken in balances with the number of receipts, tickets, etc., you have given out (this is explored further in this unit in the section on administration systems).

The final thing you must consider is whether you will expect people to pay in full immediatley or put down a deposit. If you are organising an expensive project that could incur cancellation charges or other costs, you must cover the possibility of customers not keeping to their side of the bargain. If this is the case, look at the risks involved and decide on a deposit that will cover you should people give back word. You will then need to consider when the balance must be paid and advise the customers about payment dates.

Activity	Find out which payment methods you can use for your project. Will you ask for a deposit to be paid and, if so, when will the balance be due? What will customers receive for their money (e.g. receipt, a confirmation, tickets, etc.)?

Staffing

You must consider the staffing arrangements for your project and how you will make the best use of your team and their abilities. Everyone in your group must participate in the project. This does not mean, however, everyone must be involved in every single aspect of the project. There may be some things certain team members are good at and others that one team member only feels confident to carry out. The important thing to remember is that the strengths of teamwork are that everyone contributes something different and that you can divide a very large project up and allocate tasks to people within the team so no one is overlooked.

Activity	Conduct a personal audit to assess your own skills. Divide a piece of paper into two vertical columns. In the first column, list all the skills you think you possess (be honest about this!). In the second column, try to match all the skills needed to carry out your project with your own skills.

To help you decide what you are good at, ask yourself the following questions. I am good at:

- computers
- talking to people
- reading and checking things through carefully
- organising teams
- art or design
- entertaining people
- providing ideas and problem-solving
- helping and supporting other people in the team.

This should give you a start, but there are probably many more skills you could add.

Activity	This activity builds on the personal audit you have just completed. First, list all the jobs that must be done to complete your project, then identify *all* the skills it would be ideal for the person undertaking each job to possess.

You now need to match people in your group to these jobs. Use the personal audits people have completed to match people to the various job roles. You may find that, once you have done this, there are still job roles to be allocated. If you have group members with the skills needed for these jobs, it might be appropriate to reassign job roles by swapping their jobs with others'. Alternatively, you might need to recruit additional help from outside. If you need to explore this option, make sure you include any costs it may involve in your budget and business plan.

You should also consider at this stage some of the problems that often arise when working in teams so you will be prepared for these should they occur. First, however, you must ensure all team members feel they can discuss things without being ridiculed and that you are fair in the way tasks are allocated. If people feel they can speak freely and that jobs have been given out carefully, you should be able to tackle the following problems, should they arise.

Availability

Every member of the team will have restrictions on his or her time. This might be the result of parents' rules, part-time jobs, study time needed for exams, hobbies or cultural obligations. There is no point in getting team members to agree to do tasks that will either land them in trouble or result in them letting the team down.

Money

You will all have different amounts of money you can afford to spend on the project. Some people, therefore, might not be able to afford what is being planned (for example, if you decide to go on a week's skiing holiday, it is unlikely everyone could afford this).

How comfortable people are with the tasks

People often agree to take on jobs that, in the event, they feel uncomfortable with. For example, some members of the group may not feel happy dealing with companies or asking people for money (in the case of the latter example, some cultures would view this as begging). Others might not feel confident presenting themselves in front of strangers or large groups of people. Therefore do not force anyone to do something he or she in the event is unlikely to do – if only because this person will not be very good at it and might let the team down!

There may be other things your team needs to discuss that will affect staffing arrangements, and it is better to discuss these now rather than the day before an event is scheduled to happen or a week before the project itself. If people feel free to speak at meetings and that they have been treated fairly, issues such as these should be ironed out at an early stage.

Activity	Identify the resource needs for your project, using the following headings: • physical • financial • human. Write these up in a separate report (see Figure 6.5 for an example of such a report).

Administration systems

You will need to give some thought to the way you will deal with the administration of your project (such things as keeping records of financial transactions, customer details, etc.). Administration will probably include the following.

Financial systems

You must record all payments you receive or make so that all your financial dealings can be accounted for. This will also help you to work out how much cash you have available for future spending and the likelihood of you sticking to your budget.

To record this information, you will need to design and issue simple receipts, tickets, etc. (see Figure 6.9). This might also involve keeping records of customer payments if you are taking deposits. You could, perhaps, issue payment cards to show the amount a customer has paid to date.

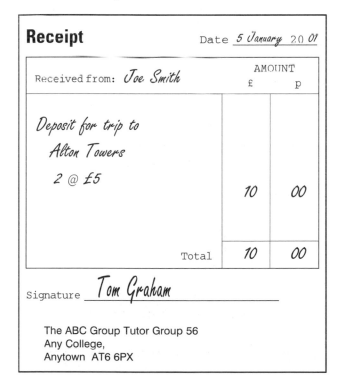

Figure 6.9   Example of a receipt

If you are ordering items through your school or college, you will probably find it uses a requisition system. This means that,

to order goods, an authorised member of staff completes a requisition form that is sent to the supplier who then sends the goods. The form is then sent by the supplier to the school or college's finance department for payment. Sometimes this system can lead to delays in goods being received (e.g. if requisition forms need more than one signature), and therefore you should check this carefully, particularly before ordering urgent items.

Customer services systems

If you are taking reservations, you will need to devise a system to process bookings. The information you might need to process a booking could include the following: the customer's:

- name
- age
- address
- telephone number
- status of booking (e.g. confirmed or on option)
- preferences or requests
- special requirements (including disabilities or special diets)
- booking dates.

There may be additional things you will need to know, depending on your product, and you might also need to consider whether or not you will be issuing a seat number or booking reference.

You must decide how correspondence with customers will be dealt with and should write guidelines about this for everyone to follow. For example, you will need to establish standard ways of producing letters and for dealing with complaints, should these arise! Base these on the sample letter in Figure 6.4, page 210.

Computer or paper-based administration systems

In an ideal world, it would be best to keep all your administration systems on a computer. However, in a project like this, you may find there are limitations in the ways you can use computers. If you share computers with other students, this could restrict the times when you can administer bookings or record payments. You also need to consider keeping your information secure, particularly if you are dealing with external customers.

Paper-based systems rely on the paperwork being easily accessible at all times for the appropriate team members. Security is again very important, and you will need to make sure you can read everyone's writing or figures for the information to be of any use to you.

Activity	Consider which administration systems you will need for your project. Next, decide which team member will be responsible for devising which administration system. Each member should then recommend which system he or she feels is the best one to use for his or her particular area of responsibility (e.g. computer or paper based).
	Put all your systems together into one administration unit that will be used by all members of the team when needed.

Timescales

Deciding on timescales is often the part of a project people do first, but there are lots of other things that must be considered prior to establishing deadlines. You should now, however, be a stage when you can start to put some dates together.

The following are some of the things you should consider when deciding on dates.

The project date

The project date is when the activity will be presented, the trip taken, the event carried out, etc. This will largely be dictated by your academic year, and it would be unwise to leave your project until it so late in the year it might be unsuccessful and, possibly, difficult to do again.

Assessment dates

Give some thought to when your tutor is going to assess the stages of your project. This will include the formal assessment of such things as your business plan and your record of involvement. It might also include observation of meetings, discussions or of your part in the project. It could involve other tutors who are assessing you in the key skills, customer service or marketing.

Meeting dates

These are the dates when you will make your major decisions about the project.

Marketing activity dates

Marketing activity dates are the dates you advertise or produce your leaflets. Include dates for market research projects and for the presentation of findings.

Administration dates

These include dates when payments need to be collected and suppliers paid. Bookings, reservations and letters of confirmation, etc., should be included here.

Staffing requirements

If you need additional staffing support, when will this be needed by?

Physical resources

The dates when these will need to be bought, hired or borrowed.

You will need to plan these out either as a year planner (see Figure 6.10) or by using a computer program. This program could be a very straightforward application (such as Excel), which you could use to list dates, activities and who will be responsible for them. Make sure you arrange the timescales in chronological order and that they are issued to all team members. Everyone must be updated about any changes, and remember this is a working document – the best examples will have many changes, additions and deletions demonstrating how you reacted to alterations to your project.

You may also find your school or college has certain dates you must consider when setting your own key dates. Look at the following:

- the timings of half-terms and bank holidays – these will have an impact on the success of your project
- when exams or external tests are taking place
- if there are any other events or projects taking place that could affect your success (especially if these are likely to attract high numbers of fellow students)

	Nov	Dec
Week 1	Market research Aims and objectives Finances and budget Contingency plans	Marketing plan Contact printers Team meeting (tutor observe)
Week 2	Identify resources Meeting with Funways	Send invoices to companies Meeting with Funways
Week 3	Write to companies Team meeting Equipment hire Write letters	
Week 4	Set up database Set up record-keeping system	
	Jan	Feb
Week 1	Start accounting for payments Design promotional material Team meeting	Reminder letters Contact local radio about feature Meeting with Funways
Week 2	Presentation of activity	Staffing plan Team meeting
Week 3	Meeting with Funways and Holiday Inn Team meeting (tutor observe)	Half-term
Week 4	Poster campaign Review of resources	Sponsorship activity Team meeting Letters to companies
	Mar	Apr
Week 1	Money to Holiday Inn Meeting with Funways Design customer feedback and evaluation forms	Evaluate activity Evaluate marketing
Week 2	Building check – Holiday Inn floor plan Staffing plan Team meeting	
Week 3	Team briefing Double check radio feature and resources	
Week 4	Last minute checks 31 March – activity	

Figure 6.10 An example project timescale

- staff events (such as parents' evenings and open days). These will put restrictions on the staff who might be involved in your project.

Finally, find out if there are any local activities or events that could affect your project, either adversely or favourably.

Legal aspects

There are many different legal aspects that could affect your project. The most important thing to remember is that, while you are responsible for running your project, your school or college will probably be responsible for the *legal* implications of your activity. Therefore, you should find out as much as possible about the potential legal issues that could arise as a result of your project, and whether or not your school or college can support you with such things as insurance or liability cover.

Health and safety

You should complete a health, safety and security risk assessment of your project. This involves drawing up a checklist of possible risks and then assessing the likelihood or possibility of these risks turning into real hazards or dangers. Obviously, different projects will involve different risks, but the sorts of things you might need to check include:

- fire exits and fire-fighting equipment
- the location of power sockets, electrical cables, etc.
- the furnishings (e.g. the carpets – are these frayed so people could trip over them?)
- first-aid facilities and the location of doctors/hospitals
- the catering facilities (for hygiene, safety, etc.)
- exits and entrances for disabled people
- the security of the site and of the equipment
- lighting (e.g. are emergency exits adequately lit?).

Remember that, if your project involves an activity, you have ultimate responsibility for the health, safety and security of your guests. If you are aware of all possible hazards, you will be able to work out how to deal with them, should such an event occur.

School or college involvement

You might also need to find out if your school or college has its own guidelines or rules relating to activities you organise, or on how its name can be linked with projects. You may need to organise a meeting with a member of the management team to discuss the following points and to find out about any restrictions your school or college might impose. Whether or not:

- prior written approval is needed from the head or principal and the timescales for this
- parental permission will be needed
- supervision is necessary for your project (for example, an overseas visit will require greater supervision than an on-site college exhibition)
- insurance is needed and whether existing policies might cover your project
- once approval is granted, you need to supply anyone with specific information (e.g. number of students and/or guests involved, your risk assessment, etc.)
- any specific wording must appear on your promotional material.

Activity	As a group, identify the legal implications of your project. Find out as much as possible about the relevant Acts of Parliament. For example: • The Health and Safety at Work Act 1974 • The Disability Discrimination Act 1955

- The Sale of Goods Acts 1979 and 1995
- The Data Protection Acts 1984 and 1998.

Find out who, in your school or college, holds responsibility for legal matters and arrange to discuss your project and its possible implications with this person.

Contingency plans

A contingency plan is basically a 'plan B'. It should provide answers to any questions that start with 'what would we do if ...'. It is, unfortunately, very difficult to find specific answers to questions like these as so many factors need to be considered. However, by considering contingency plans at an early stage, you should be in a better position to deal with tricky situations should these arise.

Activity	As a whole team, list all the possible emergencies or disruptions that could affect your event or project.
	Agree within your team contingency plans you could make to cover any emergencies or anticipated disruptions. Draw up a table listing each problem and then identify a contingency plan for each problem and the person who will be responsible for following this plan, should it be deemed necessary.

Reviewing and evaluating the project

The final part of your business plan should consider how your project will be reviewed and evaluated. There are many ways of doing this but, as this is your *own* project, you should draw the focus of the review and evaluation away from your tutor and towards yourselves. The following are methods you could consider for evaluating your project.

Self-evaluation

Self-evaluation means considering your own role and how it contributed towards the project. You could, for example, use videos or audiotapes to review how effectively you dealt with customers, etc. These could be used to produce a personal self-development plan to help you improve your skills.

Peer evaluation

Peer evaluation involves you in evaluating each other. This can be done formally through reports, questionnaires or written feedback, or informally on either a one-to-one or group discussion basis. The important thing is to listen and to take on board any suggestions but not to become defensive about criticism – use criticism constructively.

Group evaluation

This means evaluating the project as a group effort: both its success and how things, with hindsight, could have been done differently. This sort of evaluation can be done through meetings, questionnaires or written feedback.

Customer feedback

Customer feedback could be obtained informally through, for example, commendations or through discussions with customers about any problems that arose. You might also want to devise a more formal way of recording customer feedback (e.g. through the use of a questionnaire).

Performance indicators

Performance indicators are a little more scientific (for example, money collected, sponsorship raised, sales or profit/loss).

Deadlines

You should review your ability to meet deadlines. The way you stuck to (or did not stick to!) timescales is a useful way of evaluating how effective your planning was and how well you worked together as a team.

Marketing

How effective were your research, your market planning and the promotional activities you undertook?

Aims and objectives

How appropriate were your aims and objective and were these met?

Conclusions

There are many other ways of evaluating your project, and this is *your* opportunity to set *your* assessment tools for this unit. Remember, review and evaluation should not just happen at the end of the project – they must be ongoing and must result in changes to your plans as you go along. Also consider why you are reviewing and evaluating aspects of your project and how you will use the information so obtained.

Chapter 6.2 Teamwork

Creating and maintaining an effect team is a critical part of your project and will have a big impact on the success or failure of your venture. A team must contain a blend of skills and build on team members' strengths. Teamwork will also help you to generate additional evidence that will contribute towards your Key Skills. This chapter considers some of the theory concerning effective teamwork, including:

- the purpose of your team
- team structures
- the roles and responsibilities of team members
- team-building and interaction
- the factors that may influence how well the team works.

This chapter is very much based on your own participation as a member of the team, on your leadership, management and work skills, and on your attitude towards your fellow students. As certain people will observe your team meetings from time to time throughout your project (e.g. your tutor), the way you communicate with your team members is very important. Teamwork is not just about following orders. It relies on how actively you are involved in the whole project and on your ability to use initiative and creativity in your thoughts and actions.

For teamwork to be effective, you must make use of everyone in the team. It is therefore important you identify your own and each others' skills to ensure these are used to maximum effect to achieve your objectives. Look at the people in your team: are there some people who are always making their own views known? If this happens, these people might dominate the team and make all the major decisions. By contrast, are there people who never say anything, who do not volunteer and who have to be monitored by others to complete their tasks?

As a team you need to be very self-critical – not just about individuals but also about how things happen in the team. If the views of a few people are swaying the whole project, consider how to get the whole team involved in the decision-making process. You may need to ask some hard questions about why people are not contributing and what can be done to encourage their participation. It is important everyone contributes and feels he or she has ownership of the project. Look at how tasks and roles can be shared to encourage people to become involved in the activities. This will be a good learning experience that will help you when going on to work in an industry that is heavily reliant on teamwork and participation.

Purpose and structure

So what is a team? A team will:

- comprise two or more individuals
- have a common objective all team members are working towards.

Teams are to be found in almost all walks of life. For example, at work or college, teams will have been established by management for specific purposes, and there are established ways in which teams are organised. There will, for example, be an appointed leader and people who work under this leader who have specific roles and responsibilities.

Teams can be structured in different ways. The following examples might help you to decide on your own team structure.

Hierarchical

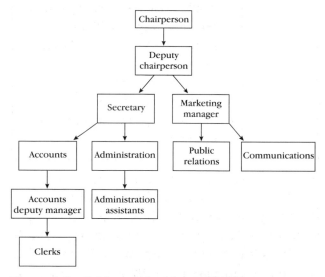

Figure 6.11   A hierarchical team structure

In this type of structure there are several levels of management and responsibility (see Figure 6.11). Lines of authority are very clearly defined but, because of these lines of authority, decision-making might be a slow process. Hierarchical structures can either be tall or flat, depending on how many layers of management there are.

Functional

In this type of structure, the management is split into areas according to the various specific roles that team members need to fulfill.

Figure 6.12   A functional team structure

Simple

You may find that, if your team is very small but there is still a need for a formal structure, a hierarchical structure might not be appropriate. For example, in Figure 6.13, there are three people only in the team. In a larger team, the secretary's position might be higher in the hierarchy than sales and marketing, but in this small team they are positioned equally beneath the chairperson.

Figure 6.13   A simple team structure

Divisional

This sort of structure is used when there are different divisions in an organisation with different areas of responsibility. The best way of demonstrating this is to look at how an overseas tour operator might be structured (see Figure 6.14). Under 'Manager, overseas operations' are four divisions, each with its own area of responsibility.

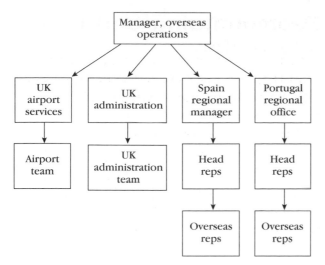

Figure 6.14 A divisional team structure

Centralised

In a centralised team structure, one person or a group of people will make the management decisions, and all other team members will just comply. This can be demonstrated by looking at the structure of a tour group (see Figure 6.15). The tour manager is responsible for making the management decisions, and all other group members share similar levels of responsibility.

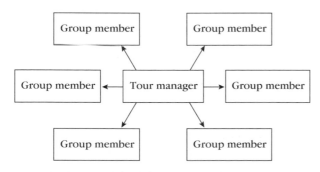

Figure 6.15 A centralised team structure

A decentralised structure is the opposite of this. For example, if each of the group members had responsibility for either a group of people or several families, then this would be what we would call a decentralised structure. Many of the management decisions are made individually.

Team members' roles and responsibilities

Now you have decided on a structure for your team, you need to sort out the specific roles and responsibilities of the members of your team. There are several reasons why it is important to do this.

- To make sure each team member has a part to play in the project and will be able to contribute both to the group and as an individual. This will give people responsibility and will make them feel a part of the team.

Activity	As a whole team, decide on a structure for your group. Justify how the structure you have chosen will help your team in the following ways: • in fulfilling its aims and objectives • in allocating and carrying out job roles and responsibilities • in making the best use of staff resources • in making communication systems more effective • for deciding on the purpose of your team.

- To share out tasks evenly and fairly so that one or two people do not end up doing all the work while others do very little. You may find that some of your job roles involve too many tasks. If this is the case it suggests more than one person is needed to do that particular job.
- To make sure it is clear who will do what. This will avoid duplication of tasks or things being missed out totally because everyone thought someone else was doing that job. It will also ensure there is no confusion within the team, and that people can work independently without being told what to do.

- To define each person's accountability and to set the boundaries people will work within. This should include a clear definition of the times when individuals should refer matters on to the team leader, the whole team or a tutor.
- To identify any tasks team members are not comfortable with, to assess whether there is any need to reallocate roles and to work out if anyone needs extra support.
- Finally, and most importantly, to ensure jobs get done and done within your deadlines.

The best way of doing this might be to write up a job description for each job role that lists each job's responsibilities and the timescales involved in that particular job. What is important is to ensure that some team members are not overloaded at one stage but then left with nothing to do at other times. This is poor time and team management and results in unnecessary stress and pressures on both individuals and the group.

Activity	Draw up job descriptions for each job role you have identified for your team and then allocate and agree roles for each member of your team. Draw as simple chart to show appropriate reporting structures and lines of authority.
	If you need to involve people from outside your group in your team, it is important you speak to them first to obtain their agreement. Produce a job description for these people as well so they know what will be required of them.

Team-building and team interaction

Before we look at factors that may influence how well a team works together, we must give some consideration to team-building and team interaction. It does not matter if your team is a well-established group who have worked together on a number of occasions before or is a group of people who have come together for the first time for this project: your project will bring your team together very quickly indeed.

Most teams or groups go through four phases of development: forming, storming, norming and performing. These are described in more detail below.

Forming

Forming (as its name suggests) is the initial bringing together of a group of people. Think back to when you first started your course at school or college and the strategies your tutor used to form you into a group. There will have been some form of induction or ice breaker, where you got to know more about each other and started to relax. You may need to adopt similar tactics with your project team to ensure you develop as a group.

Storming

Storming is the action, discussion and argument stage of development. You will all have different ideas about what you want to do and when you want to do it. At this stage, you could find there are strong individuals who try to take over the team and to dictate their views. People may fall out or leave the group, and there will be personality clashes and disagreements. Don't worry: this is what happens in newly formed teams – it always takes a while for things to settle down. The important thing to remember is that you should not take these disagreements or clashes away with you when your team meetings have ended (i.e. into your social life or into other lessons). Resolve them within the safe environment of your project team meetings.

Norming

Norming is the stage when the group begins to work together constructively. You will have settled as a group and will be progressing well with your plan. There is also likely to be less conflict between people at this stage. You will be providing updates to your other team members about progress made and will be working towards your aims and objectives.

Performing

At this stage things really begin to happen. Performing can happen at any stage in the project (for example, when a sponsorship deal has been agreed, a high volume of sales has been made or marketing material starts to appear). Performing should also, it is hoped, happen at the end of your project when all the hard work results in your project being completed successfully. This is when you can sit back to enjoy a real sense of achievement.

Teams do not all evolve at the same rate: some have relatively short bursts of storming and more of the norming, whilst others might have extended periods of disagreement. You might also find you repeat some of the stages. It might be necessary to reform the group at some stage because people leave or new people join or because of unseen external events that affect your group.

Activity

Consider the ways you could get your group through the first stages of forming and storming (if these things have not happened already!). You will need to devise strategies to overcome any problems you may encounter in these stages, as well as think carefully about any techniques you could use to smooth your transition from one stage to the next.

The following are examples of things that might have happened/ could happen when establishing your team. Some are problems that might arise, others techniques you could use. Yet others are simply processes all teams must go through. Have any of these occurred? What did you do or what could you do to overcome this particular problem? What would be the best technique to use to ensure your team goes through a process successfully?

Try to answer these questions for the points listed below. You will probably also find there are a great many other things you could add.

Forming

- Picking people to join your team or being allocated a group by your tutor.
- Your first meeting.
- Brainstorming ideas for your activity.
- Identifying your own skills and discussing these with others.
- Finding out about each others' skills.
- Splitting into teams for parts of the project (such as marketing).

Storming

- Team meetings.
- Lively discussions, debates or arguments about which activity you will pursue.
- Being advised by your tutor that a chosen activity is not possible or feasible.
- Disagreements about roles within your group.
- People who do or do not want to work with each other.
- People in the team who are not contributing.
- Domineering and forceful people who make all the decisions and who do not listen to others.
- People leaving the team or your school or college.

Factors that affect how well the team works

Some of the factors that may affect how well your team works together are as follows.

Communication

How your team is structured and your lines of responsibility will dictate to a great extent the formal methods of communication between team members. Meetings will need to have a structure to them so that people focus on the relevant issues. However, it is important the team feels relaxed and comfortable enough for all members to participate and to be involved in the decision-making.

Leadership

There are many different management styles the team leader can adopt. These range from the autocratic (which tends to be strict and authoritative) through to the democratic (which is flexible, going with the views of the members). Committee leadership tends to be in the middle (taking the popular opinion or view of the group and using this as the way forward). Think about leadership styles you have experienced so far: many will have been autocratic and few, if any, democratic. If you have been involved in groups or teams involving fellow students, these will more than likely have had a committee leadership style.

Personality clashes

Personality clashes are what we automatically think of as being one of the main factors involved in teamwork. Give some thought to the things that could be considered personality clashes in your own group. These things will probably be based on previous experiences or contact between members of the group, but could also involve people's backgrounds and even prejudices. As this is a professional project, make sure you do not allow yourself to be caught up in group dynamics – treat everyone with fairness and equality.

Access to resources

The team will need to be provided with appropriate and adequate resources if it is to perform well. This will include physical resources (such as materials, finance and equipment) and staffing resources (such as appropriate people for the roles needed within the team). Your business plan must have identified the appropriate resources for your team.

The working environment

It might be difficult to have a business-like attitude towards your project because of your school or college environment. You will need to treat the project seriously if it is going to succeed, and this includes the contact you have with internal people (staff and fellow students) and external people (suppliers, contacts, charities or sponsors). You may need to give thought to the surroundings when you telephone people (i.e. no distracting noises), to the way in which you present written information to a company or to your appearance when you visit contacts.

Chapter 6.3 Carrying out the project

You should now be at the stage where you can start on the actual activity part of your project. Your group will have been formed, you will have assessed the feasibility of the project and you will have had it approved by your tutor. You will now be taking on your allotted role within your group and will be contributing towards the success of the project. To make sure this happens, you will need to be able to:

- complete the tasks you have been allocated
- communicate effectively with the rest of the team
- deal with customers, other members of your team and any other people involved with your project politely
- support other team members while the project is being carried out
- react quickly and confidently to any problems that may arise
- keep to any agreed deadlines
- know when it is appropriate to seek help and advice from others.

You must keep a record of your involvement in the project. Keep this record going throughout the whole project – it is not something you can write up after the event is over (you will *not* be able to remember what you have been doing for the last six months). A well organised diary or journal is a good way of recording these details.

Activity	Consider *now* all the different ways you could record your involvement with your project. Make a list of these and by each one make a note of all the advantages and

disadvantages you can think of for using that method (e.g. if you were to consider using a computer one advantage would be you could easily and neatly make any necessary amendments to your entries but a disadvantage could be you might be limited in your access to the computer facilities available in your school or college).

Try to decide *now* on which system to use, and keep your log on a daily basis.

Completing your task(s)

Before you undertake anything, you must be clear about what the task or tasks involve. If you find a task needs to be broken down into smaller chunks, you might be able to do this yourself or could ask the team to help you. You must also make sure that what you have agreed to complete is something you are capable of achieving, and that the timescales are realistic. If deadlines are not met, this could have an impact on your colleagues – it is therefore better to raise any problems with deadlines at an early stage rather than leaving it until it is too late to do anything about it. Planning is extremely important. Before starting on your tasks, take some time to plan your activities, to set yourself deadlines and to consider how you will cope if there is a need to make changes.

Whilst there are some very obvious reasons why you must complete the tasks that have been allocated to you (e.g. to fulfil the requirements of this unit), it is important to your *team* that you carry out your responsibilities. Your team will lose its trust in you as an individual if you let your fellow team members down. It is also important for your own self-esteem that you fulfil and value your contribution to the overall project.

Record all tasks completed in your log or diary. This will be your main source of evidence for this part of the unit.

Dealing politely with other people

Earlier we discussed the importance of communicating effectively with all those involved in the project. This project is a business enterprise and, for this reason, you may need to take a different attitude towards your customers, team members and others involved in the project than you would when dealing with, say, your friends or family. You must make sure, therefore, that you are polite when dealing with *everyone* involved in the project. You may have already have been given advice about this, but the two important things to remember are as follows.

Always treat others as you would expect to be treated yourself. Everyone says something at one stage or another that may not be polite, but try to avoid this wherever possible. Think about how you would feel if you were on the receiving end of your comments.

Think before you speak. If necessary, pause and take a breath: don't rush in to what it is you want to say. Very often, when you give a quick response, this might not be worded in the most appropriate way or you may not use a pleasant tone of voice. However, when you have something important to say, make sure you are heard.

Everyone involved in the project is a customer and deserves the same level of politeness and courtesy. Everyone reacts

better to someone who is considerate: watch other people either at work or at school or college who are good at being polite to customers and how customers react to these people. The tactics people use to accomplish this including the following.

- *Body language.* The way you stand or sit gives off messages to people about what you might really be thinking about them. Your facial expressions might be something you also need to consider, especially if you are nervous in certain situations.
- *Your tone and pitch of voice (including volume).* When people are agitated, their voices tend to rise in volume and this is often the first sign someone is losing control. Make sure that when things are not going well in meetings or discussions you keep your voice even and that you always know what you are going to say next.
- *The use of business-like phrases and not using slang or swear words.* What you might think an appropriate response when talking amongst your friends might need rephrasing for a business meeting. Swearing or making sarcastic and abusive comments is to be avoided at all costs.
- *Consider the customers, particularly their ages and expectations.* Some people will expect to be addressed formally, for example, by their title or surname, while others will prefer you to use their first name. If in doubt, ask the customer: he or she will probably be pleased you have considered this seemingly small point.

You will find that, if you plan your tasks well, you will not place yourself under undue stress, and this will result in you being more polite towards other people. Always try to allow some time before meetings to prepare yourself so you can be more relaxed.

Activity	Think of two business occasions: one where you were dealt with politely and one where you were dealt with not so politely. As a group, and using your own experience from your two examples, complete a list of suggestions about how to be polite to other people.

Supporting other team members

You will have your own tasks to complete but there might be other people in your group who are struggling with their tasks. Always think about whether or not you can do anything to help your fellow team members. Remember, it is a *team* task you are completing.

There are, however, a few things you should consider before agreeing to offer support:

- Are you capable of helping with the task or is there someone else in the group who is better qualified or better equipped to do so?
- Do you have the time available to help or would you need to stop helping half way through, thus creating more problems?
- What opportunities present themselves in helping others? For example, helping others might make your own job role more interesting or could increase your knowledge.

It can be very rewarding to offer help and support to others, and it will also make people more likely to help you if you ever get stuck with your own tasks at some stage.

Support can also be given in a much easier way, simply through thanking people, praising them if they have achieved difficult tasks and by complimenting them on what they are doing. This will not take up much of your time but would be a good motivating factor for your fellow team members.

Reacting quickly and confidently to problems

Before studying this section it would be a good idea to reread the advice on page 196 of Unit 5 about dealing with customer complaints.

The problems you might encounter will fall into two categories: those you could have anticipated and those that, with the best will in the world, could not have been foreseen. The former type are considered first as these are the ones it may be possible to avoid.

When you put together your business plan, you considered possible disruptions and devised contingency plans to deal with these. You should review your contingency plans from time to time to assess whether or not they are still applicable. New developments may need considering and you may need new contingency plans, or some of the original possible problems on your list might have disappeared. If you have to implement your contingency plans, these will have an impact on your customers and, if the problem is addressed confidently and quickly, the customers will be reasonably satisfied. The approach you take and the way you communicate your plans will determine how satisfied the customers are.

Activity	Give each member of your group one of your contingency plans to study. Take 10–15 minutes to consider how a customer might react to this plan and what you could do to keep him or her satisfied.

If possible, take it in turns to role play explaining your contingency plans to a customer. While role playing this, try to deal with any problems or objections from the customer that might arise. Conduct these role plays in front of the whole group so the rest of the group can provide feedback.

What about problems you could not have anticipated happening? Figure 6.16 lists the steps involved in dealing with unforeseen problems.

1 Listen to the customer carefully and assess whether or not you can resolve the problem yourself. If you are able to do this, it will speed up the process and ensure the situation does not escalate. However, do not make promises you cannot keep. Make notes if you need to.

2 Apologise and empathise rather than sympathise. Make sure the customer is aware of how the problem will be dealt with. If you cannot deal with it yourself, explain this to the customer.

3 Refer the problem on either to a fellow team member who can resolve the problem or to your tutor or a responsible person at your school or college. Explain the situation to this person so the customer does not have to repeat the details of the problem.

4 Make sure the problem is shared with your fellow team members. You should discuss customer problems: discussion may reveal problems you were not aware of and that could be avoided in the future. Do not consider a problem to be a criticism of you or your team – use it as a learning experience.

Figure 6.16   The steps involved in dealing with an unforeseen problem

Keeping to deadlines

You will have identified timescales for your project and the success of your project will depend on keeping to these deadlines. If your project involves customers, it will not be possible to extend the final deadline. An event taking place on a set date cannot be changed because you are not ready or because all the arrangements have not been confirmed. If you have allowed some time

within your plan for contingency action you should be able to cope with any disruptions you anticipated. There might, however, be problems you have not identified, and so it may be necessary to work outside the school or college day or to forfeit your lunch breaks to meet your deadlines. Because this is a team activity, you are *all* responsible for ensuring deadlines are met through your own individual roles and through group tasks.

This project is likely to be different from other projects you might be undertaking as you will be taking on a great deal of the responsibility for your own time management. You will also be monitoring your own achievements and, while the team might ask you to update them on your progress, you yourself will be the main person who will be tracking how you are doing. Therefore you must give some thought as to how you will monitor your own achievements or successes as this might be something you have not had much experience in doing.

If deadlines start to become a problem, you will need to consider how realistic and achievable the original plan was. It may be you have underestimated the staffing requirements for the project or your team might be lacking in certain skills. Discuss these problems now and speak to your tutor if your project looks to be in jeopardy.

Obtaining help and advice from others

We have already looked at offering support to other people, but there will be times when you yourself will need to obtain help and advice from others. It is important you recognise this fact, that you know where your limitations lie and can identify who would be the most appropriate person to contact.

There are many situations when you would need to obtain help and advice. For example, if:

- specialist knowledge is required (for example, about health and safety or how to operate a piece of equipment or machinery)
- someone wants to know something and you do not know the answer
- the priorities change for some of your tasks and a deadline might not be achieved without help
- you lack the confidence to deal with a person or situation or feel there is a need for someone higher up than you to offer support
- you are not qualified to deal with a situation (for example, if a customer has an accident and needs first aid)

- you are unsure or have doubts about an issue and you just want confirmation that what you are doing is correct
- you need to protect yourself (for example, if collecting large amounts of cash or if you are going somewhere alone late at night).

There will be many other examples. Make sure you are aware on all such occasions of when to ask someone for help and advice. Try to create a buddy system or network that identifies people who can support each other. It is best to avoid pairing friends together for this purpose: try instead looking at the roles and responsibilities within your team and group people according to these.

Chapter 6.4 Evaluating the project

You have already identified how the evaluation will take place as part of the business plan. It is essential to keep to this once the project starts: once an evaluation opportunity has passed you by, it is very difficult to generate it again. An example of this might be collecting customer feedback at the end of a visit. You might not be able to ask people for their feedback later and, if this was done by post, the response rate might be low. You would also be risking people forgetting what they really thought about the event.

One way you can evaluate the project yourself is by your team members asking themselves the following questions:

- Did we meet our objectives?
- Were key deadlines met?
- Did our planning result in an effective performance?
- Was the project successful/effective?
- What went well and what went badly for me, individually?
- How well did the team work as a whole?
- How did working as part of a team help or hinder me?

The important thing is to remember what your reasons are for evaluating the project. Feedback from your fellow students should be something you could use for your own personal development. Listen to commendations or praise from team members and remember these for later. These comments can often be useful at job interviews when you are asked what your strong points are. You will not only be able to say what these are but will also be able to support them with the example of your project and with the feedback you have received. There might also be negative comments about your performance. Take these comments constructively: this is a good environment in which to learn about any shortfalls you might have. Once you start working in the travel and tourism industry, you may find this opportunity does not occur. Feedback from managers is often done more formally and with more serious implications.

You should be able to use the results of an evaluation to recommend how the whole activity could be improved. Consider, for example, what you would have done differently with hindsight. It is not sufficient to say that 90% of customers enjoyed the activity. You need to look at the 10% who did not and what would have made their experience more enjoyable. Once you have established what could have kept this 10% happy, you will be in a situation to consider whether or not improvements could have been made. This part of the project should be treated in a positive way: do not be disheartened by any negative comments.

Perhaps your team includes the next Richard Branson?

These can give you an insight into customers and their expectations that will help you when you enter the travel and tourism industry.

An enjoyable way of rounding off the project is to celebrate its success. You might want to do this at school or college or through a social event. A video of the project and photographs can provide a bit of light relief and enjoyment at the end of all your hard work.

Further reading and useful websites

Further reading

Weekly trade publications

Travel Trade Gazette (TTG)
Travel Weekly

Books

Code of Conduct (for social and market research), The Market Research Society, 15 Northburgh Street, London EC1V 0AH

Dictionary of Travel, Tourism and Hospitality, S. Medlik (Butterworth Heinemann, 1997)

Heinemann GNVQ Intermediate Business, C. Carysforth and M. Nield (Heinemann Eductional, 2000)

Manual of Travel Agency Practice, G. Syratt (Butterworth Heinemann, 1995)

Marketing in Travel and Tourism, V. Middleton (Butterworth Heinemann, 2000)

World Travel Guide, Columbus Press (also available on CD-ROM)

Useful websites

The following websites may be useful reference sources and many contain links to other relevant websites.
Remember that website addresses may be changed, for example if the name or ownership of an organisation is altered.

Specific websites

Alton Towers http://www.altontowers.com

ABTA (Association of British Travel Agents) http://www.abtanet.com

Atlantis Travel http://www.atlantistravel.co.uk

Bournemouth http://www.bournemouth.gov.uk

British Airways http://www.british-airways.com

British Tourist Authority http://www.visitbritain.com

Butlins http://www.butlins.co.uk

Center Parcs http://www.centerparcs.com

Disneyland Paris http://www.disneylandparis.com

Easy Jet http://www.easyjet.co.uk

English Tourism Council http://www.englishtourism.org.uk

Eurostar http://www.eurostar.co.uk

Legoland http://www.legoland.co.uk

Lunn Poly http://www.lunn-poly.co.uk

Manchester Commonwealth Games http://www.manchester2002.co.uk

Mintel Publications http://www.mintel.com

National Express http://www.nationalexpress.co.uk

Northern Ireland Tourist Board http://www.ni-tourism.com

P & O Stena Line http://www.posl.com

Scottish Tourist Board http://www.visitscotland.com

Thomson Holidays http://www.thomson-holidays.com

Travel Training Company http://www.tttc.co.uk

Welsh Tourist Board http://www.visitwales.com

Whitbread http://www.whitbread.co.uk

WTO (World Tourist Organisation) http://www.world-tourism.org

Websites of some Internet holiday companies

http://www.expedia.co.uk
http://www.connectglobal.co.uk
http://www.topclasstravel.co.uk
http://www.travel2.American Express.com
http://www.travelon.com

Other websites useful for statistics, general information and links on tourism

http://www.geoprojects.co.uk
http://www.star-attractions.co.uk
http://www.staruk.org.uk

A

ABTA (Association of British Travel Agents) 15, 34, 43
  Code of Conduct 15, 158, 197
accessibility 94, 120
accommodation 5, 23, 108
  budget 12
  grading 23
  self-catering 23, 61, 90
  serviced 23
administration 216
advertising 66, 118, 133, 136, 152
  direct response 155
Advertising Standards Authority 158
advice 191, 233
after-sales service 188
agenda 204
agent *see* travel agent
AIDA 136, 137, 189
airports 10
  UK regional 114
air travel 7, 28, 94, 114
  Australia 102
  chartered 7, 28, 100, 114
  scheduled 28, 115
  within USA 99
  see also IATA
Alton Towers 7, 91
Amadeus 13
Ansoff's product-market matrix 122
apology 196
application form 48
apprenticeships 43
assistance 192
atlas 79
attitude 170
attractions
  built 107
  event 22
  industrial 63
  leisure 22
  natural 106
  site 22
auditing
  environmental 74
Australia 101
Austria 92
awarding body vii
Ayers Rock *see* Uluru

B

Baedecker 6
bar codes 194

beaches
  blue flag scheme 63
  Caribbean 100
  features 105
benefits 187
boat operators 34
body language 179, 196
border controls 111
Boston 98
Bournemouth 65
brainstorming 204
brand 34, 134
break-even charts 212–3
break-even point 212
brochures 14, 32, 80, 136, 153–4
British National Travel Survey 33
BTA (British Tourist Authority) 24–5, 38, 58
budget
  accomodation 12
  for project 211
business
  conferences 87
  owners 68
  plan 204
  travel 31, 40
Butlin, Sir Billy 6
Butlins 91

C

CAA (Civil Aviation Authority) 33
Calgary 99
call centres 180
camping and caravanning 7
Canada 99
Canterbury 26
car
  hire in USA 99
  ownership 6
careers
  development 45
  interview 46
  office 43
  see also employment
Caribbean 100
carnivals 107
catering 12, 23, 61
  see also self-catering
Center Parcs 90
charts and graphs 83
cities 86, 93
cinema 156
climate 16, 93, 104, 120

Australia 102
  see also weather
closing the sale 187
coach travel 30
commendation 79
complaint 79, 164, 194–8
commission 36
communication 178, 190, 228, 231
  face to face 179
  skills 169
  telephone 180
  writing 181
community
  facilities 63, 70
  groups 58
competitions 156
competitive edge 164
computers 81, 192, 218
  see also Internet *and* CRS
conferences 87
conservation 63, 68
consolidation 122
consultant 56, 74
Consumer Protection Act 1987 159
contingency plans 221
costs
  fixed 211
  for project 211
  semi-variable 211
  start-up 213
  variable 211
Countryside Commission 6
crime 119
CRS (Computerised reservation systems) 8
  see also Amadeus *and* Galileo
cross-channel 5
cruises 29, 100, 116
culture 20, 64, 70, 87
currency 18, 67, 117
  exchange rates 14
  fluctuations 117
  regulations 61
  surcharge 14
customer
  attitude towards 172
  awareness 184
  children 174
  commendation 79
  complaint 79, 164, 194–8
  groups 173
  individual 173
  loyalty 42, 166

needs 79, 176, 186, 207
rapport with 185
satisfaction 165
service 34, 162, 190
service charter 195
services systems 217
types 87, 133, 173
customer relationship marketing 166
Cunard 6
CV (curriculum vitae) 46–7

D
Data Protection Act 1984 159, 192, 221
Data Protection Authority 159
day-trips 40
destination 3
  cities 86
  exclusive 118
  exotic 8
  features 93, 104
  long-haul 77, 96
  medium-haul 77
  towns 86
Development of Tourism Act 1969 24
diagrams 84
direct mail 154
Disability Discrimination Act 1995 220
discrimination 178
Disneyland Paris 8, 57, 89
Disneyworld Florida 97
disposable income 7
distance learning 43
diversification 122
door-to-door distribution 155
dress 167
duty-free 16, 28

E
ecological constraints 73
economic
  factors 117, 133
  impacts 67
economy 18, 60
education 46
Egyptians 5
EIA (environmental impact assessment) 74
empathy 197
employment 38, 41, 46, 60
  agencies 44
  generation 68
  hours of work 41–2
  interviews 50
  opportunities 41
  part-time 41
  permanent 41
  seasonal 16, 42
  temporary 41
entertainment 93, 107
environment 18–9
  working 229

environmental
  auditing 74
  education 63
ETC (English Tourism Council) 25–6, 43
  crown system 23
EU
  Package Travel Directive 16
  directives 58
European 'Grand Tour' 5
Eurostar 8
evaluation 221, 235
events 107
excursions 27

F
farm tourism 12
family values 70
features 93, 187
feedback 199
ferries 28, 115
festivals 107
films 8
fjords 92
flexible working 7
Florida 96
focus groups 143, 147, 201
food and drink 93, 107
foreign currency see currency
forests 91
formal presentation 178
France 92
funding 36

G
Galileo 13
gateway 110
gazetteers 80
grants 57
Greece 88
Greyhound buses 99
guide books 80

H
habitats 63
harmonisation 16
health and safety 220
Health and Safety at Work Act 1974 220
help 233
Heritage centres 63
hiking 91
history
  destinations 93
  travel and tourism 5
holiday
  camps 6
  centres 34
  cottages 34
  hiking 91
  niche 12
  package 8

safari 12
short break 34
theme 12
walking 91
wintersports 91
  see also tour
Holidays with Pay Act 1938 7
Horizon 7
humidity 104
hurricanes 100

I
IATA (International Air Transport
    Association) 28
illness 194
implant 32
information
  internal 149
  external 149
  qualitative 144
  quantitative 145
insurance 194
integration
  horizontal 35
  vertical 34
Internet 10, 13–4, 80, 133, 153
inflation 67
information 190
interview 50
  group 50
  nerves 50
  preparation 49
  questions 49
investors 72
Italy 89, 92

J
jewellery 167
jobs see employment

K
key skills vii

L
lakes 92
landscape 105
language
  body 179, 194
  skills 45
  training 72
Las Vegas 98
leadership 228
leaflets 153–4
legislation 15, 220
Legoland 91
leisure 22
  time 7
letter of application 48
licensing 72

lifecycle
    product 130–1
listening 186
local authorities 12, 57
local communities 56
location 132
long-haul 77, 96
Los Angeles 98
lost children 194
lost luggage 194
Lunn, Sir Henry 6

M
magazines 153
maps 83
market
    development 122
    penetration 122
    research *see* research
    segmentation 126, 138–41
    skimming 134
marketing
    communications 135, 152
    external influences 125
    internal influences 125
    mix 127, 129
    objectives 124
    place 132, 137
    plan 123
    price 134, 137
    product 130, 137
    promotion 135, 137
    telemarketing 154
Maslow's hierarchy of needs 126–7
mass market 5
meetings
    agenda 204
    minutes 206
media 118, 152
messages 191
mission statement 124, 165
money 214–6
monitoring 199
Monopolies and Mergers Commission 35
morale 165
mountains 91
Montreal 99
mystery shoppers 201

N
National Bus Company 30
national parks 6, 69, 92
National Parks Commission 6
national tourist boards 11
natural disasters 120
newspapers 66, 81
New York 97
New Zealand 102
Niagara Falls 99
niche holidays 12

North America 96
NVQ (National Vocational
    Qualification) 43

O
observation 143, 146, 201
ocean liners 28
organisations
    commercial 36
    non-profit making 11
overbooking 193
overseas representatives *see*
    representatives

P
package tours 16
    tailor made 32
Package Travel, Package Holidays &
    Package Tour Regulations 1992
    159–60
payments 214
phonetic alphabet 180
pictures 84
pilgrimages 5
place 132
performance indicators 222
personal
    dress 167
    hygiene 168
    qualities 42
    skills 45
personality
    audit 169
PEST analysis 126
    see also STEP analysis
political
    objectives 64
    unrest 119
pollution 69, 120
Portugal 89
price 134
    discounting 134
    'going rate' 134
    prestige 134
    project 213
    promotional 134
primary research *see* research
presentation 178
presenting research 82
press
    releases 155
    see also media
pressure groups 58
private sector 10, 55
    rail companies 28
problems 193, 232
product 130
    development 122
    lifecycle 130–1
profits 34, 36, 214

project
    administration 216
    aims 207
    budget 211
    conclusions 222
    costs 211
    customers 205
    evaluation 221
    feasibility 204
    marketing 208
    objectives 207
    reports 210
    review 221
    staffing 215
    tasks 230
    timescales 218–9, 233
promotion 135
public image 163
public relations 155
public sector 11, 57
publicity 64
purpose built resorts 89

Q
qualitative information 144
quality 199
quantitative information 145
questionnaires 143

R
radio 153
rail travel 29, 99, 113
rainfall 104
Raitz, Vladimir 7
receipt 217
records 192
religious beliefs 70
regeneration 62
representatives 32, 41
research
    analysis 150
    conclusions 84
    information sources 82, 84
    market 122, 126, 138, 141, 201
    objectives 138
    primary 79, 143
    secondary 79, 148, 208
    skills 78
reservations 13
    systems 8
resorts
    exclusive 118
    in the north of England 6
    over-commercialised 119
    purpose-built 89
    seaside 5
    spa 5
resources 228
    physical 209
revenue 36, 38

roads 111
roles 205
Romans 5
Rotorua 102

S
safari holiday 12
Sales of Goods Acts 1979 and 1995 15,
    221
sales
    closing 187
    presentation 186
    promotion 156
    recommendation 163
    skills 183
    support 183
    targets 183
    telesales 31, 183
San Francisco 98
sea & river travel 28, 115
seaport 110
seaside
    guesthouses 7
    resorts 5, 88
secondary research *see* research
Second World War 6
security 70
self-catering 23, 61
    see also catering
shopping 132
Single European Act 1992 16
skiing 17
slogans 66
SMART objectives 124
SME (small and medium sized enterprises)
    10
spa 5
Spain 88
sponsorship 36, 157
stakeholders 36
state control of tourism 27
STEP analysis 126
    see also PEST analysis
suggestions 201
Sun Parks activity 59
sunshine hours 104
surplus 36
surveys 143, 199
Switzerland 91
SWOT analysis 125
Sydney 101

T
taxes 57, 62, 68

team
    meetings 199
    roles and responsibilities 225
    structures 224
teamwork 43, 223
technical skills 43
technology 8, 13
telemarketing 154
telesales 31
teletext 34
television 8, 66, 152
temperature 104
terrorism 119
textbooks 80
theft 194
theme parks 90, 107
Thomas Cook 6
TICs (Tourist Information Centres) 11, 26
tolls 112
topography 105
Toronto 99
tour
    operators 30, 32–4
    package 3, 30
tourism
    definition 2
    development 55
    domestic 3, 6, 40
    economic impacts 67
    farm 12
    inbound 3, 39
    minister 27
    planning 71
    outbound 4
    sustainable 73
tourist
    attractions 22
    boards 26, 58
    councils 25
    information centres 11, 26, 136
    development 24, 27
    development agencies/companies 56
    spending by 4
    state control 27
towns 86
Trades Descriptions Act 1968 15, 158
trade papers 81
training
    colleges 43
    languages 72
    programmes 46
    schemes 43
transfers 95, 109
Transport Acts 1980 and 1985 30

transport 27, 94, 109
    public 109
travel
    air 27, 99
    agents 10, 30–1
    business 31, 40
    bus and coach 30, 109
    definition of 2
    excursions 27
    ferry 109
    package 3
    sea and river 27
    rail and train 29, 109
    tram 109
Travel Training Company 43
Turkey 88

U
Uluru 101
uniforms 167
USA 96

V
VAT (value-added tax) 211
VFR (visiting friends and relatives) 40, 99,
    101, 102
videos 81
visitors
    management 73
voluntary sector 11, 58

W
walking 91
war and civil unrest 17, 119
Washington DC 97–8
weather 94
    predictable (seasonal) 16
    unpredictable 17
    see also climate
weddings 70
Wellington 102
wintersports 91
word processing 83
work
    experience 44
    see also employment
workers
    imported 61
    unskilled 68
WTO (World Tourist Organisation) 39, 58

Z
zoning 73